HENRY KNOX'S NOBLE TRAIN

THE STORY OF A BOSTON BOOKSELLER'S HEROIC EXPEDITION THAT SAVED THE AMERICAN REVOLUTION

William Hazelgrove

Prometheus Books

Guilford, Connecticut

Ⓟ Prometheus Books

An imprint of The Rowman & Littlefield Publishing Group, Inc.
4501 Forbes Blvd., Ste. 200
Lanham, MD 20706
www.rowman.com

Distributed by NATIONAL BOOK NETWORK

British Library Cataloguing in Publication Information Available

Library of Congress Cataloging-in-Publication Data

Names: Hazelgrove, William Elliott, 1959– author.
Title: Henry Knox's noble train : the story of a Boston bookseller's heroic expedition that saved the American Revolution / William Hazelgrove.
Other titles: Story of a Boston bookseller's heroic expedition that saved the American Revolution
Description: Guilford, Connecticut : Prometheus Books, [2020] | Includes bibliographical references and index. | Summary: "During the brutal winter of 1775–1776, an untested Boston bookseller named Henry Knox commandeered an oxen train hauling sixty tons of cannons and other artillery from Fort Ticonderoga near the Canadian border. He and his men journeyed some three hundred miles south and east over frozen, often-treacherous terrain to supply George Washington for his attack of British troops occupying Boston. This exciting tale of daunting odds and undaunted determination highlights a pivotal episode that changed history."—Provided by publisher.
Identifiers: LCCN 2019054464 (print) | LCCN 2019054465 (ebook) | ISBN 9781633886148 (cloth) | ISBN 9781633886155 (epub)
Subjects: LCSH: Knox, Henry, 1750–1806. | United States—History—Revolution, 1775–1783—Artillery operations. | United States. Continental Army—Equipment and supplies. | United States—History—Revolution, 1775–1783—Campaigns. | Military weapons—United States—History—18th century. | United States. Continental Army—Biography. | Boston (Mass.)—Biography.
Classification: LCC E207.K74 H39 2020 (print) | LCC E207.K74 (ebook) | DDC 973.3092 [B]—dc23
LC record available at https://lccn.loc.gov/2019054464
LC ebook record available at https://lccn.loc.gov/2019054465

Once again to Kitty, Clay, Callie, and Careen

I return'd to this place on the 15 & brought with me the Cannon being nearly the time I conjectur'd it would take us to transport them to here, It is not easy [to] conceive the difficulties we have had in getting them over the Lake owing to the advanc'd Season of the Year & contrary winds, but the danger is now past & three days ago it was very uncertain whether we could have gotten them until next spring, but now please God they must go . . . if that should be the case I hope in 16 or 17 days' time to be able to present to your Excellency a noble train of artillery.

—Letter from Henry Knox to General George Washington
December 17, 1775

The reflection upon my situation and that of the army produces many an uneasy hour when all around me are wrapped in sleep. . . . [F]ew people know the predicament we are in.

—Letter from George Washington
January 14, 1776

CONTENTS

NOTE TO
THE READER

Sources for Henry Knox's 1775 expedition are often contradictory. Even Tom Lovell's painting of the Noble Train is suspect. It is one of the few paintings that shows how Henry Knox transported sixty tons of cannon in 1775. Lovell, an illustrator during the early twentieth century, stated that he did a lot of historical research before attempting a painting. In his depiction we see the Noble Train coming through the snowy Berkshire mountains with four oxen pulling a five-thousand-pound sled, and teamsters and militia men struggling with ropes and calling out to one another. A man in a blue tricornered hat who looks like an officer is Henry Knox. Behind are the great mountains of the Berkshires; the train of cannons on heavy wooden sleds stretches as far as the eye can see. This painting is the product of Tom Lovell's imagination after reading as much as he could about Henry Knox's expedition.

Like the Knox expedition, the painting is clouded by obfuscation. There are historians who question whether Knox used oxen to pull his cannons from Fort Ticonderoga to Concord, Massachusetts. Horses might have been used instead, which throws doubt on the impression of the painting. The snow and the cold prevented Henry Knox from writing anything other than short notes in his journal. He pulled out the ragged book along the trail as the oxen or horses puffed steam and the men rested. Knox wrote in his torn and sometimes wet journal hastily, sitting on a stump or on the edge of one of the sleds and scribbling impressions and notes. Then he was off again. Henry Knox kept the thirty-page diary at the beginning of the trip, his notes eventually tapering off by the time he reached Cambridge with the artillery. The entries largely cover logistics: who was paid and how far they traveled on a given day.

John Becker Jr., a twelve-year-old accompanying his father, John Becker Sr., a teamster in charge of the actual freighting of the cannons, kept a journal of reflections on the journey. He then gave an interview to the Albany *Gazette* in the early nineteenth century and turned over his journal, which covered his and his father's life and times during the Revolution.

Then there are the papers of Henry Knox, which include official letters and the letters between Henry and his wife Lucy. That takes care of the primary sources for Henry Knox's expedition in the winter of 1775. Every secondary source written about the Noble Train uses these sources and interprets them in very different ways, if not with entirely contradictory conclusions.

Retired Lieutenant Colonel William L. Browne wrote a small book in 1975, *Ye Cohorn Caravan*, all of eighty pages, in which he reinterpreted Henry Knox's diary and came to very different conclusions than others before him. This was a different interpretation of another military man, Thomas M. Campeau, a major in the U.S. Army who in 2015 wrote his master's thesis on the Noble Train of Artillery, painstakingly re-creating how Henry Knox and the teamsters moved sixty tons (the two men differ on the weight, as well, Browne counting 119,000 pounds of cannons using Knox's own inventory and Campeau coming in at a whopping 150,200 pounds using the Rothenberg's *Age of Warfare in the Age of Napoleon* as a guide) over a semifrozen Lake George using oxen, over the frozen Hudson River four times (the Mohawk River flows into the Hudson ten miles above Albany and Knox, and others use these names interchangeably, sometimes mistakenly identifying the rivers), and through the peaks and valleys of the Berkshire mountains. But the major differs entirely with the lieutenant colonel about how Knox procured his sleds and oxen, where he procured them, who was involved, and where and when it happened. It is as if each man interpreted two different events.

The rest of the secondary sources treat Knox's feat of transporting vital cannons to George Washington as a minor event with few details and many times in summary. There are several children's books about the Noble Train but there is no definitive source stating how it happened, so the historian, like Henry Knox during that very cold winter of 1775, must pick a path and commit to it.

What we do know—and what the military men and just about everyone else agrees on—is that during the winter of 1775, Henry Knox headed into the wilderness of Massachusetts and then New York on a knight's errand for George Washington, and two months later returned with sixty tons (most historians agree on sixty tons, or 120,000 pounds, so we will settle there) of cannons that George Washington then used to force the British from Boston and score the first American victory of the Revolution. That is the path I focused on while writing, and in a sense, it doesn't really matter if historians disagree about where Knox procured his eighty oxen and forty-two sleds or if he used more horses or more oxen. What matters is that Henry Knox, in the winter of 1775, did something that everyone said was impossible: pulling cannons with a combined weight of twenty-eight SUVs through the wilderness, over frozen lakes and rivers, and through mountains, thereby saving the American Revolution. This simple truth is the story of the Noble Train.

PROLOGUE

1775

Necessity is the mother of invention.

—English proverb

No one believed the Americans could beat the British, and many were still loyal to the Crown with Loyalists centered in Boston after the British holed up in the city, licking their wounds from Bunker Hill. The patriots had scattered into the countryside and joined the newly formed army laying siege outside of Boston. It was essentially a disparate army of farmers coalesced from the surrounding towns. The American general who assumed command of the colonial forces outside Boston had for the last fifteen years lived the life of a genteel farmer.

George Washington was appointed by the Continental Congress to lead the justly named Continental Army, a collection of colonial militias that had fought bravely at Lexington and Concord and then finally Bunker Hill. But they were not an army, and the southerner George Washington, who had named himself "his excellency," knew nothing about the New England men who would be under his command. He knew even less about how to lay siege to Boston, where the British could resupply at will from the ocean and could wait out the undisciplined colonists.

King George III had declared the colonies in rebellion and the war was "manifestly carried on for the purposes of establishing an independent empire."[1] The king then threw down the gauntlet. "I need not dwell upon the fatal effects of such a plan. The object is too important, the spirit of the British nation too high, the resources with which God hath blessed her too numerous, to give up so many colonies which she has planned with great industry, nursed with great tenderness, encouraged with many commercial advantages, and protected and defended at much expense of blood and treasure."[2]

King George sent reinforcements to America with his best generals—William Howe, John Burgoyne, and Henry Clinton—to put down the American rebellion. These would be backed up by naval forces and foreign mercenaries. By spring 1776, there would be twenty thousand British in New England. Washington had to dislodge the British in Boston, but without the use of cannons to threaten the British fleet and the city, he could do nothing.

Bunker Hill had shown that the colonists could fight, but the army was quickly falling apart from disease, expiring enlistments, desertion, and lack of money, weapons, and gunpowder. Many farmers had to return to plant the spring crops. Washington needed artillery to force the British from their stronghold, but the only cannons were in the recently taken British Fort Ticonderoga, which was 150 miles below Canada. There were three hundred miles of frozen rivers, lakes, unchartered wilderness, and mountains between Washington's army and the sixty tons of artillery. The task of bringing the cannons to Concord was deemed impossible. Many of the colonies had yet to send their representatives to the Continental Congress in Philadelphia and awaited the outcome of Boston. The British could afford to sit and wait while the Americans withered away. A sudden attack against the weakened colonial army could end the American Revolution before it began.

I

THE BOOKSELLER
AND THE GENERAL

1

FORT TICONDEROGA/ LAKE GEORGE

May 10, 1775

Taking care to dip their paddles, Benedict Arnold and Ethan Allen silently rowed across Lake George, straining their eyes in the half light. Ripples from their boats swished across the still lake in the morning silence. More of Arnold's men were supposed to be coming over. They had staggered the boats; the first wave was the Green Mountain Boys, a loosely connected outlaw militia that took orders only from its leader, Ethan Allen. This had forced Arnold to the realization that he would have to share command with the pushy Allen, if only to ensure that the two small armies didn't turn on each other.

A faint pink brimmed in the east. Soon the boats would be visible to the sentries in the fort. If the men lost the element of surprise, they could be massacred on the water. Fort Ticonderoga was perched in the corner of northern New York State. It was valuable to the Americans for many reasons, but a major one was the store of cannons at the fort. As much as sixty tons of artillery were said to be within its great walls, and the British were slow to recognize the fort's renewed strategic importance as a back door to their rebellious colonies. Overlooking a portage river connecting Lake Champlain and Lake George, British General Gage was one of the few who realized the fort's importance and instructed Quebec's governor, General Guy Carleton, to reinforce the fort before the colonists tried to capture it.

The Connecticut Militia captain Benedict Arnold also believed that the fort was vulnerable early on. The Provincial Congress of Massachusetts rounded

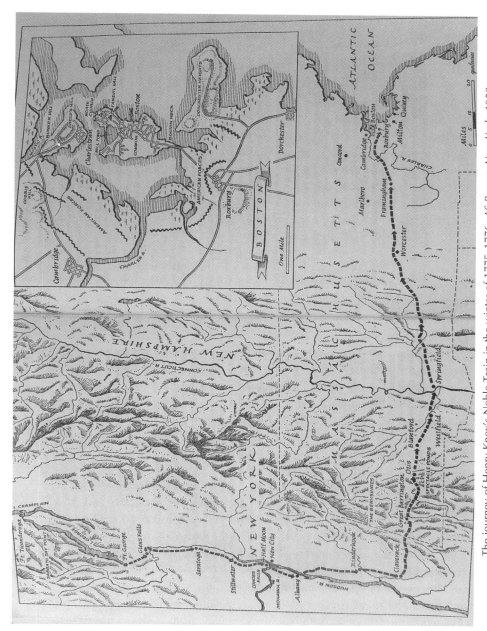

The journey of Henry Knox's Noble Train in the winter of 1775–1776. AS Barnes, New York, 1958

up the funds for Allen to attack the fort, and the Massachusetts Committee of Safety gave him a colonel's commission along with a stipend of £100 pounds, gunpowder, and the authority to enlist four hundred men. Meanwhile Ethan Allen and his one hundred Green Mountain Boys in the New Hampshire Grants territory also had become aware of the fort's strategic importance and headed north. When Arnold heard of Allen's plans, he rode so furiously that his horse collapsed. Reaching headquarters in Bennington, Vermont, Arnold learned that Allen had already headed north and was awaiting more men. Arnold finally caught up with him at Fairhaven, only to discover that Allen's Green Mountain Boys would follow only their self-styled leader.

Now they sat in two flat-bottomed boats on Lake George, a lake so pure Canadian devotees called it Lake Saint Sacrament and priests requested its waters to fill their founts for baptisms. Dawn now backlit the massive British Fort Ticonderoga, which had come to be known as the Gibraltar of North America. The fort had long been a flashpoint for France and Britain's fight for control of the continent. The French began construction in 1755, and Fort Carillon soon became Fort Ticonderoga, a pathway for the French to Britain's colonies. The British attacked on July 8, 1758, attempting to seize control. After a bloody battle in which they outnumbered the French army nearly five to one, the British were defeated, losing two thousand men in the Battle of Carillon. It was France's greatest victory of the French and Indian War.

The British returned in July 1759 and succeeded in capturing the fort. Before surrendering, the French blew up the powder magazine and the fort fell into disrepair. The strategic importance of Ticonderoga once again had become important with the outbreak of hostilities at Concord. The British realized too late that it would threaten the back of the American forces around Boston and hadn't moved to reinforce the small force of soldiers, women, and children. The fort was truly low-hanging fruit in the opening salvo of the American Revolution and a door to taking British-held Quebec.

Benedict Arnold looked at the fort again. The large black ramparts of Fort Ticonderoga were breaking the skyline. It was now or never. He and Allen conferred and decided to move ahead with the men that they had. The order was given and the boatmen began to row steadily toward the fort. Arnold pulled back the hammer on his musket as they reached the river leading to Ticonderoga and then floated toward the entrance.

The army of Green Mountain Boys reached the south gate, and Arnold reminded himself that a spy had told him that Ticonderoga was poorly defended. The musty fort was quiet, with blue smoke trailing from a pile of burning logs. Arnold rushed in as a lone sentry fled after misfiring his musket. Allen and the

Green Mountain Boys stormed the fort, waking the sleeping British in their barracks and confiscating their weapons. Lieutenant Jocelyn Feitham of the British army woke Captain William Delaplace, who demanded to know by what authority the Americans were taking the fort. Arnold quickly replied, "in the name of the Great Jehovah and the Continental Congress!"[1] Delaplace surrendered his sword and the fort fell to the Americans.

It was swift and anticlimactic as the Green Mountain Boys took to plundering and breaking into the well-stocked wine cellar. Arnold, who had been hired by the Connecticut Committee of Correspondence to bring back whatever he could find, looked for the artillery reported to be in the fort. He walked toward the walls and saw the cannons and counted 150 pieces consisting of cannons, mortars, and howitzers. Two of the cannons were five-thousand-pound Big Berthas. The black pig iron of the cannons glistened with dew and many of the mortars had rusted.

It was the only real artillery the Americans had, but two rivers, unchartered wilderness, lakes, mountains, and three hundred miles lay between the American army surrounding Boston and Fort Ticonderoga. Benedict Arnold stared at the rusting cannons, many in disintegrating wooden carriages. A lot of the cannons had not been fired for twenty years and looked as if they would never fire again. Arnold had been tasked with taking the fort, but he had no idea how to get the cannons to the men who needed them. He watched the Green Mountain Boys upending jugs of rum and turned back to the rusting cannons, shaking his head. There was simply no way to move the heavy cannons to Boston. Only a fool would even attempt it.

2

BOSTON ON EDGE

March 5, 1770

Henry Knox strutted along with his pigeon-toed gait. A heavy young man, he carried his weight like a man toting a bowling ball under his vest. It was a cold night in Boston with a hardened crust of snow on the ground. Candles flickered through frosted windows. His hard shoes clicked on cobblestones. It was still winter though there had been several thaws.

Knox walked briskly, his ponytail and scarf trailing over his shoulder. His ruffled shirt, vest, and coat were thin for the weather, and he wore another scarf wrapped around his left hand. He was all of nineteen.

Knox navigated Boston's icy, crooked streets on which he had run as a boy and then as a young man in the South End Boston gangs. A bit of rum burned pleasantly in his stomach after visiting friends. He had been on his own since he was nine, when his father, an unsuccessful shipbuilder, abandoned the family. He then joined a South End gang and found he was taller than most of the boys and stronger. The gangs battled it out in bloody fistfights, with Henry winning most of the fights and taking on the leaders of other gangs. For three years he was the toughest boy in the neighborhood.

On Pope's Night, his prowess with his fists held him in good stead. Each gang carried an effigy of the pope and the devil to Union Street, where fights broke out and the gangs tried to capture opposing effigies. The South End gang that Knox led had theirs in a heavy cart that lost a wheel. Knox put his shoulder under the axle and held the cart up while the boys fixed it, and they proceeded on to the center of town. Word spread of the strength of Henry Knox.

This was all years before. Henry ticked off the corners where he and the gang once congregated. He passed the darkened Boston Latin Grammar School he attended before he went to work to support his mother and three-year-old brother William. One of ten brothers, four of whom survived until adulthood, Henry's older brothers John and Benjamin had left years before to become merchant seamen, and Henry's new job was his salvation.

Messrs. Wharton and Bowes ran a fashionable bookshop in south Boston and agreed to hire the boy. They showed their new employee around and pointed out the books that might help his education, "volumes on mathematics and history, Greek and Latin classics, and literature—telling him that he could take any home to study. His employers said they would tutor him in the craft of binding and repairing books and teach him everything about the trade. Henry was then put to work running errands and doing chores around the shop, helping customers and making deliveries."[1] Mathematics, science, and engineering quickly became favorites and, later, military engineering. He simply could not read enough about what men constructed during times of war.

Henry took on the job with secret pride, believing he could save the family from financial ruin and restore the Knox name. Descended from crusading nobility in Scotland, William Knox was "lord of Gifford; a manor near Edinburgh in the Scottish Lowlands,"[2] and the brother of John Knox, who led the Reformation movement preaching Calvinist conversion and furthering the Protestant cause in a predominantly Catholic country led by Mary, queen of Scots. The conflict between Catholic and Protestants drove Henry's family to Northern Ireland and eventually America.

Henry's father, William Knox, sailed from Dublin in 1729 at age seventeen. William was part of a congregation that departed Derry Island for the New World and established the Church of Presbyterian Strangers on Bury Street. The strapping young man became a shipbuilder then a merchant and made money in the new economy building ships for 25 to 50 percent less than England due to the availability of cheap labor and lumber. The Irishman prospered, buying a wharf in Boston Harbor, a construction yard, and a "picturesque, two-story, wood sided home with a gambrel roof and two fireplaces on Sea Street."[3] William's home had a white picket fence and overlooked the harbor, where he could see the goods arriving that he would sell for a profit. His courtship of Mary Campbell sealed his success as an early rags-to-riches parable in Boston's rapidly evolving social structure.

The couple married, and Henry Knox was born in the new home on July 25, 1750. Henry was a rambunctious child who sought adventure at an early age. He and childhood friend David McClure attempted to "fly" by climbing onto the roof of a shed and sliding down the length of an oar to feel the sensation of flight. Knox's parents recognized early their son's intelligence. The Boston Latin Grammar School was founded a year before Harvard and counted Benjamin Franklin and Samuel Adams as alumni. Knox read verses of the Bible before the stern headmaster John Lovell in order to gain entrance.

In 1751 the Boston economy slipped into a depression after Parliament passed the Currency Act, which "prohibited the provinces from issuing paper money. The shortage of money led to a sharp drop in prices and many businesses went bankrupt."[4] When his father's business began to fail, possessions in their home disappeared as William Knox began to sell his property. The home was then sold, and Henry and his brothers moved into a smaller home when he was eight. His father, broken by the failure of his business, boarded a ship for St. Eustatius in the West Indies, leaving Henry, his mother, and his brother to fend for themselves. Years later word came that his father had died at age fifty in the Caribbean and Henry felt the abandonment keenly, swearing to himself to never abandon his own family as his father had.

In the Boston bookshop, young Henry had a big personality that filled the book-lined store, which served as something akin to a literary salon. It provided a liberal education for "clergymen, merchants, seamen, mothers, and daughters,"[5] but the military veterans who came looking for books held Henry enthralled. The old soldiers described battles with the French and the Indians in the continuing war for the Ohio River valley and exchanged tales of an expedition led by "Massachusetts governor William Shirley to capture Fort Niagara in 1755 and the victorious siege of Louisburg three years later to protect the gateway of the St. Lawrence River."[6] The soldiers kept Knox riveted in place long into the night, the voices of high adventure painting pictures against the flickering tallow light.

Knox's intelligence, ability to listen, and wit caused men like Whig leader Samuel Adams to remark that Knox was "a young gentleman of very good reputation."[7] He plunged into *Plutarch's Lives*, loving the stories of ancient battles and using his knowledge of Latin from grammar school to teach himself French. John Adams, a young lawyer, also noticed that Knox was "a youth who attracted my notice for his pleasing manners and inquisitive turn of mind."[8]

A few months before his eighteenth birthday, Knox watched a local military parade and became fascinated with a train of artillery commanded by Lieutenant Adino Paddock. Paddock, the local chair maker, had the artillery unit fire their three-pound brass cannon, shaking the windows of the bookstore. The artillery company was known as "the Train," and Knox quickly joined, learning that "to be a competent soldier encompassed more than just valor, honor, and duty, there was an underlying, dispassionate science to military art."[9]

Firing a cannon and building fortifications required understanding engineering and calculus, and Knox ramped up his study in the bookstore, poring over books like *Sharpe's Military Guide*, and borrowing other books from the Harvard library. Knox had to know how to calculate range and heading in order to hit a distant target, and he also came to understand how to transport cannons weighing several tons. The symphony of firing an eighteenth-century cannon was a dance that required precision and coordination.

A cannon crew was usually comprised of six to ten men with an officer in charge. The officer had overall command and determined the target, range, and accuracy but usually didn't participate in the actual firing. The "firer" held a linstock, which is a long wooden stick, to grip a slow match, usually a burning cord treated with potassium nitrate. The linstock allows the firer to light the cannon without getting hit by the recoil. Once everyone was in place, the careful choreography of firing the cannon was initiated. The cannon was searched with a "worm" to make sure all shot was gone. Then the barrel was swabbed with a wet sheepskin skin to extinguish lingering embers with the vent hole stopped up. A new powdered cartridge—usually black powder sewn in a fabric bag—was placed in the cannon then rammed down the barrel. Then paper or usually hay was jammed down along with the shot. The powder bag was pricked through the vent hole with a sharpened iron bar, powder poured in for priming, and "primed" shouted out. The crew then moved to firing positions with the command "make ready," and the burning match attached to the linstock was touched to the venthole and the cannon fired.

Firing a cannon appealed to the inquisitive young man in the bookstore, but it was during the far-ranging discussions under the candlelight that the real education of Henry Knox occurred. Political discussions elbowed in with the odious Townshend Revenue Acts leading the charge. The act placed a duty on "tea, glass, red and white lead, paper and paint in an attempt to raise £20,000 to pay the salaries of royal governors and crown officials as well as for British troops in America."[10] Knox must have remembered the destruction of his father's business at the hands of the Currency Act passed by Parliament, the long hand of personal disaster reaching across the ocean once again.

Samuel Adams organized a continental boycott of British goods, and the bookshop canceled orders from Boston with a subsequent drop in revenue. The young man listened to radicals like John Adams who frequented the bookstore and seeded a distrust of the British along the faint dream of independence for America. Knox's store catered to both sides of the political fence with Tories on one side and young Harvard students and professors, the "campus radicals" of Boston, on the other. Knox often met at the Green Dragon Tavern with young zealots where discussions of British tyranny swirled among coffee, tea, beer, and wine. But his final evolution was about to come.

Henry Knox turned the corner, passing down the winding streets, where a whiff of the harbor lingered in the air, the scent of dead fish and the tar used on the ships. The moon shone brightly and at times he saw his shadow on the snowy cobblestone streets. Lately Knox had been thinking of starting his own bookstore after having worked in the trade for eleven years. His own bookstore would be a revelation, but the Parliamentary Acts had kicked off another boycott of English goods, and he could order no books from London. He could do nothing until Britain lifted the odious tax on all imports.

Knox made his way down the streets without lamps. He could see very well with the crisp snow lapping the window crests and the ruddy glow of candles against frosted glass. It was 9:00 p.m. and the streets were empty. There had been much talk of not being out after dark. The "lobsterbacks" were up in arms over the beating of several soldiers by workers at the Gray's Rope Manufacturing factory. Knox didn't think about the warnings. He was a fighter and he had proved it many times in the street gangs. Now, at six feet tall, broad shouldered, with a heavy build that topped 250 pounds, he had the booming voice of a sailor and saw no problems he couldn't handle.

Boston had been simmering ever since the Massachusetts House of Representatives had responded to the Townshend Acts with the boycott of taxed goods. The British countered by sending the fifty-gun warship HMS *Romney* into Boston Harbor along with four regiments of British soldiers. Knox had watched the smartly dressed soldiers march into town as Boston became an immediate flashpoint for confrontations between the redcoats and Bostonians. Two regiments eventually left Boston in 1769 but the Fourteenth and Twenty-Ninth Regiments remained. Life in the city had changed. "Boston had become an armed camp and spectacles such as public floggings for military deserters became frequent at the Commons. The British commanders ordered that a cannon be placed directly in front of the Massachusetts Provincial House, which had been converted into a barracks."[11]

Knox heard the urgent low voices in the bookstore and their talk of rebellion and independence from Britain. This excited the young nineteen-year-old who felt the passion of the "Sons of Liberty," as many called themselves now. "Like many in town, Knox seethed at this threat to his freedom." He became friends with many in the Sons of Liberty including "Benjamin Edes and Jonathan Gil, publishers of the *Boston Gazette*, and Paul Revere, the silversmith and sometime dentist."[12]

Knox continued, hearing the soft crunch of his shoes. The clear strike of church bells rang in the frigid air. It was a call of distress for fire, and he began to run toward Provincial House, where the British were waking up along with the town. The catalyst for the ringing bells was a young wigmaker's apprentice named Edward Garrick who had yelled at a British officer, Captain Lieutenant John Goldfinch, while crossing King Street, "There goes that mean fellow who had not paid my master for dressing his hair!"[13] The debt had been settled, but Private Hugh White, standing guard in front of the Customs House, heard Garrick. White had been involved in the Gray's Rope fight before and called out to the boy that he should be more respectful of officers and then shouted, "Show me your face!"[14]

"I'm not afraid to show my face to any man," Garrick shouted back, approaching White and poking him in the chest with his finger.[15]

The British soldier swung his musket, clubbing Garrick in the head with the stock. The boy fell to the ground, stunned, then jumped up and ran off. A witness who saw the redcoat strike the boy rang the fire alarm that brought Henry Knox and fifty other Bostonians on the run. Knox ran into the square, his breath puffing into the cold night. He saw Garrick return with friends and begin throwing snowballs at Private White.

"There is the soldier who knocked me down," Garrick yelled.[16]

Knox felt his heart throb. There had been fights in the last few months between the British, the townspeople, and Loyalists. Several people who found themselves on the wrong side of quickly gathered mobs had been tarred and feathered. Loyalists and soldiers had become targets ever since the Boston Tea Party and the Intolerable Acts. Boston was a loaded keg of gunpowder, and it was only a matter of time before the flint was struck. More snowballs, sticks, bottles, stones started to pelt Private White, who loaded and primed his musket.

"The lobster is going to fire!" another boy yelled out.[17]

Knox turned and ordered the boys to leave the soldier alone. Henry then turned to the soldier. "If you fire, you must die for it!"[18]

It was an amazing moment. Knox put himself in the middle of the fight, but it was a British law that deemed capital punishment for any soldier who fired on civilians without an explicit order. The crowd had grown with some holding torches. The frightened British soldier backed up to the Custom House. "I don't care," he yelled to Knox. "If they touch me, I'll fire!"[19] He then retreated to the door of the Custom House and, pounding on the wood, shouted, "Turn out the Main Guard!"[20]

A servant rushed from the custom house to the British barracks and screamed, "They are killing the sentinel!"[21]

Six soldiers with fixed bayonets from the Twenty-Ninth Regiment led by Captain Thomas Preston rushed to White's aid. Knox persisted, telling the captain that if the soldiers fired, it would be death for them all. He shouted at the regimental commander, "Take your men back again, if they fire, your life must answer of the consequences!"[22]

The crowd shouted at the soldiers, moving closer: "Lay aside your guns and we are ready for you. . . . Come on you rascals, you bloody backs, you lobster scoundrels, fire if you dare. We know you dare not!"[23]

"I know what I am about," the captain yelled at Knox as his men loaded their muskets.[24] Several soldiers pushed back against the colonists, now numbering eighty. The six men formed a semicircle around Private White as the crowd continued to grow to two hundred and began to throw more snowballs, taunting the soldiers. Knox felt all the anger that had been swirling around the bookstore during the last year rushing out and catching fire like flames starved for oxygen. The crowd continued to taunt the soldiers, daring them to act.

"Fire! Fire!"

"You are cowardly rascals," another man shouted, "for bringing arms against naked men!"[25]

Torches gave the scene a lurid cast. Knox knew the pent-up passions that had begun well before the Boston Tea Party had erupted into the open. Richard Palmes, a local innkeeper, approached Captain Preston with a cudgel and asked if the muskets were loaded. Preston assured him that they were but that the soldiers wouldn't fire unless he ordered them to. The match to the American Revolution would be a heavy stick thrown at British Private Montgomery.

Private Montgomery fell to the street and dropped his musket, shouting for his men to fire. He picked up his musket while Palmes swung his cudgel at Montgomery and then at Captain Preston. The British muskets flashed with fire in the cold darkness. Captain Preston was clubbed to the ground by Palmes, and the crowd began running for their lives. Henry Knox heard a second round of shots and saw smoke rolling out across the town square. He saw the first man killed in the American Revolution, a mixed-race former slave, Crispus Atticus, who had been shot in the chest with two balls. The owner of the rope factory, John Gray, died next with a clean shot to the head. Mariner James Caldwell was hit in the back twice by two musket balls and died instantly. Eight more people were wounded with Samuel Maverick, an apprentice ivory turner, dying a few hours later, and Patrick Carr, an Irish immigrant, lingering for two weeks before expiring.

It was over in seconds. Henry Knox stared at the snow laced with blood. All the talk in the bookstore and the loss of his father's business and subsequent abandonment meant nothing compared to the blood in the snow on the Boston street. It was his baptism of fire, and Knox felt a deep hatred for the British he hadn't known before. The British were already reloading as Preston told them to stand down, striking their flintlocks with his hand. Knox tried to help with the wounded being dragged away, leaving rivers of blood across the snow. The entire town had awoken now to the news that the British had fired on the townspeople and many were dead. Bostonians ran to the intersection of King and Exchange Streets to stare at the carnage.

Knox heard a townsman say that five thousand people were massing on a nearby street as battle drums beat throughout the city. "To Arms! To Arms!"[26] The cry engulfed the young bookseller as Massachusetts Lieutenant Governor Thomas Hutchinson rushed into the street to plead with the gathering mob to return to their homes and let the law take its course. He told the British to return to their barracks as well. "The law," he pleaded, "should have its course," and he would "live and die by the law!"[27]

Knox later told magistrates what he had witnessed. Preston and the other soldiers who had fired were arrested later that night. The next morning, Henry went to a town meeting at Faneuil Hall along with twelve hundred others, where a statement was written demanding the British troops leave Boston. It was the first known organization of rebellion that Henry Knox attended. Samuel Adams along with a committee of fifteen were sent to meet with the lieutenant governor. The Twenty-Ninth Regiment, which had been involved in the shooting, was ordered to leave Boston, but the Fourteenth Regiment remained.

Knox watched in amazement as patriots from the surrounding towns of Roxbury, Charlestown, Braintree, Dorchester, and Cambridge descended on Boston with muskets at the ready.[28] It was a dry run for what would happen at Concord and Lexington, and by nightfall ten thousand rebel colonists were in and around Boston. The British pulled further back to the barracks at Castle William Island in the harbor.

Knox attended the funeral of the four Bostonians on Thursday, March 8, with twenty thousand people marching down Main Street. "Shops were closed, and bells tolled in slow solemn cadence not only in Boston but neighboring towns . . . at 4 p.m. several hearses formed a procession on King Street at the scene of the tragedy. They proceeded up Main Street followed by fifteen to twenty thousand mourners, who marched four and six abreast through the narrow lanes."[29] The *Boston Gazette* noted, "The distress and sorrow visible on every countenance, together with the peculiar solemnity with which the whole funeral was conducted, surpass description."[30] The bodies were held in a burial vault until the spring thaw. Paul Revere produced a famous engraving of the Boston Massacre showing the British shooting the unarmed citizens of Boston.

Knox returned to the bookstore, and on April 12, Parliament repealed all the surtaxes on goods from America, acknowledging the effectiveness of the boycott. The boycott ended in Boston, and the young bookseller could now order books from London. Henry Knox was ready to leave the bookstore of Wharton and Bowes and strike out on his own; the rebel bookseller would now have his day.

3

HIS EXCELLENCY

July 15, 1775

His Excellency George Washington stared at the HMS *Cerberus*, a twenty-eight-gun British man-of-war that had brought Generals William Howe, John Burgoyne, and Henry Clinton to Boston. The ship was peacefully at anchor in the harbor of Long Wharf, along with three other ships that had had fifty guns or more. They were proud ships with gleaming brass and bright red British flags flapping in the sea wind.

Washington sat astride his white horse with his reddish hair, his fair complexion sunburnt as it usually was, a long aquiline nose, and pale blue eyes that became cold in seconds. At forty-three, he had a few defective teeth and cheeks slightly scarred from smallpox. He was six feet, two inches, with long, powerful thighs, and he weighed 190 pounds. He was in his prime but tired, not having slept since he arrived, trying to catch up all the business of assuming command of an army comprised of a collection of colonial militias.

George Washington was magnificent to look at, and although some thought his title, "his excellency," ridiculous and overblown, it did seem to fit. He had a commanding quality that people recognized quickly. Some might have called it arrogance—and many did—but no one could deny the mantle of leadership that sat on his shoulders. James Thatcher, a doctor present for Washington's arrival in Concord, recorded his impression of the new general who was to command what was then called "the army of the United Colonies."

His excellency was on horseback, in company with several military gentlemen. It was not difficult to distinguish him from all others. His personal appearance is truly noble and majestic, being tall and well proportioned. His dress is a blue coat with buff colored facings, a rich epaulet on each shoulder, buff underdress, and an elegant small sword, a black cockade in his hair.[1]

A physician from Philadelphia, Benjamin Rush, noted that Washington had "so much martial dignity in his deportment that you could distinguish him to be a general and a soldier from among ten thousand people. There is not a king in Europe that would not look like a valet de chamber by his side."[2] What the two doctors didn't know about the imposing general was that he had grave doubts about what he was about to undertake. In fact, George Washington "did not feel certain that the Americans could win a war with Britain or even that they could force the British to an accommodation of American liberties."[3]

Washington had not been at Concord, Lexington, nor the slaughter of Bunker Hill with its thousand British casualties. He didn't even know about Bunker Hill until he arrived or the baptism of fire that the men under him had experienced. He simply saw disarray, an army of disparate colonial militias and farmers fresh off the fight and now facing the full might of the British army.

The planter from Virginia had accepted the appointment like a reluctant bride unsure about the marriage but willing to go through with the ceremony. He had responded to Congress with mild protest, "My abilities and a Military experience may not be equal to the extensive and important Trust."[4] George Washington had been retired from the military, but there was honor here, a word Washington used frequently, and he felt it would bring dishonor upon himself, his wife, and his friends to refuse to lead the fight of the American Revolution.

George Washington, for the last fifteen years, had been living the life of a genteel Virginia planter with all the trappings of wealth and status his wife's money could deliver. His military background was spotty. "His only prior experience had been in backwoods warfare—a very different kind of warfare—and most notably in the Braddock campaign of 1755, which had been a disaster. He was by no means an experienced commander. He had never led an army in battle, never commanded anything larger than a regiment. And never had he directed a siege."[5]

The man on horseback staring toward Boston had not had a military career that would warrant his appointment as commander of the newly named Continental Army. He had been consumed for the last two decades with the expansion of his plantation, crops, horses, the finest bourbon, and the best tobacco. John Adams had written to his wife after he put Washington forward to command the Continental Army: "This appointment will have great effect in cementing and securing the union of these colonies."[6] He went on to predict that Washington would become one of the greatest generals the world has ever known. John Adams might have been shocked to know Washington's greatest desire at one time was to become an officer in the British army. The problem was that the British didn't want the young officer who had proved several times that he was inept as a commander.

George Washington was born 1732 to a Virginia planter. His was not a wealthy family, and when his father, Augustine Washington, died in 1743, he left his wife and two sons ten thousand acres and not much more. George had seven years of private tutoring for schooling and none in "Latin or Greek or law, as had so many prominent Virginia patriots."[7] He lived with his older brother, Lawrence, at Mount Vernon, along with his mother, Mary Ball Washington. She was not a pleasant woman by all accounts, quarrelsome and bitter about her lot in life, and young George would have liked to get away. As a young man Washington was clumsy and awkward. His large hands and feet often got in his way, and he was keenly aware of his lack of wealth and distinguished lineage. He was determined to remake himself and turned to books for instruction. *Youths Behavior or Decency in Conversation amongst Men* was a manual Washington read to smooth out his rough edges: "In the presence of Others sing not to yourself with a humming noise nor Drum with your fingers or feet. Shake not the head, feet or legs, roll not the eyes, lift not one eyebrow higher than the other, wry not the mouth, and bedew no man's face with your spittle, by approaching too near him when you speak."[8]

Washington developed a strong writing style and a head for mathematics that allowed him to become a surveyor of land at sixteen. He liked to dance, enjoyed parties, and a common quote of the time could have been applied to him: "He liked his glass, his lass, his game of cards."[9] He was passionate about acquiring land, going West and returning in 1748 with fifteen hundred acres. When he turned twenty-one, he "owned several thousand acres, he had leased Mount Vernon (which would soon be his), he was a major in the militia, and he was the surveyor of his county."[10]

But Washington craved fame and fortune, and the fighting between France and Britain over control of the continent gave him an opportunity. After an expedition by order of Virginia's governor to challenge French claims on the Allegheny River valley in 1753, he published a diary, *The Journal of Major George Washington*, which brought him fame in America and Europe. In 1754, the twenty-two-year-old was assigned to take the fort at the Allegheny and Monongahela Rivers, Fort Duquesne. It went badly, but Washington discovered something: he did not have the typical fear that other men did in battle. "I heard the bullets whistle and believe me there is something charming in the sound," he wrote in a letter later printed in a London magazine.[11]

A final debacle ultimately tarnished the young officer. He and a British officer, Thomas Gage, took part in General Braddock's ill-fated attempt to take Fort Duquesne. Seeing the undisciplined rabble of colonial soldiers did not fit with his ideals of an officer in a military force, and Washington realized he wanted out of the colonial militia system. He wanted an officer's commission and made overtures to the British but was flatly refused. Perhaps the British simply didn't see George Washington as officer material. The irony is that Washington would endeavor to create his own version of the British army that had spurned him.

The only real military success that would justify the Continental Congress choosing Washington to lead the American army was his appointment in 1755 as colonel of the Virginia Regiment. It was an opportunity to organize a thousand paid, full-time soldiers. The twenty-three-year-old Washington proved a stern taskmaster with floggings and hangings of deserters that rivaled his British counterparts. But the "blues," as they came to be called because of their colorful uniforms, gained respect on the frontier in defense of the colony. Colonel George Washington's regiment came to be regarded as the "toughest" and "best trained" soldiers in the colonies. Governor Dinwiddie said of the regiment, "If it should be said that the troops of Virginia are irregulars, and cannot expect more notice than other provincials . . . I must beg to differ and observe in turn we want nothing, but commissions from His Majesty to make us as regular a corps as any upon the continent."[12]

So Washington had his army and was pulled in once again to the French and Indian War with another assault on Fort Duquesne with General John Forbes. Though Forbes was open to Washington's suggestions, it was ultimately a British show. "Surly and recalcitrant throughout the planning of this arduous campaign, he seemed almost disappointed when after hacking their way through the wilderness the British Army discovered that the French had burned and left the fort."[13] There was no credit for this "victory" for the young colonel. Washington soon after announced his retirement from the military and in 1758 married Martha Dandridge Custis, "an attractive extremely wealthy widow with two children, to whom he gave his full devotion."[14]

Washington became the landed planter of Virginia nobility with "54,000 acres, including some 8,000 acres at Mount Vernon, another 4,000 acres in Virginia's Dismal Swamp, nearly all of which he had acquired for speculation."[15] George Washington now enjoyed the life of the English gentry in Virginia. He had a stylish green coach built to his specifications in London, where he ordered his books, clothes, shoes, and even Moroccan leather slippers. He fit the description of an English gentlemen described in a popular English novel, *The Expedition of Humphry Clinker*, who was "obliged to keep horses, hounds, carriages, with suitable numbers of servants and maintain an elegant table for the entertainment of his neighbors."[16] Washington also had a passion for theater and attended plays in New York up to seven times. His favorite play was *Cato* by Joseph Addison, which had a line that Washington invoked more than once during his command: "Tis not in mortals to command success, but we'll do more, Sempronius, we'll deserve it."[17]

Washington had committed to expanding his home the year before he took control of the Continental Army. The expansion would double its size, and he supervised every aspect of the construction. Washington had "an abiding dislike of disorder and cared intensely about every detail."[18] A library, a two-story dining room, and a grand room for entertaining conferred Mount Vernon a regal air as befitting its master. Washington insisted on perfection, and even during the heat of battle, he sent letters home with specific instructions for his manager, Lund Washington: "I wish you would quicken Lamphire and Sears about the dining room chimney piece as mentioned in one of my last letters as I wish to have that end of the house finished before I return."[19]

Washington seemed to have the ability to focus on whatever he was doing to the exclusion of all else. Fox hunting became an obsession, which was the sport of choice among the Virginia gentry. Thomas Jefferson wrote that Washington was "the best horseman of his age,"[20] often riding for eight hours in the saddle, leaping over fences, and staying in the lead until the kill. "Found a fox in Mr. Phil Alexander's Island which was lost after a chase of seven hours," Washington wrote in his diary in 1772.[21] The next day he wrote, "Found a fox in the same place again which was killed at the end of six hours."[22] That he was an intensely physical man is known. Washington was said to possess great physical strength, besting some young men throwing an iron at Mount Vernon further than anyone else without even removing his coat. He was a man who was intensely competitive.

Washington didn't progress as a leader of much more than a plantation of one hundred slaves at this time, although "the fifteen years from 1759 until 1774 were quiet but important, nonetheless. When they began, Washington was a disappointed officer, an ambitious man, jealous of his honor and reputation, inclined to self-pity, sensitive to slights, selfish and self-seeking, in short still immature."[23] There was the public role, as well, which included the House of Burgesses; later, he became a member of the Continental

Congress. "In these years he met the requirements of patrician leadership; concern for the community informed by balance and judgement in making decisions. Those qualities had been identified by the second Continental Congress in Philadelphia."[24]

Now Washington felt the warm breeze off the ocean while staring at the British ships that could lob cannon balls into the middle of his army. He was facing the greatest power on earth with a collection of colonial militias just barely held together. He had left his beloved Mount Vernon to stare down the gun barrel of the British warships that could destroy his army, which had fallen to fourteen thousand men. The original estimate of twenty thousand men had proved a fiction after desertions, disease, and enlistment expirations had taken their toll. Only fourteen thousand men could be called fit for service, and British General John Burgoyne's branding of the American army as a "rabble in arms" was not far from his mind as Washington evaluated his men.

Appraising the colonial soldiers, Washington experienced déjà vu. Here, as in the wilds of Pennsylvania, uniforms were nonexistent. Many soldiers were without shoes or with shoes that were long worn out. Conditions were unsanitary. Disease was rampant. The food was poor. Many times Washington doubted his decision to take command of such a disparate group of men masquerading as soldiers. On paper, he referred to the men as "raw materials" for an army but not as soldiers. The men were living in an assortment of hovels; some were in wigwams. "Some are made of boards," the minister William Emerson wrote, "some of sailcloth and some partly of one and partly of the other. Others are made of stone and turf and others again of brick and others brush. Some are thrown up in a hurry . . . others are curiously wrought with doors and windows."[25] In a letter to his cousin, Washington once described the New Englanders as "a dirty and nasty people."[26]

Staring at the British ships in Boston Harbor with the knowledge that General Howe would continue to bring in reinforcements and that he and the Continental Army were facing the best trained troops on the planet—an army he had desperately wanted to join himself twenty years before—Washington could fall back on only two convictions. The first was that he had been chosen by providence to lead the Americans in their struggle for liberty and independence from the British. He would sum this up in his own words this way: "But as it has been a kind of destiny that has thrown me upon this service, I shall hope that my undertaking it is designed to answer some good purpose."[27] The good purpose being God's will. Washington's second conviction was one his own men must possess in order to endure what was ahead: "a love of the 'glorious cause'": the defense of the liberties of Americans.

In a sense, the outbreak of hostilities rescued George Washington from a life of obscurity as a successful Virginia planter. He saw now that his entire life had led to this moment, and his destiny was to lead the Americans in the possible formation of a new country. Love of the glorious cause ultimately would sustain him and his men in the dark days ahead. Washington knew he had been destined for something great but had not found the quest commensurate with his ambitions. Now he was to lead the fight to create a new nation out of whole cloth.

When George Washington arrived, he took up residence in the home of the president of Harvard, Samuel Langdon, and later moved to a Georgian mansion when Langdon's home did not fulfill his expectations. He noted the men were not "possessed of the absolute necessity of cleanliness," a petty observation but one that reveals the gulf between the Virginia plantation owner and the hard-scrabble New England soldiers.[28] But beyond his immediate dismay over the state of the army was the military situation.

> Had a seagull's eye view been possible, one could have seen the whole American army and its fortifications strung out in a great arc of about ten miles around the landward side of Boston, from the Mystic River on the northeast to Roxbury to the south, with British redcoats camped on the slopes of the Boston Common and manning defenses at the Neck and within the town and on Bunker Hill, and at the center of the town, the Province House, headquarters for the British command, could be readily identified by its large octagonal cupola and distinctive gold weathervane of an Indian with a bow and arrow.[29]

In short, the British held Boston with what was reported to be eleven thousand troops, and Boston was accessible to the mainland by a half-mile causeway—the Neck—which made the city more like an island. The British controlled the sea and could shell the Americans at will and bring in reinforcements and supplies. They had built barricades to keep the Americans out, and the Americans had built barricades to keep the British in. This was a siege, and Washington had not one engineer and no artillery to speak of. Shortly after his arrival, he became convinced that a British attack that could decimate his army was imminent. "We scarcely lie down or rise up, but with the expectation that the night or the day must produce some important event," wrote one of Washington's staff.[30]

The army George Washington was facing was a conventional eighteenth-century fighting force trained to fight in the prescribed aristocratic tradition in which armies met on the field of battle to minimize losses and enable swift victories. There were two groups who did the fighting: "the aristocracy who provided the officers, and an underclass, peasants, vagrants, the dregs who filled the ranks."[31] The common soldier, or dregs, was looked upon as unreliable, so harsh discipline was used ensure that they would fight under the aristocratic officers. There was no overriding national cause to motivate the soldiers; the only motivation was the point of their officers' bayonets or muskets. There were rules of engagement as well. Operations were conducted mostly in the summer when the weather was hospitable; winter campaigns were nonexistent. "Winter quarters were carefully selected to permit a reasonably comfortable existence and opportunities for renewal of the men and weapons."[32] Victories in battle were usually not followed up on and pursued by the army, as they risked a later defeat if the enemy turned on the army. Combat was not pursued if it could be helped. The type of total war involving civilians that would be fought in the Civil War and World Wars I and II was still a hundred years in the future.

Drill was looked upon as an end to itself. The dregs were taught not to think, and drilling was the perfect tool to get men to think as one—or not to think at all. Firing weapons was also tightly choreographed.

> Troops ordinarily moved in columns, places in the column corresponding to places in the lines from which fire was delivered. The British, along with most European armies, fought with their infantry deployed in lines three deep, the front rank kneeling, the center with each soldier standing with his left foot inside the right of the man kneeling in front, and the rear rank with each soldier placed with his left foot in the right of the man ahead in the center.[33]

No one fired until ordered. Discipline was preeminent.

Washington knew this very well and admired European military doctrine, but the new "citizen soldiers" he inherited were not dregs or aristocrats nor were they of military doctrine. They were an army of colonial militias bounded together loosely by a common cause. This did not exist in the European theater of war, and this loose devotion to the "glorious cause" could be snuffed any minute, Washington believed, if the "rabble" were not converted quickly into a unified army.

George Washington didn't fit into the new army he had inherited. The farmers and townspeople who made a stand at Lexington were a far cry from the wealthy planter who took up residence in Vasall House on Cambridge's Tory Row after rejecting the home selected for him, which simply wasn't grand enough. John Vasall was a wealthy loyalist who, fearing for his life and his family, headed for Boston where other loyalists had fled. The patriots controlled the countryside now, and loyalists often traveled at night to reach the safety of the British-controlled city.

Washington moved the elegance of his old life into the command center of his new one. "Virginia hospitality more than lived up to its reputation at Cambridge. Purchases included quantities of beef, lamb, roasting pig, wild ducks, geese, turtle, and a variety of fresh fish, of which Washington was especially fond, plums, peaches, barrels of cider, brandy and rum by the gallon, and limes by the thousands to fight off scurvy."[34] There was a complete domestic staff with a "steward, two cooks, a kitchen maid, a washerwoman, eight others whose duties were not specified and included several slaves, plus a personal tailor for the commander."[35] This would be the nerve center of the Continental Army where the new general conferred with his officers, entertained dignitaries and politicians, dispatched letters to Congress, and handled the innumerable organizational duties that go with running an army.

The hardscrabble Yankees might have wondered what a man like George Washington thought of them. Best they didn't know. A week after arriving he wrote Richard Henry Lee, "The abuses in this army, I fear, are considerable and the new modeling of it, in the face of an enemy, from whom we every hour expect an attack, is exceedingly difficult and dangerous."[36] Apart from the loose bonds of colonial militias on temporary duty, Washington detected another weakness: the prejudice of the Virginia planter class for the New England soldiers. Bluntly, he found "an unaccountable kind of stupidity in the lower classes of these people," which "prevails but too generally among the officers of the Massachusetts part of the army which are all the same kidney with the privates."[37]

Washington saw the detriment of the men electing their own officers in the local militias. Many of the officers would have to be relieved, as they "curry favor with the men by whom they were chosen and, on whose smiles, possibly they think they may again rely."[38] He needed officers who could command, not necessarily those who were liked or popular with the men. Washington's first action had been to take a count of the soldiers and determine how much ammunition the army possessed. The initial count came back at sixteen thousand men, of which two thousand were not fit for service. Washington believed he needed twenty thousand men for the siege of Boston.

Then came sobering news. In August Washington learned that the army had less than ten thousand pounds of gunpowder. This meant enough gunpowder for only nine rounds per man. No gunpowder was produced in the colonies and little more was expected soon from secret shipments from Europe. When Washington heard this stunning news, he couldn't speak for a half hour. An army could not fight without gunpowder and certainly not lay siege to a city without artillery or powder to fire the cannons. Everywhere Washington looked, he saw disorder and chaos and catastrophe. He later wrote, "Could I have foreseen what I have and am like to experience, no consideration upon earth should have induced me to accept this command."[39]

Then there were the mounting deaths from camp fever, which included dysentery, typhus, and typhoid fever. Typhoid resulted from food or water contaminated with human feces. It was a disease that killed many, "characterized by a raging fever, red rash, vomiting, diarrhea, and excruciating abdominal pain."[40] The men relieved themselves wherever they liked and open latrines leaked into the camps. The summer heat brought more disease, and Washington quickly imposed strict regulations, requiring pits for the "necessities" to be located farther out of camp and establishing a routine of reviewing the troops and the condition of the camps daily. Like his Virginia regiment, he imposed severe punishment for offenses: floggings, rides on the wooden horse, and hangings for desertions.

There were no uniforms, of course, and Washington had no resources to change this. Men wore "heavy homespun coats and shirts, these often in tatters from constant wear, britches of every color and condition, cowhide shoes and moccasins, and on their heads, old broad brimmed felt hats, weathered and sweat stained, beaver hats, farmer's straw hats, or striped bandannas tied sailor fashion."[41] The weapons were varied as well, with muskets and fowling pieces dominating. The flintlock musket was the most common and most deadly: "A single-shot smooth-bore muzzle-loading weapon that threw a lead ball weighing about an ounce and which could inflict terrible damage."[42]

Most muskets were five feet long and weighed ten pounds. The barrels were not rifled, and accuracy was not great, but they could be loaded rapidly and fired. A good soldier could get off four rounds in a minute. Washington immediately directed major generals to wear purple ribbons across their chests and brigadiers to wear pink ribbons. He, too, wore a ribbon, but there was no mistaking George Washington. He ordered the men to build better defenses and often rode about inspecting the work. Often, he would look toward Boston with his spyglass. The British held Bunker Hill and Charleston, which had been burned nearly to the ground. The only thing they didn't hold was Dorchester Heights.

Washington turned and stared toward the cliffs of Dorchester, "a high windblown no man's land," which overlooked the harbor and Boston itself. Artillery placed upon the heights would command the city and the harbor and force the British to leave or face annihilation. He wondered why the British had not chosen to occupy the Heights. They knew there was no danger from the Americans, who had no artillery to rain havoc down on the city.

Still, Washington felt he must do something, lest disaster end the war for all of them. Gouverneur Morris, a New York statesman who knew Washington well, said later that "boiling in his bosom were passions almost too mighty for man . . . his first victory . . . was over himself."[43] George Washington was a man who liked to attack, and siege warfare was unfamiliar to him.

Remaking the army required strict discipline. Washington began the courts-martial at once for sentries leaving their posts and anyone caught fraternizing with the enemy. Desertions were occurring at an alarming rate, with many men returning home to tend to their farms. Some returned when they felt their home life was under control. Washington dealt harshly with all desertions. Men swimming in the Charles River were now required to cover their privates, especially if ladies were crossing the bridge to Cambridge. Infractions of all sorts were dealt with by lashings and, for the more serious offenses, hangings. Reverend William Emerson wrote later, "There is a great overturning in the camp as to order and regularity. New Lords new laws. . . . The strictest government is taking place. . . . Everyone is made to know his place and keep in it or be tied up and receive . . . 30 or 40 lashes. . . . Thousands are at work every day from four till eleven in the morning. It is surprising how much work has been done."[44]

The independent colonial militias didn't like having their freedoms curbed, and fights broke out among men who hailed from different colonies. The men who had fought at Bunker Hill had yet to integrate into the Continental Army, as Congress had named them. When a fight broke out between riflemen from Virginia and fishermen from Marblehead, Washington himself became involved in breaking it up. Israel Trask, a boy of ten, remembered the incident years later: "With the spring of a deer he leaped from his saddle, threw the reins of his bridle into the hands of his servant, and rushed into the thickest of the melee and with an iron grip seized two tall, brawny, athletic, savage looking riflemen by the throat, keeping them at arm's length, alternately shaking and talking to them."[45]

Washington immediately put the men to work digging new defenses, but he really wanted to attack the British with a knockout blow, though he knew he did not have the resources. The hunger for glory still unfound haunted him, and Washington fought back against his doubts as well as those of his men with the grand design of action.

> He might have recognized the dangers of an undisciplined army, but Washington was driven by a desperate need to prove himself. Even though it might not be justified militarily by what he found in Cambridge and Roxbury, he wanted to attack. . . . Half of him wanted to create an altogether different kind of army—a painstaking process that required time and patience. The other, more impulsive half wanted to "destroy" the British army with a cataclysmic thrust and be done with it.[46]

George Washington kept his eyes on the British ships in Boston Harbor. He knew he had to dislodge the regulars before they became too reinforced. He immediately put the soldiers to work digging new breastworks. The British were doing the same, and he could hear their clipped English voices on quiet nights. He felt an old resentment, the hopes of a young man dashed. There would be not a little revenge for the army that had spurned him twenty years before. But how to get the British out of Boston was the question. Action was what was needed, "a speedy finish," as he had confided to his brother. He would get the defenses in order then assemble his war council. Congress had been very clear that there was to be no attack without consulting his war council. There was a risk that the British would burn Boston if he attacked, but as Washington later wrote to the governor of Rhode Island, "No danger is to be considered when put in competition with the magnitude of the cause."[47]

The new general turned in his saddle and stared again at the green cliffs of Dorchester Heights. The warm breeze from the ocean lifted his hair. He heard a distant bell from one of the British ships. He knew how indomitable the British military machine was and later commented on America's chances in the spring of 1775: "It was known that . . . the expense in comparison with our circumstances as colonists must be enormous, the struggle protracted, dubious, and severe. It was known that the British were in a manner inexhaustible, that her fleets covered the ocean, and that her troops had harvested laurels in every quarter of the globe . . . money the nerve of war was wanting."[48]

The cliffs of Dorchester shone bright with the last rays of sun. Washington had no way of knowing that after the battle of Bunker Hill, British Major General Henry Clinton in a council of war suggested moving immediately to occupy Dorchester. He told Commander-in-Chief Gage that possession of the Heights "was absolutely necessary for the security of Boston as they lay directly on our water communications and more seriously annoyed the port of Boston than those of Charleston." Clinton would later write "that if the King's troops should be ever driven from Boston, it would be by rebel batteries raised on those heights."[49] Gage did nothing, though, and the Heights remained unoccupied.

George Washington turned, adjusting himself in his saddle. He slowly headed back to camp. He shook his head. What he couldn't do with some artillery and a first-rate military engineer.

4

THE REBEL
BOOKSELLER

April 24, 1775

Henry Knox, in a white ruffled shirt and vest, stood behind the high desk in his bookstore and looked anxiously for his wife Lucy. She was late, and he wondered if she had been discovered. He watched the British soldiers talking to the Tory ladies who frequented his store. He had just lit the oil lamps and the tallow candles. Knox basked in the warm light and the scent of tobacco, feeling a sense of pride once again, even as he was about to leave everything he had ever known. With the harbor blockaded by the British, he couldn't even bring books in anymore. It was dispiriting. He had done so well in a short amount of time.

The London Bookstore had become a literary salon in Boston for the fashionable crowd of officers and Tories. Literary subjects, debates, and discussions about the topics of the day echoed off the plank floors and the lines of books Knox ordered from London. It was April 22, 1771, and Knox had just turned twenty-one when the publishers Edes and Gills posted an announcement in the *Boston Gazette*: "This day is opened a new London Bookstore by Henry Knox, opposite Williams Court in Cornhill Boston, who has just imported in the last ships from London a large and very elegant assortment of the most modern books in all branches of Literature, Arts and Sciences and to be sold as cheap as can be bought at any place in town."[1]

More British officers entered Knox's store. He watched as they looked around the shop and then their eyes slowly settled on him. People liked Knox. He was young and handsome, gregarious, impressive in size, and with a quick wit. The ladies flocked to his store, and their perfume graced the well-lined shelves of shiny new volumes on all subjects, but if someone were to take an inventory, he would find an inordinate number of books on military history and military engineering. People read vociferously in the eighteenth century, and the titles Henry Knox brought to his store revealed a broad range of tastes:

> Millan's *Army List*, Buckner's *Practicable Method to Enable Deaf Persons to Hear*, Caverhill's *Experiments of the Causes of Heat on Living Animals*, Fordyce on *Venereal Disease*, Haller on *Irritability*, Hunter's *Elegant Treatise on the Teeth with Plates*, Millar on the *Asthma and Whooping Cough*, Manning on *Female Diseases*, Pott on the *Hydrocele*, Rowley on the *Cure of Ulcerated Legs without Rest*, and a pamphlet entitled, "Indolence, Intemperance and Vexation—The Causes of All Our Chronic Diseases."[2]

During Knox's time, it was traditional for booksellers to put their names on the title pages of books, participating in the publishing and acting as distributor. The first book with Knox's name was *Some Thought on the Names of the Days of the Week—In a Letter to a Friend*.[3] Although Knox had become friendly with the British officers, he also felt their rapacious stares. There had been two recent battles at Lexington and Concord, and though Knox was generally well liked by the occupying force of British soldiers, it was known that he was a rebel sympathizer. He knew it was only a matter of time before he was arrested. Knox smiled at the soldiers. *Show that all is well. All is well.* He and Lucy were to be in the store to show that nothing was amiss. The British knew that patriots all over the city were sneaking away to join the colonial army outside the city, and those who were caught could be imprisoned or hanged for treason.

Knox didn't want to leave. It broke his heart. He had buried his mother just four years before, but she had lived to see him open his store. He had supported her and his brother William since he was nine. Her fifty-three years had been ones of toil, but Knox took solace that she saw him become a successful owner of a popular bookstore. He quickly outgrew his first store at Williams Court and moved to a larger store near the center of Boston. Knox brought a native sense of resourcefulness to bookselling, beating out the seven other bookstores for customers. He advertised heavily with notices around town and came up with the unheard-of idea of using blurbs from the literary magazine *Critical Review* to sell books. He also lowered the prices of his books below the agreed publisher's level. This upset other bookstore owners, but Knox believed that poor people should have the opportunity to buy books as much as the rich.

Knox was not only a bookseller, but "an importer, distributor, publisher, and binder."[4] Besides books, Knox sold "patent medicines, flutes, bread-baskets, telescopes, dividers, protractors, and wallpaper."[5] A friend, Henry Burbeck, later said that "Knox's store was a great resort for the British officers and Tory ladies who were the vogue of that period." The irony that the British were his best customers was not lost upon Knox. He was a rebel bookseller and was known as such, but, in the eyes of the British, this only elevated his store as a fashionable bohemia and gathering place for ladies. Knox adopted the manners and culture of his patrons. Though he had the build of a heavyset sailor—six feet tall with a booming voice and broad shoulders—"his seemingly innate appreciation of truly fine things became more and more accentuated by his prolific reading of the books in his store until his culture, though necessarily superficial, appeared almost as thorough as that of many of his English Educated patrons."[6]

Knox looked again for Lucy, keeping the bandage tight around his left hand. He wondered if the British were aware that he cofounded the Boston Grenadier Corps. It was not uncommon for the colonies to have their own militias to fight the Indians, but the men who drilled under Knox and orderly Sergeant Lemuel Trescott were training to fight the British. Knox often put the bookstore in the care of his younger brother William in the evenings and "drilled the men . . . choreographing their movements and training them to load and fire cannons and perform battle maneuvers as well as to use a sword, bayonet, and musket."[7] Their uniforms were smart, and Knox led the men before all the Boston citizens. It was here that he met Lucy Flucker. She had seen him in the parade with his handkerchief wrapped around his left hand, a signature associated with Henry Knox that disguised the damage caused by a hunting accident on his twenty-third birthday.

Knox glanced down at his hand and saw the fowling piece discharge again, blasting away the fingers of his left hand. From that moment in 1773, he hid his missing pinky and ring fingers with colorful scarves. It made him more dashing in the eyes of Lucy Flucker, but not so much in the eyes of her father, Thomas Flucker, the royally appointed secretary of Massachusetts. Thomas Flucker was a fierce, high-minded Tory who had no sympathy for the rebel cause and who counted the upper echelons of British society as his friends. "He had served on the governor's council, the upper house of the legislature, which was patterned after the House of Lords from 1761 to 1768 during the controversies over the Sugar Act, the Stamp Act, and the Townsend measures as resistance to Parliament grew."[8]

That his daughter should fall in love with a rebel bookseller of no background was nightmarish to Flucker. But the plump, vivacious, intelligent Lucy Flucker did just that. British officers vied for the attention of the seventeen-year-old with the "bewitching face" who hailed from a prominent family. Lucy appeared at Knox's bookstore after seeing him in the parade, and he immediately discovered not only her charm but her independent mind. "Lucy was distinguished as a young lady of high intellectual attainments who was very fond of books—especially of the books sold by Henry Knox."[9] Henry would often miscount change while talking to the cultured young woman. "As time went on, the talks between Henry and Lucy became more frequent and ardent, and often she was seen to blush under the keen looks of his gray eyes."[10]

One friend later summed up Lucy during this early period of their courtship as "very fond of books and especially the books sold by Knox, whose shelves she had frequent recourse."[11] They might have been a society couple were it not for Knox's political leanings and his background. Lucy loved his hardscrabble roots, his pluck, the way he supported his family since he was nine. From Lucy's privileged background, Knox was the clean breath of air she had been waiting for, and she even admired his missing fingers, seeing them as war wounds. Knox fell in love with the beautiful girl possessed with the culture he lacked.

Lucy took on Knox's political views in opposition to the Tory household her father had created. In 1773 four ships loaded with heavily taxed tea sailed into Boston harbor. This was King George's attempt to tax something that he thought might not be objectionable to the colonists. He was wrong: the colonists saw the Tea Act as an affront to their very liberty. By law the tea had to be unloaded by December 16 and the duty paid. The *Dartmouth* was the first ship to arrive, and the captain went to a townhouse meeting of eight thousand people. Knox's grenadiers were appointed to guard the ship to keep anyone from unloading it during the night. Knox was in plain sight of other British vessels, and it was clear whose side he was now on. This was in direct opposition to Lucy's father and other conservative Tories who saw the rebels as treasonous.

That night, young men disguised as Mohawk Indians tossed the tea into Boston Harbor. No one is sure if Knox participated in the Boston Tea Party, but it is safe to say that he and his men provided cover to the men dumping the tea. Massachusetts Governor Hutchinson believed war was inevitable and sides had to be chosen. Thomas Flucker threatened Lucy, invoking dire consequences if she married Knox: she would be destitute, ostracized, married to a traitor to Great Britain, and reduced to begging for help from friends. "He bluntly laid the future before her. . . . If she married this humble bookbinder, she could anticipate a future of poverty . . . one day she would undoubtedly watch as her siblings traveled in fine carriages and attended elegant banquets and enjoyed all that a life of privilege had to offer."[12]

Worse, in the event of war, Knox would be fighting Lucy's own brother, who had just enlisted in the British army. Henry wouldn't blame Lucy if she cut off their courtship. Not only did her father pressure her, but friends warned that she would be cut off if she married the rebel bookseller. Amazingly, this young woman withstood threats of poverty, loneliness, and outright hostility for marrying the man she loved. But Lucy Flucker loved Henry Knox with the very essence of her soul, and no sacrifice was too great.

Still, it was dangerous. They had to meet secretly, and as tensions increased, Knox feared that he would be arrested and Lucy would suffer from her association with him. Notes were passed covertly, and in public they kept a polite friendship. Knox wrote furtive letters in 1773 while enduring a toothache:

> I have been upon the upmost rack of expectation for above two hours past, expecting some message from you. . . . Is there anything I can say or do that will affect it. If there is a command, it shall be done. If my assurance of the most perfect disinterested love that ever filled the breast of a youth, if the most sacred promises of the continuation of that love with interest, as time increases upon it will tend to raise your spirits you have them, and God Almighty is my witness that if all the riches of the world were in my possession they should back my assertions. My tooth by the help of two or three jerks of the Doctors is past giving me pain.[13]

Lucy and Knox frequently rendezvoused in coffeehouses at night away from the prying eyes of her family. "To the coffee house tomorrow evening? Do you ask me? Or is it only like the banner affixed at the head of your letter? N-N-N-No. . . . Let me hear from or see you. I could write a volume to you, but I write so much in a hurry that as your woman is waiting, that you could not read. God have you in his kind protection is the desire of your Henry Knox."[14]

The couple considered eloping while Lucy pressured her father to accept that she loved the bookseller. Knox wrote her anxiously on March 7, 1774, imploring for news and declaring his love.

> What news? Have you spoken to your father or he to you upon the subject? What appearance has this to our grand affair at your house at present? Do you go to the ball tomorrow evening? I am in a state of anxiety heretofore unknown. I wish the medium of our correspondence settled, in order to which I must endeavor to see you, when we will settle it. . . . My only consolation is in you, and in order that it should be well grounded, permit me to beg two things of you with the greatest ardency: never distrust my affection for you without the most rational and convincing proof—if you do not hear from me in a reasonable time, do not lay it for my want of love, but want of opportunity, and do not, in consequence of such distrust, omit writing to me as often as possible.[15]

Knox inhaled sweet perfume as several beautiful Tory women passed him in his bookstore. He watched the British officers and played the obsequious bookseller, getting a book for a lieutenant and stationery for another. He must betray nothing or the game would be up. Even Knox himself could not believe that he was to leave all he had known.

Finally, faced with Lucy's intransigence, Thomas Flucker gave his consent and the couple set their wedding date for June 20, 1774. Flucker then tried to bring his future son-in-law to heel by securing Knox a commission in the British army as a lieutenant. The old Tory believed that Knox's radical beliefs stemmed from a desire to serve in the military and that service in the British army would swing him away from the dangerous path of a rebel. Knox turned his fiancée's father down, and Flucker realized the young man's convictions ran deep and predicted a troubled life for the young couple. And Knox had to admit that the patriarch's predictions came true quick enough.

Soon after the Boston Tea Party, the British Parliament passed the Coercive Acts, forbidding commercial ships in the harbor. This affected Knox's business, since Boston citizens approved a boycott of English goods. All of Knox's books originated from London, and he quickly couldn't pay his creditors. Business dropped and his main supplier "the London bookselling firm of Wright and Gill notified him that 5 percent interest would be tacked on his 350 debt."[16] Still, Knox believed in the boycott and even helped enforce it. It was during a drill with the Boston Grenadier Crops that he saw the British ships enter the harbor carrying four regiments and General Gage, who was to replace governor Hutchinson. When Gage disembarked, he noticed Knox's soldiers and was impressed with their military precision.

The occupying force began drilling in Boston Commons as Knox and Lucy prepared for the wedding and Henry fought for the survival of his business. He pleaded with his creditors the day before the Port Act went into effect, blocking off Boston Harbor. Knox wrote to Wright and Gill, predicting a swift end to the proclamation:

> If the act to block up this harbor should continue in force any length of time, it must deeply affect every person in trade here, and consequently their correspondents on your side of the water. But it is expected the British merchants will see their own interest so clearly as to induce them to exert their whole influence in order to get so unjust and cruel an edict repealed.[17]

What Knox didn't know was that his future father-in-law was working to enforce the shipping ban and monitoring the now-defiant Massachusetts Assembly.

In effect, he was killing Knox's business and working with General Gage, who could close the assembly if he deemed it as working against British interests. On June 1, 1775, Gage gave Thomas Flucker the order to shut down the Massachusetts Assembly. Flucker found the doors locked at the legislature and read the order outside the doors, buttressed by a crowd of Tories. When the doors opened, it was too late. Sam Adams, John Adams, Thomas Cushing, and Robert Treat Paine were headed for the Continental Congress meeting in Philadelphia.

Thomas Flucker returned to Governor Gage enraged over his treatment and incredulous that in three days his daughter would marry a bookseller with known affiliation to the rebels. Knox would always remember that on the day of their marriage, June 20, the British soldiers marched through the streets and the militias prepared for war. Knox was now twenty-four and Lucy was eighteen. A friend composed a poem dedicated to Lucy, which paid tribute to putting love over self-interest.

> Blest tho she is with every human grace
> The mein engaging, and bewitching face
> Yet still on higher beauty is her care
> Virtue, the charm that most adorns the fair[18]

As predicted, Lucy's family treated her as an outcast as did her friends. The young woman who risked everything to marry a rebel bookseller didn't care. She was in love with Henry Knox and he was in love with her. But Knox was in trouble. He had a business to run and tried to not let his politics interfere. His father had abandoned his family because of his failing business, and Knox didn't want to repeat his failings. He tried to maintain commercial ties with Tories and Loyalists, but the rebel bookseller was on borrowed time.

Things moved quickly. Knox believed war was inevitable and wrote to a New York bookseller, "The new acts for regulating this government will, I perfectly believe, make great difficulties. The people are in no disposition to receive an act pregnant with so great evils. What mode of opposition will be adopted, I do not know but it is the general opinion that it will be opposed, hence the key to the formidable force collecting here."[19] Knox began watching the British drills and took notes. He noticed another observer, a Quaker from Rhode Island just seven years older than himself, Nathaniel Greene, who would become one of his closest friends.

Nathaniel Greene harbored military aspirations. He worked at the family foundry in Rhode Island for a time, then, in opposition to his Quaker teachings, he organized a local militia, the Kentish Guards. Despite a lame knee that caused a lifelong limp, Greene wanted to lead men in battle and shared Knox's political beliefs and military interests. The two often talked late into the night at a local Whig gathering spot, the Bunch of Grapes. Neither man knew how important their association would be to the Revolution, but they were caught in the hotbed of patriotic fever sweeping through Boston that had reached a boiling point after the arrival of Gage's soldiers.

General Gage knew of Knox's reputation as a grenadier and had secretly issued orders prohibiting him from leaving Boston. His bookstore came under surveillance, and Knox's suspicions that he might be arrested were confirmed when friend and patriot Paul Revere came to his store and they started a ruse of arguing in front of the British and the Tories. Revere let Knox know secretly that British spies had approached him seeking information about the rebel bookseller. Knox quietly began telling his grenadiers to begin slipping out of town.

Most of his company left Boston while other colonists smuggled out gunpowder, ammunition, and other supplies in the basements of homes outside Boston. Knox became involved with a network of spies keeping tabs on what was happening outside Boston. Gage and many Tories noted that the homes of suspected rebels had been closed and heard rumors that militias were preparing for battle outside of Boston. Gage fortified the 120-yard isthmus of Boston Neck with twenty-eight cannons.

Knox assisted some more customers, still keeping an eye on the door for Lucy. The candles and lamps in other storefronts flickered out in the darkness. There was a buzz in the air. People knew that the war had started but what did it mean? Should they go on with business as usual? Would there be a quick end with a brokered peace? Once Gage had sent 260 soldiers looking for powder in Cambridge on September 1, the fuse had been lit. Gage's men had taken the town's powder magazine and two cannons. Although no shots were fired, the militias had formed and it was only a matter of time. Knox knew that if he left Boston he would be tracked down and arrested for treason. If he joined the militia, he would be abandoning his wife, his business, and his brother.

Henry felt constrained by circumstances and his sense of duty. His business was dying but he couldn't leave yet. He still held hope that differences between Britain and her colonies might be resolved. In 1774 he wrote book distributor Thomas Longman in London that he couldn't meet his payments:

> I had the fairest prospect of entirely balancing our account this fall; but the almost total stagnation of trade, in consequence of the Boston Port Bill, has been the sole means of preventing it, and now the non-consumption agreement will stop

that small circulation of business left by the Boston Port. It must be the wish of every good man that these unhappy differences between Great Britain and the colonies be speedily and finally adjusted. . . . I cannot but hope every person who is concerned in American trade will most strenuously exert themselves, in their respective situations, for what so nearly concerns us.[20]

However futile it might have been, Knox was pleading for his business, essentially asking his distributor in London to lobby against the prohibition of trade from Boston.

Bostonians were now smuggling in provisions from small boats in the harbor. Food was becoming scarce, but Knox, whose business was close to bankruptcy, managed to continue to eat well and his weight increased to 280 pounds. On February 1, 1775, another Massachusetts provincial congress met and began planning for war with defenses to stop British aggression. Homes of patriots who had left Boston were broken into and looted. Soldiers broke down the doors of suspected rebels and smashed windows and tore apart homes looking for military contraband. On February 27, the British captured a colonial arsenal at Salem.

The end was nearing, and Knox ran his final advertisement for Knox's London Bookstore in the *Boston Gazette* on March 20, 1775. The advertisement talked of a pamphlet written by a student at Kings College in New York, Alexander Hamilton: "Just published and to be sold by Henry Knox in Cornhill, price 1 s. 6 d. The Farmer refuted, or a more impartial and comprehensive view of the dispute between Great Britain and the Colonies, intended as a further vindication of Congress."[21] It was a final shot across the bow for Knox. He had not carried many Tory pamphlets, but he pushed Hamilton's treatise, which proclaimed, "That all Americans are entitled to freedom is incontestable on every rational principal."[22] He might as well have posted a sign that the Rebel Bookstore was now open. Knox was on borrowed time and he knew it.

The evening of April 18, the British left Boston in large numbers. Knox immediately noticed that many of the British officers who frequented his store were gone. If only to spy on him, they came with regularity, but now the streets were empty. He heard the British were collecting boats in Boston Harbor. At 11:00 p.m., seven hundred British soldiers boarded the boats to cross the harbor, reassemble on the other side, and march toward Concord. Paul Revere rode to alert the towns as "church bells rang, guns were fired, and flares shot into the night sky as patriots tried to rouse the inhabitants along the road to Lexington."[23]

The next morning Knox saw a contingent of twelve hundred Welsh soldiers—the Forty-Seventh and Thirty-Eight Regiments—march out of Boston along with two cannons, singing "Yankee Doodle" to taunt the patriots. News soon came that shots had been fired at Lexington and that seven colonials had been killed and nine wounded. Wounded British soldiers straggled back into Boston.

The war had begun, and Knox knew he would have to join the fight. Lucy demanded to go with him if he left Boston. His brother William agreed to watch the bookstore, and they made their plans. On Thursday morning, April 20, Knox heard news of the battle at Concord, where the Americans lost ninety men but the British suffered three hundred casualties from colonials picking them off on their way back to Boston. Munitions had been destroyed and five hundred pounds of cannonballs had been thrown in the river, but Sam Adams and John Hancock had escaped capture. There was no time to lose; Knox knew they had to leave Boston as soon as possible.

The door to Knox's bookstore swung open. There was Lucy, her long brown hair flowing against her shoulders, her full figure swaying. A few Tory women glanced at her and immediately turned away. They talked in low voices and Knox made a show of business as usual for the few officers still in the store. Knox greeted his wife and spoke in her ear, agreeing quickly to meet at their home after he closed the store. They loudly said their good-byes before Lucy left, and Knox looked at his watch then prepared to close shop. He felt as if he was being watched, but there was nothing he could do. He escorted the last customer out, a woman who had been looking for a book of poetry, then snuffed the last candle, stepped outside, and turned the lock in the door. Knox paused, glancing into the darkened bookstore, and wondered if he would ever see it again.

He hurried home, taking a circuitous route through alleys and back streets, before reaching his house, glancing over his shoulder, and closing the door. Lucy met him in the darkened house, where they quickly dressed in disguises. Lucy had a hooded coat and she sewed his sword into her petticoat. They said good-bye to his brother, William, then slipped out the back door of their house. Boston was eerily quiet as they made their way through the cooling air. The cobblestone streets were deserted. A bell rang down at the harbor, and Knox reassured Lucy that it was nothing, though he couldn't be sure.

They held hands and hurried for the waterfront, wooden-heeled shoes tapping on the cobblestones, keeping watch for any British guards. Knox knew that if they were caught, they would be imprisoned for treason or possibly hanged. They slipped down streets he had frequented as a boy, and he remembered the long-ago night of the Boston Massacre, which convinced him that America and Britain would have to part eventually.

The sour smell of fish lingered by the docks. He heard the call of a British sailor aboard one of the anchored men-of-war. Then silence. A small dinghy bobbed in the water. William had placed it there and told Knox the exact location. Henry helped Lucy into the boat and she sat facing him. He positioned the scarf on his left hand, then clunked the oars against the locks. Knox nodded, waited, then began to slowly row the dinghy into the harbor, dipping the oars ever so slowly into the glassy water.

The few candles in Boston's windows seemed unnaturally bright to Lucy. She stared at the only home she had ever known and wondered if she would ever see her sisters Hannah and Sally or her brother Thomas again. Her father barely spoke to her, and now she was leaving with the man for whom she had sacrificed everything. Lucy listened to the swish of the oars, watching the ripples angulating out from their boat into the dark syrupy water.

They headed out of the harbor, and Knox stared back at Boston. A lone candle burned high in the church steeple in the center of town. Since he was nine, he had been on his own and fought his way toward owning a business and marrying a girl from a prominent family. He had been living a developing American Dream, and now he was leaving one world for another. All that he held dear was in the boat with him. The rebel bookseller rowed in the darkness, feeling the cool air on the water, keeping his eyes on the British ships, silent and massive. Knox realized then that the American Revolution had begun, and he was staring not at Boston, but a new republic, born out of the darkness of the Old World.

5

THE FRUSTRATED GENERAL

October 24, 1775

In the breaking light of morning, George Washington raised the telescope he had just taken from his manservant Billy Lee and watched the British fortifying their breastworks. He looked magnificent atop his white horse with his sword and blue tunic with the swooping brocade of his coat and his tricornered hat. He had come from a meeting with his generals where he proposed an immediate amphibious attack against the British.

Washington quickly made his case: winter was coming, the troops were deserting, enlistments were expiring, gunpowder was in short supply. Sitting outside Boston and waiting for the British to attack was not an answer. George Washington craved action and as he had confided in his brother: "The inactive state we lie in is exceedingly disagreeable."[1] He wanted a "speedy finish."

This was the duality of George Washington. A plodding, meticulous man who planned carefully lived within the renegade who embraced bold action as a tonic to his own doubts about the army and his role as commander. Abigail Adams had observed of Washington that "if he was not really one of the best-intentioned men in the world, he might be a very dangerous one."[2] George Washington carried in his psychological knapsack the seeds of his own failure and was saved many times by others who recognized his approach as reckless. "No danger is to be considered when put in competition to the magnitude of the cause," he wrote to the governor of Rhode Island.[3] One great action might finish the war. His dramatic plan to use flat-bottomed boats to cross Back Bay and attack the British, he explained to the eight gathered generals on September 11, 1775, "did not appear impractical though hazardous."[4]

The council of war that had convened was "three major generals, including the venerable Israel Putnam . . . and four brigadiers."[5] The only man who was not a New Englander and the only one with true military experience was General Lee, a veteran of the French and Indian War and a former British officer. Lanky with a long hooked nose, rough manner, and unkempt uniform, Lee was a fighter among men and had done a little of everything. He had married an Indian chief's daughter and served with the British in Spain and then as an "aide de camp to the King of Poland."[6] He loved dogs and always had two or three with him. Clergyman Jeremy Bellnap described him as "an odd genius . . . a great sloven, wretchedly profane."[7]

His Indian name, "Boiling Water," betrayed his notoriously short temper, his moodiness, and his blunt manner in speaking. Washington thought he had the best military mind in the army as "the first officer in military knowledge and experience we have in the whole army."[8] He requested Lee as his second in command, a position Lee tolerated, thinking Washington's moniker, "his excellency," was perfectly ridiculous.

Major Artemas Ward was the opposite of Lee: "a heavy set, pious looking Massachusetts farmer."[9] He too was a veteran of the French and Indian War and had command of the army until Washington's arrival. Lee viewed Ward as having "no acquaintance whatever with military matters,"[10] but Ward was competent and operated on an even keel to Lee's sporadic impulses. Washington had Lee take over the left wing of the army, Putnam in the center, and Ward oversaw the right wing, which included the Heights.

The assembled brigadiers were William Heath and John Thomas of Massachusetts, John Spencer of Connecticut, and the newest member, Nathaniel Greene. These were all citizen soldiers who found themselves rapidly advancing in the army when war broke out. Thomas was a doctor who had served in the French and Indian War, William Heath was a wealthy farmer, and John Sullivan was a lawyer from Boston who had also served in the Continental Congress. John Spencer was the oldest; his troops referred to him as "Granny."

Washington pointed out to his council that winter was coming and troop enlistments would continue to expire with men leaving the army every day. He cited the lack of firewood and gunpowder, arguing that when winter came, they would be forced to wait until spring to attack the British. Washington felt they had just enough gunpowder for the attack and conceded that "the hazard, and the loss that may accompany the attempt, nor, what will be the probable consequences of a failure," also should be entertained.[11] Washington, straining to be even minded, at times hurt his own best arguments. The generals in his war council saw only disaster: "Unless they caught the tide exactly right, the men in the boats could have been stranded on mudflats a hundred yards or more from dry ground and forced to struggle through knee deep muck while under withering fire."[12] The slaughter might have exceeded that of the British at Bunker Hill. Washington accepted the decision of his council but continued the construction of the boats, noting that "all the generals upon the earth should not have convinced me of the propriety of delaying an attack upon Boston."[13]

This was the young man who had charged into the Pennsylvania wilderness years before, just managing to sidestep disaster. Washington continued biding his time, reinforcing his defenses, and trying to discern what the British were up to. Using his telescope, Washington could see that the British were dismantling Boston, using homes for firewood, hounding the populace to ferret out the rebels. Already General Howe, newly arrived from Britain, had tried to use smallpox as a weapon against the Americans, sending the sick from Boston, obliging the Continental Army to take them in. Washington saw his own army melting away with expiring enlistments and no money to pay his soldiers. "The paymaster has not a single dollar in hand," he wrote John Hancock, pointing out that without money, "the army must absolutely break up."[14]

George Washington considered the possibility of getting the guns from Fort Ticonderoga. On May 10, 1775, Ethan Allen and Benedict Arnold had stormed the British-held Fort Ticonderoga. Washington had been told there were "78 serviceable cannons . . . 3 howitzers and 30,000 musket flints."[15] He had then sent Benedict Arnold to attack the British in Quebec and authorized the use of small boats, or "privateers," to harass the British ships. He was doing anything he could to prepare for an attack that could decimate his weakened army.

In October, Washington proposed another plan to his war council. They had met in his headquarters along with Benjamin Franklin in front of a roaring fire. Again, the risks were deemed too high. General Lee later wrote James Warren, president of the Massachusetts Assembly, "Things hereabouts remain in pretty much the same situation. . . . We look at their lines and they view ours. . . . They want courage to attack us and we want powder to attack them and so there is no attack on either side."[16]

Bad news followed with a dispatch informing Washington that the British had burned the town of Falmouth and turned out the entire population. It was a type of warfare Washington saw now as "proof of the diabolical designs" of the British ruler, along with the revelation that Dr. Benjamin Church, his surgeon general and a member of the Provincial Congress, had been revealed to be in the pay of the British as a spy.[17] He was a classmate of John Hancock and a leader of the Patriot cause from the early days. A letter had fallen into the hands of Nathaniel Greene who took it to Washington. The deciphered letter spelled out his years of treachery.

Washington lowered his telescope. He just saw a British officer staring back at him with a telescope, and he didn't want to become a target for a British sniper or an artillerist. He had received a letter from Congress on October 23, 1775, authorizing him to go after the cannons in Ticonderoga. His war council had resoundingly rejected the idea. "It almost certainly would fail and at a time when embarrassment to the army would embolden the British and the Tories. The expenditure would divert badly needed funds to a hopeless cause."[18] There were a lot of reasons not to pursue the cannons three hundred miles away, not the least of which would involve crossing the Berkshire mountains, rivers, lakes, and an unforgiving wintry wilderness. Still. . . .

Washington handed the telescope back to Billy Lee, reined his horse around, and headed back to his headquarters. King George III had declared the colonies to be in open rebellion and had replaced General Gage with Major General William Howe. "Washington knew that all hope for reconciliation with Great Britain had been snuffed out."[19] The prudent side of Washington sided with his council. Getting the cannons from Ticonderoga might be a disaster. But the bold stroke, the ingenious move had great appeal to the Virginian who had left his wife and his home, Mount Vernon, risking virtually everything for a cause that might result in him being hanged for treason by the British. The one reason to pursue the feat of transporting sixty tons of cannons from a fort three hundred miles away was the young man of substantial girth that Washington had met on July 5. He had been walking along a road outside of Concord with a colorful scarf wrapped around his left hand.

6

THE BOOKSELLER
MEETS THE GENERAL

May 16, 1775

Knox and Lucy made their way through the countryside of Boston to the town of Worchester. Lucy pleaded to go with Knox to join the army, but Henry was adamant. Tories abounded and they could easily be given away, and the army was no place for a pregnant woman. Lucy had told him in the darkness that she was with child, and for Henry Knox it cemented his belief that he was fighting for a just cause. He wanted his daughter or son to grow up in a free country where liberty was guaranteed, and no man or woman should fear arrest, imprisonment, or execution by an occupying force.

He arranged for Lucy to stay with friends in Worchester and left with the knowledge that he was going to be a father. Knox entered "Camp Liberty" and found the patriot army in disarray. The Cambridge encampment had swollen to 13,600 men after the Massachusetts Committee of Safety had put out the call for other militias to assist in the siege of Boston. Knox reported to the headquarters of Artemas Ward, recently named commander of the colonial forces. Henry was not impressed with the "chaotic collection of hunters, farmers, unemployed seamen and tyros."[1] Knox proceeded through the camp and "noticed men coming and going as they pleased. . . . There was no system to channel food and no allowance for hygiene. The camp stank from lack of sanitation. Many men had no rifles, and others had only fowling pieces that discharged buckshot."[2]

The nearly fifty-year-old Ward had fought as a lieutenant colonel for the Massachusetts militia and had been "appointed brigadier general in charge of the provinces militia in 1775."[3] He was trying to organize the army before the British marched out of Boston and attacked. Ward knew Henry and already saw him as a military engineer. It is curious that Ward should regard Knox as an engineer at this point. He must have been aware of his drilling of the local militia and the artillery train and his study of military engineering. Knox wanted to be more involved directly and suggested he might be better used to help design and build fortifications.

He immediately noticed the patriots had not erected any defenses along the road leading from Boston Neck, which was the only road out of Boston. This was where the British must pass, and Knox picked the town of Roxbury to build his defenses. "Henry drafted plans for a redoubt on a hill overlooking Roxbury and put men to work digging encroachments and building fortifications that could help repel a British attempt to leave Boston."[4] It was during this time that Knox first heard of Ethan Allen and Benedict Arnold's success in taking Fort Ticonderoga in upstate New York with its cannons. Knox instinctively knew that the cannons should be brought immediately to Boston, even though Fort Ticonderoga was three hundred miles away with rugged wilderness between the army and the fort.

Henry was put to work training and educating soldiers on the firing of artillery. Dr. Warren and the Committee of Safety, knowing Knox's background as the owner of a Boston bookstore, requested that he "be applied to for supplying the Colony Army with military books."[5] There was little Knox could do while the British occupied Boston, and he recommended books from Harvard college. He would slip away when he could to visit Lucy, who was now staying with John Cook in Watertown. Then he returned to train gunners on artillery newly arrived with a company from Providence. The twelve cannons weren't much, but it was all the colonial army had. At least soldiers could learn how to fire a cannon.

British General Gage had posted an order that all rebels lay down their arms and take an oath of allegiance or be deemed traitors. This was followed with a British plan to take the heights overlooking Boston, Bunker Hill. The Americans occupied the hill and waited as the British crossed the harbor with three thousand men in twenty-eight barges. Knox was in Roxbury when the British bombardment began. He responded with his few cannons but was quickly overwhelmed by the superior firepower. The British ships rained cannonballs on the American position. Knox was impressed by "the British gunners aboard the battleships as the 68-gun *Somerset*, the 20-gun *Lively*, the 36-gun *Cerberus*, the 34-gun *Glasgow*"[6] fired upon the colonials. The British also had mounted artillery on Copp's Hill a mile away and sent well-aimed cannonballs into the

American position then shelled the town of Charleston from ships and batteries, incinerating the entire town within hours. From Roxbury, Henry Knox saw the Battle of Bunker Hill play out.

> Knox watched as the sea of red clad troops formed a battle line and began the march up the green slope of Breed Hill. After the British neared the crest, a loud volley from colonial guns shredded their ranks and sent the British in retreat, stumbling among the tall grass and fallen bodies. The king's men made a second assault but were again repulsed by the muskets of colonials. On the verge of abandoning the battle, the British received news that the colonists were out of powder.[7]

General Howe then ordered a bayonet charge, and brutal hand-to-hand combat broke out as the colonists ran. The loss of 1,150 British against 441 patriot soldiers boosted American confidence even though the British eventually took the hill. Many of the dead were friends of Knox, and the Americans lost an able general in Dr. Joseph Warren. After Bunker Hill, Knox believed more than ever that the American army needed artillery if they were going to fight the British.

George Washington arrived on July 3 to take command after twelve days of travel. The meeting between the former Boston bookseller and the new general fresh off his planation in Virginia occurred on July 5 along a road outside of Cambridge where Knox was walking back toward camp. Washington was riding on his white horse in a hail of dust with General Charles Lee when they asked Knox to accompany them on their inspection of the Roxbury fortifications he had erected. Henry Knox followed the resplendently attired general who had come to save the American Revolution.

"General Washington fills his place with vast ease and dignity and dispenses happiness around him," Knox later wrote to Lucy. "Yesterday, as I was going to Cambridge, I met the General, who begged me to return to Roxbury again which I did. When they had viewed the works, they expressed the greatest pleasure and surprise at their situation and apparent utility to say nothing of the plan which did not escape their praise."[8]

What did Washington see in the man who "walked in a slightly odd pigeon-toed fashion with his legs bowed outward and his paunch . . . bulging under his vest"?[9] Washington desperately needed talented men who knew their way around artillery and military fortifications. Perhaps he was taken with the young man's confidence and his encyclopedic knowledge gained by reading books about military fortifications. Beyond that, Washington knew the fate of his army rested on finding young energetic men who could step into the shoes of commanders. Knox might have even been one of the sons Washington never had.

Knox always addressed Washington as "your excellency" and was unfailingly loyal. Both men were intensely physical, rugged individuals who did not shirk from hardship. Knox's deep reading on all things military impressed Washington, and the general valued his insights into the needs of the new army. Henry Knox was only twenty-five, and Washington liked to surround himself with confident young officers. Still, it was amazing that this New England bookseller should become one of George Washington's closest generals and the man most instrumental in the siege of Boston.

But for now, he was assisting General Washington with whatever he needed. In a July 9 letter Knox wrote Lucy "that he had to run off to wait on the commander in chief."[10] Two days later, he followed up with "The new generals are of infinite service in the army. They have to reduce order from perfect chaos."[11] There were not enough New England officers, and none other than John Adams began lobbying for a position for Henry Knox. He sent the Massachusetts Committee of Safety a list of men, including Knox, who "are well qualified for places in the army, who have lost their all, by the outrages of tyranny, whom I wish to hear provided for . . . they could be Captains or Brigade Majors."[12]

Meanwhile, Knox tried to mollify his pregnant wife, who was staying with strangers in Worchester. Painting a picture of his daily life, Knox explained why it was hard for him to slip away:

> I have written to the dear Idol of my heart every day that I have been here except yesterday when no opportunity offered. . . . I go to Roxbury and Cambridge in the morning and return here every evening for the sake of Mr. Jackson's company. We are here in a very decent private house, Mr. Cooke's near the bridge. I shall endeavor to set off for my dear girl tomorrow in the morning if possible. If not, on Wednesday afternoon and reach home on Thursday. Believe me, my dear, nothing in the world should detain me from you but absolute necessity. Did I not think I was doing my oppressed country an essential service; I should have come home to my lovely girl before this?[13]

The truth was that Knox would see Lucy less frequently as he was drawn into the army. His letters become testaments of his love, attempts to keep his young wife's spirits up since she could no longer see her family or her husband. "I wrote to you to who is the animating object of my life but had not opportunity of sending it. Therefore, to make my promise good and agreeable to my own inclinations, I attempted to talk to my Lucy this morning, but alas forty miles away she can't hear me. . . . Indeed my dear girl, I love you too well to be separated from you at all."[14]

By now Henry Knox was regularly dining with George Washington and his generals, Charles Lee, Israel Putnam, William Heath, Nathaniel Greene, and Horatio Gates. General Washington had clearly taken Knox under his wing, inviting him and Lucy to dine with him on September 22. On a table set with silver candelabra, Virginia ham, and a fine claret, Lucy charmed Washington and his wife Martha with the refinement that the hardscrabble Knox lacked. The young, energetic couple appealed to Washington, who liked pretty women with a flair of wit. Lucy left the next day, just before the British began shelling the American camp.

The shelling by the artillerymen was not as accurate, and Henry bragged to his brother in a letter, "Let it be remembered to the honor and skill of the British troops, that they fired 104 cannon shot at our works at not a greater distance than half point blank shot—and did what? Why scratched a man's face with splinters of a rail fence!"[15] Knox was feeling more confident in his role as an unofficial commander of artillerymen, and it was a foregone conclusion that Henry would be offered some sort of position in the army. He was disappointed to learn from Sam Adams that he was being considered for lieutenant colonel position rather than full colonel.

Knox, though of no rank at all, was hurt by the slight. He later wrote Adams:

> I have the most sacred regard for the liberty of my country and am fully deter-
> mined to act as is in my power in opposition to the present tyranny attempted to
> be imposed upon it, but as honor of the comparative, I humbly hope that I have
> as good a pretension to the rank of colonel as many now in the service. . . . If your
> respectable body should not incline to give the rank and pay of colonel, I must
> be to decline.[16]

The brash young Knox thought he should be propelled to the upper ranks of the army as his friend Nathaniel Greene had been elevated to general. The army increasingly became one comprised of very young men; Washington knew the optimism of young officers would be essential when facing the superior might of the British army. Knox need not have worried about his commission. George Washington saw him as a key commander and needed to replace the arthritic artillery leader, Colonel Richard Gridley. After meeting with his council of officers, he wrote Congress, "The council of officers are unanimously of the opinion, that the command of the artillery should no longer continue in Colonel Gridley and knowing of no person better qualified to supply his place, or whose appointment will give more general satisfaction, have taken the liberty of recom-mending Henry Knox."[17]

Amazingly, Knox was to become a colonel in the artillery corps without ever serving in the army. This was a testament to George Washington's ability to see hidden talent, but it also shows how adept Henry Know was at ingratiating himself with those who could show him favor. He had a big personality, and as one French admirer said of Knox, "it is impossible to know him without esteeming him or to see him without loving him."[18] This son of a failed shipbuilder with scant formal education who had made himself into a merchant then educated himself in the doctrines of military theory and practice appealed to Washington, who lost his father at an early age and fought his way up through the aristocracy of Virginia.

A shrewd hand was at play. When Knox was told he was to be commander of the army's artillery, he asked where the artillery was, to which Washington deadpanned that there was none to speak of. Worse than that, America had not one foundry to produce cannons and had but one regiment of 635 artillerymen and a dozen heavy guns. It may well be that George Washington knew that if there was one man resourceful enough to retrieve the cannons from Ticonderoga, it was Henry Knox. One could make a case that Knox's proposal to get the cannons at Ticonderoga was what George Washington wanted to hear.

It made sense that Knox would suggest getting the cannons; as the newly commissioned commander of the artillery, he was the commander of nothing without cannons. The letter arrived from Congress on October 23 authorizing the use of the cannons at Ticonderoga and greenlighting the expedition to the fort. But how to do it? "The fort was 300 miles away from Washington's army, separated not only by distance but rolling hills, winding rivers and lakes. The roads along the way were seldom used and not worn solid by heavy traffic, much less the tonnage of cannon."[19]

Washington's war council wanted no part of bringing the cannons from Ticonderoga, pointing out that the undertaking would fail and become an embarrassment to the army at a time when they were desperately trying to increase enlistments. The money would be wasted and could be better used for gunpowder and munitions. Washington listened to their protestations but went his own way. The letter from Congress was the rubber stamp Washington needed to fund the expedition. After overruling his war council, he gave Knox $1,000 in Continental currency and on Thursday, November 16, orders

to take stock of supplies in the artillery corps and to inventory its needs, then to proceed first to the New York Provincial Congress and then to Albany to prepare and send supplies to Cambridge. He was then to go to Fort Ticonderoga in upstate New York and if need be, going all the way to St. Johns in Quebec if needed, to gather as many cannons and as much ammunition as he could cart back with him.[20]

Recovering any cannons and munitions was essentially a scavenger hunt. In the young Knox, George Washington might have seen himself twenty years before when he charged into Indian-held territory to demand that the French abandon their forts on land claimed by the British. He also knew that Knox possessed a supreme confidence in his abilities and that, as a Bostonian, he was fighting to liberate his own hometown. Washington understood the risks of setting off in winter to bring back cannon through the wilderness, but he also saw no other alternative. Necessity was the mother of invention, and he was facing a supremely armed foe that he could not dislodge with muskets and fowling pieces alone.

Lucy was none too happy when Knox broke the news. Her husband assured her it was not a dangerous undertaking; however, the separation could be long. He tried to cushion the blow, telling her that he would stop in Worchester to visit on his way West. Washington then gave Knox letters of introduction and a formal request to the New York Congress to assist him any way they could. Knox was designated a "squire" or "an experienced engineer" in the letters while his commission wound its way through Congress.

Essentially, Henry Knox, the twenty-five-year-old bookseller from Boston, was going after the only known cannons in order to turn the tide of the war against the British in the fledgling American Revolution. It was no different for Knox than reading up on a military operation and trying out those very same theories in drills after closing the bookshop. The American Revolution was a citizen soldier revolution, and, commission or not, a citizen was about to embark on a hazardous, near-impossible journey to retrieve sixty tons of cannons, howitzers, and mortars during what would be one of the worst winters on record.

Washington and Knox had their livelihoods, their families, their very lives on the line. Both men would have to gamble on youth, ego, strength, boldness, and fortitude. The bold move would become a hallmark of George Washington's legacy, but in 1775 in Boston he was just beginning to explore the boundaries of being a leader of an American army poised to take on the greatest power on earth.

Washington wrote to Knox before he left and tipped his hand, the usually unflappable general showing that he was running out of time and options. "The want of them [the cannons] is great, that no trouble or expense must be spared to obtain them—I have wrote to General Schuyler, he will give every necessary assistance that may be had and forwarded to this place, with the utmost dispatch."[21]

Knox knew time was of the essence. A train of British artillery had arrived in Boston along with reinforcements from five Irish regiments. The British would continue to reinforce and would move on their own timetable. Washington was more convinced than ever that they would attack when the colonials were at their weakest point. He gave Knox orders for General Schuyler to provide Cambridge with "powder, lead, mortars, cannon, indeed of most sorts of military stores. For want of them, we really cannot carry on any sort of spirited operation."[22]

Washington's council of officers thought it folly, but few knew the dire circumstances the American army was in. At the end of November, only 2,540 men had reenlisted, and Washington reported that "our situation is truly alarming and of this General Howe is well appraised. . . . No doubt when he is reinforced, he will avail himself of the information."[23] He would later write to his former adjutant Joseph Reed: "Could I have foreseen what I have and am like to experience, no consideration upon earth should have induced me to accept his command."[24]

The war would rest on one man, a former Boston bookseller with no experience at all in moving anything. Though Henry Knox would be commissioned as colonel of the artillery in Philadelphia by the Continental Congress while he was gone, the young man setting out to retrieve the cannons was a former bookseller now tasked with saving the American Revolution.

7

THE HEIGHTS
OF DORCHESTER

November 1, 1775

If Knox returned with the cannons, there was only one logical location for them. The Heights of Dorchester were windy cliffs overlooking Boston and the harbor. From here, cannons could lob shells into the city and menace the British ships docked in the harbor. After the bloody fight for Bunker Hill, the British and the Americans assumed that the next place of attack would be Dorchester. For the British, it made sense to the take the Heights, if only to keep the rebels from occupying them. General Howe knew the Americans possessed no artillery, but after Bunker Hill he wasn't in a hurry to spill British blood again.

In a letter to London he asserted, "We are not under the least apprehension of an attack on this place from the Americans."[1] Then in a meeting with his general staff, Howe asserted that if the colonials made a move on Dorchester Heights, "we must go at it with our whole force."[2] The original plan for the British called for taking the high ground in Charlestown and the Dorchester peninsulas. This plan changed with the Battle of Bunker Hill and its one thousand casualties. Still, even when Gage was in command, a council of war meeting at Province House zeroed in on the taking of the Heights. Major General Henry Clinton proposed they move on Dorchester immediately. He proclaimed that taking the Heights was "absolutely necessary for the security of Boston, as they lay directly on our water communications and more seriously annoyed the port of Boston than those of Charlestown."[3] But General Gage made no move and one can assume he felt no threat from an army that possessed less than a dozen artillery pieces.

The same could be said of General Howe when he took over. The Americans had made no move to occupy the Heights, and so each side kept a wary eye on the position. It was not a state secret. Loyalists in Boston questioned why the British had not moved to take it. A prominent loyalist in Boston, Justice Peter Oliver, wrote, "It has often been wished that this hill had had proper attention paid to it and it had been repeatedly mentioned that it was of the last necessity to secure such a position, but the general answers were that there was no danger from it, and that it was to be wished that the rebels would take possession of it, as they could be dislodged."[4]

Why waste men on Dorchester Heights when the colonials could do nothing with it? Even if they did, the British would merely take it back. This was General Howe's approach to the siege of Boston: the rules of European engagement would apply first and foremost, and war was not fought in winter but in spring, summer, and early fall. Winter was for the army to rest and to prepare for the spring, when the war would commence again. Besides, they would be in Boston for only a short time, as New York was where the seat of war operations should take place. The British had deemed Boston a sideshow. According to men like British General Grant, they should abandon the city then burn it and head for New York. In fact, Howe received orders from London to abandon Boston before winter, but it was too late. Winter had come. Besides, there was no real threat. It was time to make the best of conditions as they were. For the British gentry officer class, this meant dining and the theater while the Boston populace suffered.

Firewood had passed £20 a cord and trees were cut down all over the city to heat Boston's homes. Even the Liberty Tree at the corner of Essex and Orange Streets was sacrificed, producing fourteen cords of wood. Houses, barns, old ships, wharves, porches, and just about anything else that could burn was used for firewood. Many of the Bostonians had fled, leaving the Loyalists to occupy the town and try to protect their property from looters. "In all there were about 4,000 civilians under siege, at least half of whom were women and children. . . . They were hurting from shortages of all kinds, the poor inevitably suffering the most."[5] Food was in drastically short supply; even horse meat commanded exorbitant prices.

But General Howe and his officers snuggled in for a long winter and appropriated the Old South Church to be used as a riding ring. The pews were destroyed, and the floor covered with dirt, hay, and horse manure. To the British, who believed that the meetings in the church had been the heart of the insurrection, this was a fitting end. General Howe liked evening entertainment and allowed his "redcoat gentry" to partake. "We have plays, assemblies, and balls, and live as if we were in a place of plenty,"[6] wrote one officer. Faneuil Hall, named by the patriots "the cradle of liberty," was turned into a playhouse "for amateur productions of Shakespeare and original farces, with officers and favored Loyalists taking parts."

In a bit of irony, Sally Flucker, Lucy Flucker's sister, took the lead in *Maid of the Oaks*, a satire written by General Burgoyne. So while her pregnant sister hid in the countryside with her husband, who was readying for a journey into the wilderness to retrieve cannons that would force the British from Boston, Sally was on the stage performing a farce for the very people who wanted to hang her brother-in-law.

That was not to say General Howe was not a fighter. At Bunker Hill, he was in the front lines and liked to tell his troops before battles: "I do not in the least doubt but that you will behave like Englishmen and as becomes good soldiers."[7] But he was used to assumed rules of engagement and saw no reason to engage an enemy that in his estimation would eventually surrender to the might of the British military. "He had far greater experience than George Washington and had better equipped and better trained troops and the ships of the Royal Navy riding at anchor in the harbor."[8]

William Howe graduated from Eton and a year before his eighteenth birthday had a commission in the Duke of Cumberland's Light Dragoons. His two older brothers had paved the way with military careers. George Augustus Lord Howe had been killed in the French and Indian War and was revered in England as one of "the bravest and best loved British officers of the time."[9] Richard Admiral Lord Howe had enlisted in the navy at fourteen and, like his brother William, was a member of Parliament and had the ear of the king.

Richard and William were wealthy and had connections to the very top of British society. Their mother, rumored to be the illegitimate daughter of King George I, smoothed the way for her sons in London society. The brothers were "staunch Whigs and had a decided resemblance, a rather gloomy dark look, with dark eyes, heavy lids and a swarthy complexion."[10] Horace Walpole said William Howe was "one of those brave silent brothers who was reckoned sensible, though so silent that nobody knew whether he was or not."[11] He had expressed no real interest in serving in the war with America, but if the king wanted him to go, then he would cross the ocean.

During the French and Indian War, the young colonel had taken a division of infantry and charged up the embankments at Quebec to clear the way for General James Wolfe, who would later defeat General Montcalm and the French. At the Battle of Bunker Hill, he had led his troops, saying he would never ask them "to go a step further than where I go myself."[12] He led the men up the hill three times until he was the last man standing in the final assault with bodies lying all around him.

Howe, just two years older than Washington, now faced a general with much less experience and with an army that had very little experience as well. General Howe's soldiers were better trained, better equipped, and he also had the very best of Britain's generals in support of his operations. General Clinton and Burgoyne were like Howe, aristocrats with stellar military careers. Clinton was Howe's second in command. Fat, short, and sometimes petulant, Clinton had grown up in America—his father, Admiral George Clinton, had been governor of New York—and he understood Americans. The only problem was that Clinton and Howe didn't get along, nor did they work well together.

For all his military experience, Howe knew little about the man he was facing or his army. He had no spies or sources of intelligence about what the Americans were doing. He didn't know that Washington's army was unraveling as enlistments expired or that the army was perilously short of gunpowder. He simply had no consideration at all of George Washington. His assumption of British military superiority kept him from considering who might face him on the other side of the fortifications. Even though Bunker Hill had been a stunningly bloody battle, Howe assumed that once British force was brought to bear, the Americans would fold quickly.

If Washington had one advantage, it was that he had nothing to lose—the bold stroke was always a possibility. Howe, despite being a brave man in battle, was by nature a phlegmatic, slow-to-act, procrastinator who enjoyed the comforts of winter camp. Why not enjoy oneself as best one could? Dorchester Heights was a barren, icy, windswept cliff that would remain so. The winter of 1775 was proving to be brutal. The British regulars were freezing in their tents, and some men froze to death standing watch. The soldiers were not used to New England winters that clamped down on the land like an icy lid. General Howe, smoking his cigar, drinking his brandy, would have been astounded to learn of a bookseller who was heading into the wilderness to retrieve sixty tons of artillery. Moreover, he wouldn't have believed it.

II

THE EXPEDITION

8

STARTING OUT

November 17, 1775

The Knox expedition was composed of militia men, teamsters, sleds, oxen, and horses, which Knox assembled as he journeyed north. Sleds of wood and iron pulled through snow with oxen was the most efficient and logical way to move the artillery over the three hundred miles of roads, trails, wilderness, ice, and mountains. The artillery train changed shape and composition along the way as Henry Knox continually improvised and made do with available resources in order to deal with the hardships encountered on his expedition.

What history has handed down to us is a train of forty-two sleds and eighty oxen with ninety militiamen and forty-five teamsters. This was the most expeditious way to move men and material in eighteenth-century America and the only way to get the cannons from Fort Ticonderoga to Concord. This was based on the assumption of snow for the sleds and frozen lakes and rivers to support sixty tons of men, beasts, and cannons. The story of the expedition is one of deviation, adjustment, and creative solutions based on this simple plan—or, in other words, how it really happened.

On November 17, 1775, the Knox expedition left Cambridge. Henry Knox rode out of camp in the crisp New England sunshine, breathing the cold, clean air of raw adventure, riding ahead of a train of men along with his brother William. Less than six months before, he had been a Boston bookseller. Now he led an expedition to retrieve cannons for the American fight for liberty and to deliver it to His Excellency George Washington to force the hated British out of his hometown of Boston. Knox wanted to shout thanks to the heavens that providence had put him in such a position.

But Lucy Knox did not share his joy. Pregnant, living with strangers in the rural town of Worchester, separated from her husband for long periods of time, cut off from friends and family, and unsure whether she would ever see her own parents again, she couldn't be blamed for questioning her decision to marry Henry Knox. She had received his letter but was unsure what it meant.

> I lodged at Barker's and arrived here Yesterday in the most violent N. East Storm that I almost ever knew. Keep up your spirits, my dear Girl, I shall be with you tomorrow night and don't be alarmed when I tell you that the General has ordered me to go the West as far Ticonderoga, about a three week's journey. Don't be afraid, there is no fighting in the Case. I am going upon business only. My only regret will be to leave my love who I am sure be as easy as possible under the circumstances.[1]

Although he knew he would be gone months, Henry Knox told his wife that he would be gone only three weeks, a lie to placate his lonely young bride. Lucy wasn't above guilting her patriotic husband and reminding him of the situation he had left her in. Months after his baby was born, Lucy sent him a letter dripping with recrimination.

> Is my Harry well. Is he happy? No, that cannot be when he reflects how wretched he has left me. I doubt not, but the plea of his little girl as he used to call me, must sometimes draw a thought from him tho surrounded with gaiety and scenes of high life. The remembrance of his tender infant must also greatly affect him when he considers it at so great a distance from his father, its natural guardian in a place exposed to an enraged enemy and almost defenseless.[2]

Lucy had not been happy for some time. She was a large woman and the pregnancy only exacerbated her condition. Abigail Adams said, "Her size is enormous, I am frightened when I look at her."[3] Around the army camp she had tried to dress the part of the lady, regaling in fashion among the homespun creations of the Continental soldiers, but this only made her stand out more. Dr. Manasseh Cutler, the army chaplain, wrote that her hair was piled "up at least a foot high, much in the form of a churn bottom upward, and topped off with a wire skeleton in the same form, covered with black gauze, which hangs in streamers down her back. Her hair behind is a large braid confined in a monstrous crooked comb."[4] It was actually "the modish pouf newly popularized by Marie-Antoinette," but this made her all the more incongruous among the rugged frontiersman.[5] And now she had received a letter that said Henry was coming to see her and then leaving again for Fort Ticonderoga.

Boston meanwhile had been steadily ravaged by looters, including Henry's beloved London Bookstore. His brother William Knox slipped out of Boston in October to join the army. Knox tried to secure his brother a commission, mentioning it to General Washington and General Lee, who assured him that there would be no difficulties. Henry preferred to have his brother in the artillery with him.

William now rode behind Henry for the journey to Fort Ticonderoga along with forty-two militiamen. The food for the journey consisted of George Washington's requirement for each soldier: "One and a half pounds of flour or bread, one pound beef or fish or ¾ pound of pork, and one gill of whiskey or spirit or one and half pounds flour, one half pound pork or bacon, one half pint of peas or beans and one gill of whiskey."[6] The soldiers usually slept six to a tent and created a "mess," or eating unit. The $1,000 Henry carried was to purchase provisions and to hire the necessary teamsters and oxen to ferry the cannons back to Boston. Henry planned to stop in New York along the way and purchase supplies for the army there.

Washington had ordered Major General Schuyler to assist Knox in any way he could. Originally promoted for the Canadian campaign, Schuyler was technically the commander of the northern Continental Army headquartered in upstate New York and responsible for the army from Canada to New York City and western Massachusetts. George Washington had hatched a plan to attack the British in the Canadian city of Quebec using two different points of attack. The first army followed the St. Lawrence River, and the second approached through what is today Maine.

The campaign against the British in Canada proved a disaster. Benedict Arnold commanded a regiment of Connecticut militiamen and reached Quebec from the south, while Schuyler and General Richard Montgomery were to sail up the Hudson past Fort Ticonderoga, attacking garrisons along the St. Lawrence River. Washington's plan culminated in Schuyler and Arnold joining up in Quebec to attack the city. Nothing went right. Schuyler became ill and handed off command to Montgomery and then went to Albany to run the logistics of the campaign. On December 1, the Americans were repulsed, and Montgomery was fatally wounded. Arnold took over and fought a rearguard action, retreating from the city. This news was yet another blow to Washington, who thought Quebec lightly defended. But in a strange irony, the failed Canadian campaign enabled General Schuyler to assist Knox.

Schuyler supplied Arnold's army with food and provisions using teamsters and oxen to move the bulk of the war materials. Utilizing teamsters or wagon wranglers who used sleds, horses, and oxen to haul the cannons would be the heart of the Knox expedition. Besides being involved in the eventual procurement of animals and teamsters, Schuyler also performed a more important task: protecting Knox's convoy from Indian attack.

For the Canadian campaign, Schuyler had established peace with the Iroquois Indians, who had sided with the British against the French. The general invited the chiefs to Albany and had signed peace treaties ensuring that Iroquois would allow the rebels attacking Quebec as well as the Knox expedition to pass unmolested.

This was no small thing. The atrocities on both sides were horrific. According to the 1775 Phips Proclamation in Massachusetts, King George III of Britain called for "subjects to embrace all opportunities of pursuing, capturing, killing and destroying all and every of the aforesaid Indians."[7] The colonists had obliged, and Indian men, women, and children were massacred to make room for expanding settlements. Conversely, the Indians would strike with vengeance, raping women, burning colonists alive, burying men up to their waists with their own genitalia in their mouths. The men of the Knox expedition would have been an easy mark for the Indians were it not for Schuyler's negotiations.

The Knox brothers and the militiamen traveled on horseback along the New England roads with the trees already ripped bare by brisk November winds, reminding Knox of the deep winter they would soon face. They were to stop first in Worchester, where Knox would see Lucy. Snow was already falling. The Amherst Road they followed was like many roads during colonial times: trails that had been widened slightly to accommodate horses and wagons. The truth was that most people didn't travel in 1775. Travel was dangerous, expensive, and done primarily by government officials. Henry Knox was not unusual in never having left the town in which he was born.

After Worchester, Knox would proceed to New York City to requisition what they could for the army before heading into the wilderness and Fort George on the south end of Lake George. From there they would cross the lake to Fort Ticonderoga, retrieve the artillery, turn around their train of oxen and horses, and haul the cannons back to Boston. Knox had optimistically written Lucy that it was "a three week's journey," intimating that he would be back soon after. He would do the same with Washington, predicting a speedy month-long journey.

Optimism might have been a necessary personality trait for anyone attempting to bring back heavy cannons across frozen Lake George, the Hudson and

Mohawk Rivers, and more importantly, the Berkshire mountains. The mountains were a southern continuation of the Green Mountains of Vermont, extending from the Housatonic and Hoosic River valleys in western Massachusetts to the Connecticut River valley in northcentral Massachusetts and to the foot of the lower Westfield River valley in southcentral Massachusetts. Henry Knox would have to drag the cannons up and over an elevation of 2,841 feet. Knox, having never left Boston, had no idea what lay ahead, but for now he had a personal mountain to climb as he entered Worchester on November 20 to say good-bye to his pregnant wife.

It was there Knox began to keep a diary of logistical entries interspersed with impressions of the land he traversed. On November 20, he wrote, "Paid Miller of Worcester to leave with his wife two seven dollar one six-dollar continental bill."[8] Knox added members to his caravan as he needed them, and Miller was a man he would use for "expresses"—hand-delivered messages—among other things. Miller was a hearty man who was not afraid to brave the wilderness to deliver Knox's communications. Knox left the equivalent of $20 with Miller's wife for her husband's services.

Henry intended to bring back the cannons the same way he had learned to shoot a cannon: by reading up on it and then simply doing it. He had no concrete idea about how to haul sixty tons of iron to Concord, Massachusetts, using sleds, oxen, and teamsters. Knox's brash, can-do spirit was beginning to wear Lucy down. It had begun to dawn on her that she was now married to a military man who would be largely absent from her life for the duration of the war. To be sure, Henry invoked the "cause of liberty" to his wife's complaints as he explained his mission. She undoubtedly questioned how he would transport the cannons across lakes and rivers and through mountains in the dead of winter. She stared disbelievingly as her husband again reassured her: "Don't be afraid, there is no fighting in the case. I am going on business only."[9] And had he any training in moving such cannons? None. Perhaps he then outlined his journey north to her. From Worchester he would go to New York City, then Albany, entering New York state, on to Half Moon, Stillwater, then Saratoga, and, passing Glens Falls, he would arrive at Fort George.

He would cross Lake George to Fort Ticonderoga (hopefully it would not be frozen yet), then he would sail up a small river to the fort. He would procure the cannons and return with them on the lake (if it had not frozen) in various boats (which he did not possess) and then transfer them to sleds and oxen (of which he had none). If there was snow (which there was not), he would reverse his journey and haul the thousands of pounds of iron and brass along roads and trails across the Hudson River (praying the river was solidly frozen under five-thousand-pound cannons) four times. He would then climb the sheer Berkshire mountains (God willing) and continue across the frozen wilderness of Massachusetts (if there was snow), back through Worchester, and on to Cambridge, where he would deliver it to His Excellency George Washington—that is, if they weren't attacked by Indians, the British, or Loyalists and as long as they didn't freeze or drown, should a lake or river give way under the thousands of pounds of iron cannons.

Lucy, staring at Knox in the flickering candlelight, recognized that this bordered on insanity, even for a man like Knox known for his volubility, his bluster, his overpromising. Nonetheless, a day later he waved to his pregnant wife from astride his horse, heading off to save the American cause at Boston. Lucy Knox, who had known no hardship during her life until her marriage to the man disappearing into the stark, early winter landscape, must have considered whom she really married, a man whose fortunes were now tied forever to the American Revolution, win or lose.

9

ON TO NEW YORK AND ALBANY

November 20, 1775

The Continental Congress made Henry Knox the chief of the artillery for the Continental Army. Knox's biggest booster, John Adams, ensured that his predecessor, Colonel Gridley—whose age and health had impaired his abilities, leaving many to doubt whether he could create an artillery branch out of whole cloth where none existed—would step aside as chief of the artillery. The twenty-five-year-old with his head bent against the cold, riding along the Albany road that at times seemed to disappear into a white void, had no idea he was now the commander of the artillery of the Continental Army.

It was here that Knox and his party "while passing though Marlboro, Massachusetts . . . were caught in the most violent northeastern storm he had ever seen."[1] Driving rain, snow, and wind combined with plummeting temperatures to force the men to hunker down. This proved to be just a taste of the forbidding winter of 1775 that awaited them. British sailors introduced to northeasters in Boston were in awe of the power of the winter storm.

> This sort of storm is so severe that it cannot even be looked against, and by the snow freezing as fast as it falls, baffles all resistance—for the blocks become chocked, the tackle encrusted, the ropes and sails quite congealed, and the whole ship before long one cake of ice. . . . The sentinel on shore is frequently found frozen to death upon his post, though relieved every half hour.[2]

The men emerged from the storm soaked and chilled to the bone. Henry Knox's diary survives as a crumbling, yellowed book of parchment with almost indecipherable script. His initial entries marked the date and distance of their progress in the shaky script of a quill pen. Henry Knox had never left Boston, but he cannot be faulted for writing so little, as he was enthralled to be headed for New York. There is a bit of the wanderlust in his later entries.

> Nov 20 Went from Westchester to go to New York, Reached Western that night 38 mi[les].
> Nov 21 From Western to Hartford 44
> 22 from Hartford to New Haven 40
> 23 from New Haven to Fairfield 28
> 24 from Fairfield to Kingsbridge 56
> 25 from Kingsbridge to New York 14[3]

The Knox expedition moved swiftly without sleds, oxen, or cannons to slow them down. They reached New York on November 25. Colonel Alexander McDougal of the First New York Regiment met them, and Knox presented his letters from Washington identifying him as an "an experienced engineer" and requesting any artillery that could be spared. Like Knox, McDougal had been a merchant before the war and had a small store. He promised to meet with the New York Provincial Congress to request the heavy cannons but agreed to send smaller cannons with shells and ammunition. In a letter sent later from Fort George on December 5, Knox gave Washington a report on the New York trip:

> May it please your Excellency,
> I arrived here last Saturday morning and immediately made inquiry whether Col. Read had done anything in the business with which I was charged—I found that his stay had been short during which time the Committee that sat during the recess of the Congress could not be gotten together so that he went away without being able to forward the business in the least. Yesterday the Committee met and after having considered your excellency's letter to them Col. McDougal waited upon me and gave such reasons for not complying with the requisition of the heavy cannon. . . . He has promised me that he will use his upmost influence in the Congress which meets tomorrow and has no doubt of success, that 12 exceedingly good Iron 4 pounders with a Quantity of Shells and shot shall be sent to Camp immediately and also he promised the loan of two fine brass six pounders cast in a foundry in this city.[4]

Knox had secured some cannons from McDougal, and although it wasn't what Washington wanted, it was the best they could do for now. To say that Knox was on a scavenging mission for the army would not be untrue. He continued exploring in New York and discovered a foundry that might be used to cast cannons. On November 27 he let Washington know of the new foundry. "I very sincerely wish your excellency have been acquainted with this circumstance and charged me with a commission to have a number cast for the camp. . . . If you should think proper to have some done and will give orders to Colonel McDougal or some other gentlemen of this city—the foundry will execute one in two days after he shall receive the orders—and in any number in proportion."[5]

The lack of foundries in America was of concern. The Americans simply had no way to produce cannons to fight the British, so Knox's excitement at finding a foundry is understandable. Washington had hoped that he might shortcut Knox's mission if McDougal could spare some of his big guns. Henry wrote Washington that McDougal "gave such reasons for not complying with the requisition for the heavy cannons as would not be prudent to put it on paper."[6] More than likely, McDougal did not want to leave New York vulnerable by shifting her guns to Boston. He knew that New York was the next target for the British. This meant that George Washington, who needed big guns to shell the British ships in the harbor and Boston, would be dependent on the cannons Knox brought back from Fort Ticonderoga.

Knox was in awe of the city. He later wrote Lucy his first impressions of New York:

> New York is a place where I think in General the homes are better than in Boston. They are generally of brick and three stories high with the largest kind of windows. Their churches are grand, their colleges and workhouses and hospitals most excellently situated and exceedingly commodious. Their principal streets much wider than ours. The people—why the people are magnificent in their equipages which are numerous in their house furnishings which is fine. In their pride and conceit which are inimitable, in their profaneness which is intolerable, in their want of principal which is prevalent. In their Toryism which is insufferable for which they must repent in dust and ashes.[7]

Henry Knox, the Boston bookseller, interpreted New York as a more Tory-dominated town than Boston. Boston was a hotbed of patriots committed to the glorious cause. But the country was nearly evenly divided between those who wanted to break with the mother country and those who wanted to reconcile with her. The fight at Boston was crucial for the wavering colonies that had not sent representatives to the Continental Congress and were waiting instead to see which way the revolutionary winds would blow.

Knox left New York on November 28 and headed for Albany. His diary tracked his progress again:

28 Left New York the Tuesday following and reached Crapton's Ferry 39½ miles
29 from Crapton's Ferry to Poughkeepsie 44
30 From Poughkeepsie to Livingston Manor 40
Dec 1 From Livingston Manor to Albany 40 miles
2 Stayed at Albany[8]

Knox arrived in Albany on December 1. He was so impressed by the city that he prophesized that "Albany from its situation, commanding the lakes and immense territories westward must one day be, if not the Capitol yet nearly to it of America."[9] Knox didn't meet General Schuyler, whom Washington had sent to Fort Ticonderoga to take inventory for Knox. Knox assumed he would bump into Schuyler on his journey northward. Schuyler wanted to ensure that the cannons would be safely transported to the Continental Army, which desperately needed them. Although Knox had undoubtedly read up on how to transport heavy artillery, Schuyler had done it—and what's more, he had just the man to head up the job: teamster John Becker Sr.

General Schuyler and John Becker knew how to transport sixty tons of iron and brass across frozen lakes, rivers, and mountains. The truth was that Henry Knox would depend on Schuyler and others to deliver the cannons he had promised Washington. He had no real contacts of his own and only vaguely understood the use of oxen and horses to haul heavy equipment. The controversy among historians regarding whether Knox used primarily oxen or horses to haul the cannons starts here. Oxen clearly had some advantages. They could pull heavier loads longer than horses. The sheer weight to be hauled dictated oxen as a first choice. However, throughout the journey, fresh horses and oxen would be substituted as animals gave out, which made the composition of the expedition a hybrid. The bearded teamster John Becker recommended that sleds and oxen be used to do the heavy lifting to drag the cannons. "The sleds were vital to Becker and his teamsters to transport the heavy guns back to Cambridge."[10] He had worked with General Schuyler before, moving freight for the colonial army, and proved to be a godsend for Henry Knox. Becker had the hands-on experience Knox lacked. "Becker was a vital contributor to Knox's success because he was the subject matter expert on animal transport, carpentry, and was the single point of contact for all the teamsters joining Knox's expedition. . . . [The term] teamster was used interchangeably for the modern day contractor who worked exclusively with animal push cart wagons."[11]

Becker already had proved his worth to Schuyler many times while moving freight. John Becker Sr. hailed from the New York area; his son John Becker Jr. would accompany his father and keep a detailed journal. Later, when he was in his sixties, the younger Becker would write an account of moving the cannons through the wilderness for an Albany newspaper. His journal impressions at age twelve would come down through the ages as one of the few primary sources for the Knox expedition:

> The year of my birth was that of the introduction of the stamp act," he wrote fifty years later. "What advantage a piece of paper possessed, because it bore certain marks upon it, more than any other piece without them, seemed quite a problem with the honest yeomanry of the day. . . . My father told me that I had commenced my career in a stormy period, and that the unsettled times, would probably have an injurious effect upon my prospects.[12]

Becker Jr recounted his father's participation in the French and Indian War and the moment, years later, when the town received the news of the battle of Lexington. "I will remember, notwithstanding my youth, the impressive manner with which in my hearing, my father told my uncle, that blood had been shed at Lexington."[13] He also recounted the connection to General Philip Schuyler:

> The startling intelligence spread like fire among the congregation . . . after the morning discourse was finished and the people were dismissed, we gathered around General Philip Schuyler for further information. He was the oracle of our neighborhood. We looked up to him with a feeling of respect and affection. . . . He confirmed the intelligence already received and expressed his belief that an important crisis had arrived which must sever us forever from the parent country.[14]

John Becker Sr. was a patriot to the cause, and this surely influenced his decision to assist in the hauling of the cannons. However, he had no illusions about what the colonies were up against by fighting Britain. "I remember afterwards hearing my father remark, that among the most influential and the best educated part of the community great anxiety was felt as to the termination of the struggle, for a conviction seemed to prevail that we were unable to sustain ourselves against the armies and navies of England."[15]

When war broke out, Becker Sr. was elected captain of the local militia but declined citing a lack of experience "for a station involving so much responsibility." His son also began to see the hardships that would ensue when "the drum and fife resounded on all sides, and persons of reflection began to consider the consequences that would follow an appeal to arms."[16]

Becker Sr. eventually took on the job of moving the cannons and "would be the head contractor in charge of the 45 men (teamsters he would use for the journey)."[17] It was in Albany that a firm plan for moving the cannons was established between Schuyler and Becker:

> Becker preferred to move heavy equipment over rough terrain on either wagons, or sleds, drawn by yoked oxen. On rough terrain he had teams of carpenters create a system of ropes and pulleys to pull the heavy loads up and then used them to prevent the equipment from running out of control when moving downhill. This system explains why additional men were needed to conduct the movement. This procedure took a long time and was exhausting work, but it was work Becker knew how to do.[18]

Henry Knox would have to trust Becker and Schuyler, as he knew nothing of moving heavy equipment. It was determined that eighty oxen would be required and forty-two sleds. In 1775, two oxen were harnessed to a single yoke to drag farm equipment or, more commonly, plows. Schuyler and Becker would round up the sleds and oxen while Knox continued northward to Fort Ticonderoga. Confusion regarding when and how these sleds and oxen were to be delivered led Knox to talk to others about procuring sleds and the draft animals, as well.

General Schuyler clearly took the lead on the main logistical problem of Knox's expedition: how to move what would be 120,000 pounds of artillery. No mechanized component existed to assist the men, so Schuyler and Becker devised a plan in which sleds on runners pulled by horse or oxen would transport the cannons, some of which weighed 5,000 pounds.

But this plan required snow. If there was no snow, the rough, rutted roads would be virtually impassable. General Schuyler might have harbored doubts about the heavyset young man who came to move the lifeblood of the revolutionary army three hundred miles through mountains and across frozen lakes and rivers. Schuyler and Becker had known each other for years, and most recently had been handling logistics for the campaign in Canada. The men would take Knox under their wings in order to ensure—to the best that they were able—the success of his mission. But this is all still to come; now Knox had to get to Fort George.

On December 3, 1775, Knox's expedition left Albany. His party, according to Major Thomas M. Campeau's *Noble Train of Artillery*, had doubled in size. Schuyler already had headed for Fort Ticonderoga, so the question is, how did Knox learn of Becker and Schuyler's plan to move the cannons? He had picked up additional teamsters who would assist with the oxen and sleds. We can only speculate that some intermediary informed Henry—since he was well aware by now—of the number of sleds and oxen the expedition would require. Knox, his colorful trademark scarf wrapped around his left hand, waved his men on. He was ready to recover his cannons and headed straight north. He would later write Lucy, "We shall cut no small figure in going through the country with our cannon, mortars and drawn by eighty yoke oxen!"[19]

This was pure Knox.

10

WASHINGTON ON ICE

December 2, 1775

One cannot blame George Washington for jumping up and down in frustration on the ice of Back Bay. Enlistments in the American army were due to expire on January 1, and he wanted to strike a blow while Henry Knox journeyed to Fort Ticonderoga. He would have to cut down thousands of trees to keep his troops warm through winter and the "paymaster did not have a dollar in hand."[1] His inexperienced soldiers, "dragged from the tender scenes of domestic life," were, in his view, "unaccustomed to the din of war."[2]

The general of the American army might have been throwing a tantrum. He was frustrated. He had sent Henry Knox to retrieve the cannons from Fort Ticonderoga on November 16 but had not heard from him. His army had dwindled to thirty-five hundred with no end in sight as enlistments expired. He had no gunpowder to speak of and he had just received news of the disaster at Quebec. It was worse than believed. Washington ordered the attack to eliminate threat from the northern border, but things went badly from the start. Washington was so confident of a victory that he had instructed Benedict Arnold and General Montgomery to "forward blankets, clothing, and other military stores captured in the conquered city."[3] It was Washington's first campaign as commander of the army, and he looked forward to a quick feather in his cap. Arnold's trek through the Maine wilderness toward Canada quickly turned into an endurance test. The army was "slowed by heavy rains, swollen streams, and fierce rapids. Starving troops devoured soap and candles and gnawed on boiled moccasins."[4]

The weakened army finally reached Quebec and met General Montgomery's army. With enlistments soon to expire in the twelve-hundred-man army, the attack commenced, and the heavily fortified British stopped the colonials cold with cannon fire and volleys of timed musket barrages. The Americans lost four hundred men; British casualties were minor. Washington was devastated when he received General Schuyler's letter. "I wish I had no occasion to send my dear general this melancholy account."[5] This was a severe setback for the new general: his first offensive failed miserably and his own war council held no confidence in his plans to attack the British. Vexed, Washington went down to Back Bay to see if the ice had formed sufficiently to permit troops to move across it. His valet Billy Lee held the reins of his horse while Washington jumped up and down. He had written earlier to his adjutant Reed, pouring out his thoughts:

> I have often thought how much happier I should have been if, instead of accepting of a command under such circumstances, I had taken my musket upon my shoulders and entered the ranks, or, if I could have justified the measure to posterity and my own conscience, had retired to the back country, and lived in a wigwam. If I shall be able to rise superior to these and many other difficulties which might be enumerated, I shall most religiously believe that the finger of Providence is in it, to blind the eyes of our enemies; for surely if we get well through this month, it must be for their want of knowing the disadvantages we labor under.[6]

Washington was convinced that General Howe would attack once he learned of the weakened state of the American army. In fact, Howe did know of Washington's disadvantages from the steady stream of deserters joining the British army. But Howe saw no advantage to attacking in winter when reinforcements were on the way that would clearly overwhelm the rebels. Glimmers of terrorizing the colonial populace crept into the British strategy to subdue the rebellious colonies as the British shelled the towns in Massachusetts after warning inhabitants to evacuate their homes. The British army incinerated three hundred homes, causing Washington to reflect to General Schuyler in a letter that the British had "acted with every circumstance of cruelty and barbarity which revenge, and malice would suggest."[7]

Frustrated, Washington received congressional approval to arm colonial vessels with an enticement of a booty of one-third the value of whatever the privateers captured. "Before long six such ships, dubbed 'George Washington's Navy,' prowled the Eastern Seaboard marking the birth of the U.S. Navy."[8] In late November Washington's Navy hit pay dirt.

The British brig *Nancy* was captured with two thousand arms and accompanying ammunition, which Washington called an "instance of divine favor."[9] In the hold of the ship was a store of material that would have made Henry Knox very happy. There was "3,000 round shot for 12 pounders, 4,000 shot for 6 pounders, 10,500 flints, 2,000 muskets and 31 tons of musket shot."[10] It was an astounding infusion of war supplies.

The general demanded the new sailors to behave as impeccably as his soldiers. Invoking his own sense of honor, Washington instructed the privateers, "whatever prisoners you may take, you are to take with kindness and humanity as far as it is consistent with your own safety."[11] With nothing else to do but watch the British, Washington took on the issue of excessive drinking. The problem was a rum quota that was recognized as a means of keeping up the men's spirits, especially in an attack. Washington wrote John Hancock: "benefits arising from moderate use of liquor have been experienced in all armies and not to be disputed."[12] Still, he handed out lashes many times for public drunkenness.

In addition to the war for independence, Washington also understood he was in a public relations battle with the British. Many Americans did not support a break from Britain, and many of the colonies watched events in Boston to see if the winds of change would blow the way of independence. For this reason, there could be no abuses on the part of his army with the citizenry, and Washington was merciless to men who stole or looted homes. One man was "to receive thirty-nine lashes upon his bare back" for stealing some cheese.[13]

Still, all the good public relations in the world achieved nothing without adequate enlistment. By the end of November, Washington was down to thirty-five hundred men, and he wrote his brother, "No man, I believe, ever had a greater choice of difficulties and less means to extricate himself from them."[14] Soldiers abandoned his army for bounties promised by state militias. Washington couldn't compete as he had no money in the coffers to pay any of his soldiers.

There was no turning back, but there was no offensive, either. The only bright spot for Washington at this time was the arrival of Martha Washington on December 11. Realizing he couldn't return to his beloved Mount Vernon in October, Washington sent for Martha to join him in Cambridge. Like Lucy Knox, Martha Washington was stressed by the separation from her husband and the uncertainty of the outcome of the war. The trip from Virginia to Cambridge would take almost a month, and the dutiful husband had left the decision up to his wife. "I have laid a state of the difficulties . . . which must attend the journey before her and left it to her own choice," he wrote to his brother Jack.[15]

Martha put off the trip until November 17, 1775—the same day Henry Knox departed—then finally piled into the carriage to join her husband in Cambridge. "She traveled luxuriously; her clothing packed in elegant leather trunks studded with brass nails. She brought along five household slaves tricked out in the livery of Mount Vernon. On this arduous northward journey, Martha discovered her sudden elevation in the world and that she had left obscurity behind forever."[16]

When she finally reached Cambridge and joined her husband, Martha quickly adopted to camp life. She was instrumental in canceling a ball to which she had been invited that she viewed as too lavish and instead took out her needles and began knitting socks for the soldiers. Washington had to entertain many visiting dignitaries and Martha relieved him of social responsibilities by offering "oranges and wine to guests and heartier fare for midafternoon meals."[17] Martha was not a highly educated woman herself, yet she could win over cultured, educated women who came calling. Mercy Otis Warren, a "prolific bluestocking who wrote poems, plays, and histories," visited with Martha and later told Abigail Adams, "I took a ride to Cambridge and waited on Mrs. Washington at 11 o'clock where I was received with that politeness and respect shown in the first interview among the well-bred and with the ease and cordiality of friendship of a much earlier date."[18]

George Washington wasn't a man with close friends; there were few with whom he could unveil his private fears about the course of the war. Martha could take the edge off. "Mrs. Washington is excessively fond of the General and he of her. . . . They are happy in each other," Nathaniel Greene wrote his wife.[19] Martha put on no airs and was affable to soldiers and officers alike. Mary Warren wrote that her warmth could "soften the hours of private life or . . . sweeten the cares of hero and smooth the rugged pains of war."[20]

The Washingtons' lives had been turned upside down since George had left Mount Vernon the previous May and both were adjusting. The British continued to shell the American camp indiscriminately from Boston, and Martha had to adapt to a world she had never seen before. "I confess I shudder every time I hear the sound of a gun," she wrote to her friend Elizabeth Ramsay, "I have never seen anything of war, the preparations are very terrible indeed. But I endeavor to keep my fears to myself as well as I can."[21]

The Washingtons loved to share humorous moments. Eighteen-year-old Joseph White came to headquarters for orders from Washington, having adopted the fake rank of an officer. Washington smelled the ruse and asked White, "Pray sir, what officer are you?" The eighteen-year-old claimed to be an assistant adjutant in the artillery regiment. Washington raised his eyebrows. "Indeed . . . you are very young to do that duty." White didn't miss a beat and responded, "I am young, but am growing older every day."[22] White later said that Washington turned to his wife and both smiled.

George Washington needed the release of humor. America wavered in the balance, many considering the price paid for independence from Britain as too high. An article appearing in the *New England Chronicle* signed by "A Freeman" laid out the argument for independence and freedom. The article took aim at Washington's troops, whose enlistments were expiring with many electing to go home.

> Never was a cause more important or glorious than that which you are engaged in, not only your wives, your children, and distant posterity, but humanity at large, the world of mankind, are interested in it, for if tyranny should prevail in this great country, we may expect liberty will expire throughout the world. Therefore, more human glory and happiness may depend upon your exertions than ever yet depended upon any of the sons of men. . . . We expect soon to break off all kind of connection with Britain and form into a Grand Republic of the American United Colonies, which will, by the blessing of heaven, soon work out our salvation, and perpetuate the liberties, increase the wealth, the power and the glory of this Western World.[23]

But of eleven regiments, or about ten thousand men, only a thousand had agreed to stay on and reenlist. George Washington had to do something soon or all could be lost through nothing more than attrition. Washington jumped up and thundered down on the ice again in Back Bay. It was frozen, but he noticed long slender cracks rippling out in every direction. Like the American Revolution, its commander was indeed on thin ice.

FORT GEORGE

December 4, 1775

The man on whom George Washington was depending was now leading his men north. Historians are divided about exactly how Knox traveled to Fort Ticonderoga and with whom. The version that seems to be accepted by most historians today suggests that he and his brother William left Albany and headed north with the militiamen. Another version had William and Henry picking up another forty-five teamsters in Albany through the efforts of Schuyler and Becker. According to a third version, Knox left Albany at the head of oxen, men, and sleds: "On the 5th of December, with General Schuyler remaining in Albany, Knox's complete party of 90 men, 80 yoked oxen, 42 empty sleds, and supplies for both men and animals left for Halfmoon, New York"[1]

The famous painting by Tom Lovell depicts the latter version of Knox's expedition traversing the Berkshire mountains. In the painting, the oxen pull the sleds, with militiamen on each side and an officer on horseback whom we can presume to be Henry Knox. The oxen are two to a yoke, which was standard for the time, and the cannons are disassembled, with their carriages also on sleds. This version is accurate insomuch as this is how the train of artillery *eventually* will be transported. And for the purposes of a story, the last version is the neatest and easiest to handle for both reader and writer.

The truth is that Knox picked up some teamsters in Albany through Schuyler and Becker, but the oxen still had to be rounded up and the sleds built. Forty-two sleds capable of hauling thousands of pounds of iron and floating across rivers and lakes weren't just laying around. Nor were eighty head of oxen. The number of oxen and sleds required didn't come out of the air but was determined by Schuyler, and Knox repeated them in his letters. Knox did not speak with Schuyler, but he did speak with someone who informed him that eighty oxen and forty-two sleds would be required. Who this person might have been has been lost to history. Nonetheless, there's an expectation that oxen and sleds will be delivered to Fort George when Knox returned with the cannons over Lake George.

Knox's journey was undeniably serendipitous, mirroring his own personality. There was no road map for his expedition; he had to make it up as he went along. General Schuyler and Becker were experienced in moving freight, but Knox's mission differed logistically. The cannons were being transported a great distance, and the five-thousand-pound cannons required new methods of hauling over mountains, frozen lakes, and rivers. It would take time to bring all this together: men, sleds, oxen, and horses. Henry Knox apparently left Albany with a vague promise of the oxen and sleds. It makes sense that teamsters would join Knox's party at this point and the sleds and oxen would follow.

Knox and his men headed north along the Hudson River for Halfmoon, New York. The cold and wind were brutal with snow slowing their progress. "At Halfmoon the group had to cross the Mohawk River over its small bridge. This bridge would not be used on the return trip as it could not support the cannons."[2] Here, another substantial snowstorm hit, and the men had to fight their way through blinding snow and wind, following old trading trails used by Indians and fur traders. These roads were often only muddy paths in the forest.

Twelve-year-old John Becker Jr.'s account of traveling these roads with his father to transport goods from Fort George and Fort Ticonderoga offers an impression of what it was like to travel in 1775:

> The weather was cold and disagreeable; the roads were very bad and the whole business to me vexatious. A luckless urchin I considered myself, to be thus perched on top of a wagon, jolted to death, with the air penetrating to my very vitals. Yet, we traveled at the rate of twenty miles a day and after bestowing our cargo at Albany, we turned our faces towards Saratoga and our own firesides. Ere we arrived a snowstorm commenced and covered the ground to a depth of several inches.[3]

Knox's own diary centers on mileage and dates:

Dec 3 Rode from Albany to Saratoga 35
Dec 4 Set out about 10 o'clock from Saratoga to Fort George, 30 miles which
    place we reached at 2 o'clock.[4]

At this point, events become murky, throwing into doubt Schuyler and Becker's promise of sleds and oxen. On the way north, Knox acted on his own to procure sleds and oxen, stopping in the town of Stillwater. Retired Colonel William L. Browne in his book, *Ye Cohorn Caravan*, writes, "It also becomes clear in later correspondence that Knox first discussed the arrangements for strong sleds and draft animals with George Palmer in Stillwater on this trip north, although he made no mention of it in his diary at this time."[5] The truth was that even with teamster Becker stepping in to orchestrate, Knox still felt that it was up to him to procure the sleds and oxen for the cannons and was isolated from any communication except for "expresses," messenger-borne missives sent back and forth across the wilderness.

Knox and his men fought through the storm until they saw the outlines of Fort George. The fort sat on the southern end of Lake George. This would be the staging area for the cannons, where they would be loaded onto the waiting sleds and oxen. Knox and his men reached the fort on December 4 at 2:00 p.m. and realized it was too late to attempt to cross the thirty-eight miles of open lake to reach Ticonderoga. Knox decided to stay the night in the fort and set off in the morning.

John Becker Jr., the teamster's son, described the fort as

> a post which was designed by Colonel Montresor and called his Folly. I shall not in this place describe it but of the garrison of which this detachment had been a part, I would mention that they were downright oddities. Their blue coats with white flarings were tarnished by the smoke of the pine knots which it was the fashion to use in the double capacity of fire and candle. A more somber family I think I never saw.[6]

These remote forts, such as Fort George and Ticonderoga, quickly became outposts of endurance for their inhabitants. Often not resupplied for months, the isolation, long winters, lack of fresh food, scurvy, and sickness turned some of these eighteenth-century forts into enclaves resembling prisoner-of-war camps. Knox found himself in a one-room cabin, where he sat down and wrote a letter to Lucy the next day. He huddled near the smoky fireplace, adjusting the tallow candle on its rickety table, and blew on his fingers, writing with cold ink blotting from his quill. Fort George was not warm, and Knox wrote his wife, whom he hadn't seen for a week straight since the war began, blowing continually on his fingers to warm them.

> My dear Lucy,
> I arrived here yesterday. I shall go this day over Lake George to Ticonderoga—
> I have been exceedingly well since I left you—I have in God you keep up your

spirits and are in perfect health. I am now in the greatest hurry; the battle's waiting for me. Having an opportunity to write to General Washington by General
Schuyler, I took this opportunity to the dearest object of my affections—believe I
think continually of you. God preserve you.[7]

The interesting point is that Knox gave the letter to General Schuyler, who
just returned from Fort Ticonderoga. Schuyler, who was heading south, would
deliver Knox's letter to someone who would then get it to Lucy. Here by the
flickering fire was also where Knox met Lieutenant John Andre, who was being
taken south in a prisoner exchange between the armies. The fur trading trails
were common routes used to bring prisoners from the northern forts of Crown
Point and Ticonderoga. John Becker Jr. and his father not only freighted cargo
but prisoners as well. The boy wrote of bringing two Indians and a Frenchman
from the British Fort Crown Point:

> On our return a Frenchman and two Indians were placed under our care. They
> had been taken prisoners, and for some purposes or other were sent down to
> Albany. The Indians were very sulky. They could not speak the English language
> and appeared unwilling to make any attempt. The Frenchman claims a place in
> my memory, from being one of the lowest class of habitants as well as the filthiest.[8]

Andre, the captured British soldier, was a member of the British Seventh
Regiment stationed at Fort Chambly on the Sorel River in Canada. Knox and
the young man hit it off, discovering a common love of literature, politics, philosophy. It was as if he was back in London Bookstore discussing the topics of
the day. Knox was careful not to discuss his mission with the prisoner, but to
find someone well-versed in the middle of the wilderness was a tonic to the vol-
uble Knox. They lay before the fire all night talking and parted in the morning
with feelings of high respect if not mutual admiration. In a surprising turnabout,
five years later Knox would sit on a court-martial that would sentence Andre to
hang for his association with Benedict Arnold as a British spy. Such were the
ironies of war, which placed duty many times over one's personal feelings.

At some point on December 5, Knox wrote George Washington of his progress thus far and about meeting General Schuyler:

Fort George Dec. 5, 1775
May it please your Excellency
I arrived here yesterday and immediately got ready to go over the lake this
morning but General Schuyler arriving here before day prevents my going for an
hour or two. He has given me a list of those stores on the other side from which I

am enabled to send inventory of which I intend to forward to camp—the Garrison is too weak at Ticonderoga the conveyance from the fort to the landing so indifferent and the passage across the lake so precarious that I am afraid it will be ten days at least before I can get them on this side of the lake—when they are here the Conveyance from here will depend entirely on the sledding—if that is good they shall immediately move forward—without good sledding the roads are so much gullied it will be impossible to move a sled—General Schuyler will do everything possible to forward this business.[9]

So, what can we conclude from this letter? "Knox was awakened by Schuyler's arrival and certainly its wording suggests that he has received the latest information on weather conditions at Ticonderoga from the General as well as the list from which he could compile the inventory. . . . It implies the general spent most of the night traveling on the lake."[10]

Knox also had been told there was sickness at the fort and anticipated a ten-day round trip to transport the cannons to Fort George. It would seem Schuyler was returning from Ticonderoga with an inventory of supplies listing the cannons and equipment he intended Knox to take back to Massachusetts. General Schuyler was well acquainted with Fort Ticonderoga after using it as a staging area for the failed assault against Quebec in August. He knew firsthand the number of cannons and the shape they were in, and it was here that he clearly informed Knox of his and Becker's plans for the sleds, oxen, and horses. Knox did not tell Schuyler of his earlier meeting with George Palmer about providing oxen and sleds. One can only assume that Knox was still unsure where these sleds and oxen were to come from. Clearly someone had made plans for Knox's oxen and sleds when he wrote to Lucy, "We shall cut no small figure in going through the country with our cannon, mortars and drawn by eighty yoke oxen!"[11] In the final part of the letter, Knox acknowledged that he would be crossing the open lake with thousands of pounds of iron, which, it seemed for the first time, tamped his enthusiasm for the endeavor.

Knox recognized the folly of using sleds to move the cannon should the snow not materialize. He told Washington the men of Fort George were too weak to help him, so he had to use hired men. Henry was ready to cross Lake George, but the nagging questions about the sleds and oxen remained. Apparently, Knox's meeting with George Palmer in the town of Stillwater did result in Palmer's promise to procure the eighty oxen and forty-two sleds. Knox seemed to be playing both ends against the middle by backing his hand with Palmer in case Schuyler didn't come through. The problems Knox encountered in obtaining the sleds and draft animals would ultimately show that Henry Knox's grasp has exceeded his reach.

But for now, December 5, Henry Knox was finally headed for Fort Ticonderoga with the belief that his oxen and sleds somehow would be delivered to Fort George by the time he returned with the cannons transported on boats. Knox and William boarded the boats with a third of his men for the lake crossing. Henry also had hired additional men for the crossing. "Since Fort George had a small port, it was easy for him to hire some local boats and boatmen to take him and his team by water to Fort Ticonderoga. The two men Knox hired were Captain Johnson and his 43 men and Mr. Holmes and his 12 men. These men came from Crown Point which was a port city on Lake Champlain just north of Fort Ticonderoga."[12]

Knox needed men familiar with the lake to get the guns down to Fort George from Fort Ticonderoga. Lake George, also called the Queen of the American Lakes, laid along the direct land route between Albany and Quebec at the southeast base of the Adirondack Mountains. The native Americans originally named the lake Andia-ta-roc, and James Fenimore Cooper called it Horican in his novel *The Last of the Mohicans*. The 196-foot-deep lake extended thirty-two miles, draining into Lake Champlain and the St. Lawrence River basin and eventually the North Atlantic Ocean. The vista that Knox would see on his crossing included Black Mountain, Elephant Mountain, Sugarloaf Mountain, and Sleeping Beauty Mountain. He passed some of the 170 islands that filled the lake, their sizes ranging from the size of a car to miles across.

Though the lake was thirty-two miles as the crow flies, Knox would record thirty-eight miles in his diary. This was more accurate as a straight course was nearly impossible with the islands, wind, and currents. Diane Struble swam the length of Lake George in 1958 and logged forty-one miles. "Knox's boatmen would hug the west shore as the normal lee shore thus avoiding as much adverse wind as possible."[13] If the wind died or turned against them, the only alternative was to row across the wide lake.

On stormy days with whitecaps tipping the waves, the lake resembled an inland ocean. At this point there was little snow, but the temperature was falling and the lake had iced in, leaving an open channel only in the middle. In addition to the thirty-eight-mile sail across the lake in the narrow channel of water, Knox faced a three-mile trek up to the fort itself on Lake Champlain. The danger was that the lake could freeze completely before Knox returned with the cannons.

The small fleet set out in the morning with Knox watching the dark, swollen sky. Ever since Ethan Allen and Benedict Arnold had taken the fort from the British, the guns of Ticonderoga had been a tantalizing key to unlocking Britain's grip on Boston. If the weather cooperated, they could return to Cambridge in three weeks, but this depended on Palmer or Schuyler and Becker delivering the oxen and sleds on time. Knox needed snow for his sleds and worried there might not be any. The roads were too primitive and gullied to drag the sleds without snow, but too much would impede their progress. Right now, Knox had to concentrate on getting the cannons out of Fort Ticonderoga and down into the boats.

Knox procured three different types of boats for transporting the cannons. Gondolas were fifty-five-foot-long scows with "one mast with a sail and were also capable of being propelled by poles when necessary."[14] The most prevalent boat was the flat-bottomed bateau, which was capable of hauling heavy weight. Knox would put the heavy brass cannons on a bateau, since it could carry a five-thousand-pound cannon. The piragua was an oversized canoe capable of carrying weight no more than two thousand pounds. These were not small boats: the gondolas were fifty-five feet long, the bateaux sixty to seventy-five feet, and the piraguas thirty to forty-five feet.

Henry Knox, in the center of his fleet in a piragua, stared out across the snowy icebound lake with a biting wind blurring his eyes. The men rowed out to the center of the water lane to catch the wind. Knox noted with pride that his little armada of forty-five boats filled his line of vision. He wrapped his scarf around his hand and put his hand on William's shoulder. The wind howled down from the north and blurred his eyes again. The sails filled. Knox stood and raised his arms wide, his scarf rippling from his hand. They were on their way to get the cannons of Fort Ticonderoga.

12

FORT TICONDEROGA

December 5, 1775

Ticonderoga comes from the Iroquois word *cheonderoga*, which means "be-tween two waters" or "where the waters meet." The fort built by the French near the south end of Lake Champlain was constructed by a Canadian-born French military engineer, Michel Chartier de Lotbiniere, over a two-year span between 1755 and 1757 during the French and Indian War. The original name of the fort, Carillon, honored a French officer Philippe de Carrion du Fresnoy, who built a trading post in the seventeenth century. The name also was attrib-uted to the rapids of the nearby river, which sounded like the chiming bells of a carillon. Construction was slow, and most of the work was done during the warm months of the year, when troops traveled from Fort St. Frederic and Canada.

The walls were built first, along with the four main bastions. The outer walls were seven feet high and fourteen feet thick and ringed with a dry moat that was five feet deep and fifteen feet wide. The walls were initially constructed of squared wooden timbers with earth between each log, then reinforced with stone from a nearby quarry. The fort was initially armed with cannons brought from Fort St. Frederic and Montreal. There were four storehouses, three bar-racks, and a bakery that could produce sixty loaves of bread a day. A powder magazine was burrowed deep in the bedrock under the center of the main building. On the southern wall a wooden palisade was constructed between the lake shore and the fort. This was the main landing where supplies and troops would enter.

After completion, French General Montcalm criticized the fort's construction, citing the height of the buildings as too tall and easy to hit with cannon, the powder magazine leaked water, and the masonry was poor quality. The real problem was the location: nearby hills overlooked the fort and attackers could lob cannonballs within it. William Nester later studied Ticonderoga, noting its small size for a "Vaunan" style fort with only five hundred feet across and small barracks that could hold only about four hundred soldiers and deemed it hard to defend.

By the time the Americans took Ticonderoga, it had fallen into disrepair with only a skeletal contingent. It wasn't as strategically important to the British as it was during the French and Indian War, when it guarded the principal waterway on Lake George and Lake Champlain. After the Treaty of Paris and the French detonated the powder magazine, the fort slowly fell into disrepair. In 1775 a garrison of British soldiers (two officers and forty-six men) and twenty-five women and children occupied the fort when Ethan Allen and Benedict Arnold stormed in during their early morning raid. Arnold and Allen departed and Ticonderoga was left with a small contingent of sickly men who now watched the strange fleet approach from the ramparts.

John Beck Jr. in his journal described another fort, Crown Point, where he and his father freighted supplies for the Americans. The similarities between the two forts are striking:

> It was a very strong fort, built of stone, with four bastions, a dry ditch, and a covered way to the lake. In the northwest corner of the fort stood the citadel, also built of stone, and in shape an octagon, four stories in height. This was erected on arches and was mounted with 20 pieces of cannon. Around this was also a dry ditch, and the entrance was secured by a drawbridge. The walls were ten feet thick and the roof was shingled. The fort also contained a chapel and several wooden buildings. . . . In 1775 it was quite defenseless with but one sergeant and twelve men.[1]

Henry Knox would later write in his diary, "We set sail from Fort George over the lake about 10 o'clock and having an exceedingly fine passage reached the landing place belonging to Ticonderoga about half past five and immediately went up to the Fort Ticonderoga, 3 miles the length of the lake being 38 miles."[2] The sentries who watched Knox's fleet approach could hardly believe anyone would undertake such a mission in winter. The shores of Lake George were frozen to the middle and large chunks of ice floated in the narrow stream of open water.

Knox sailed to the north end of Lake George and then proceeded up the river three miles to the fort situated on Lake Champlain, guarding the narrow river portage between the two lakes. The two access points were a road to the fort and the river, but Knox's diary entries suggest that the main landing point for the flotilla was on Lake George and not the river. Knox presented his orders from George Washington and General Schuyler. The men of the fort stared at the scraggly, bearded fat man as their disbelief turned into incredulity. Knox needed all the help he could get to transport the cannons and painted a picture of George Washington waiting for the cannons at Boston to dislodge the British. After explaining his mission, Knox headed off to inspect the cannons. What he found was not encouraging.

Most of the 150 cannons were unusable due to years of exposure to the ravages of northern winters. Knox discerned only fifty-nine salvageable cannons and made a quick inventory of what he would transport to Concord. He clambered over the frozen cannons, many of them separated from their disintegrating carriages, rusted and corroded, having not been fired for many years. Knox was anxious. He had to get the cannons to the boat landing before the lake froze over completely. Evidence of Schuyler's work was evident; Knox "began the move so promptly and later reported that the armament was all but removed from mounts and carriages, which would have to be fabricated in Cambridge, indicates that General Schuyler had anticipated him and following his own instructions to be ready to ship what he could afford to lose from the defenses of the fort, ordered the guns to be readied."[3]

Many carriages were shipped along with the cannons, but many of the disintegrating carriages were left behind and would have to be built in Cambridge. Knox's final tally of artillery was extensive, though he dismissed two-thirds of the cannons as unusable. Historian North Callahan notes discrepancies in the number of cannons taken:

> Knox sorted out three score usable pieces, ranging from 4-pound to 24-pound guns as well as howitzers and mortars. Authorities differ as to just how many guns were brought from Ticonderoga: Freeman says 66, Spaulding 55, Perry 78, and the Commonwealth of Massachusetts states in 1925 House Document Number 219, that there were 58 pieces. The inventory of Knox himself, however, sets the number as 59 . . . besides the mortars and howitzers there were in the assembled artillery, some cohorns, which were really a type of small mortar named for their Dutch inventor, Baron van Coehoorn. In general, the artillery pieces ranged from one foot to eleven feet in length from 100 to 5500 pounds in weight.[4]

According to the inventory Henry Knox later would leave with his brother William at Fort George the total weight came to 119,000 pounds.[5] Major Thomas M. Campeau, in his 2015 thesis on the Nobel Train, put the weight much higher using contemporary estimates of comparable cannons, coming in at 150,000 pounds.

BRASS
2 Cohorn—5$\frac{7}{10}$ in. 1,000 lbs. (total)
4 Cohorn—4½ in. 2,000 lbs. (total)
1 Mortar—4½ in. 500 lbs.
8 Cannon—3 Pounder 3$\frac{1}{20}$ in. 4,800 lbs. (total)
3 Cannon—6 Pounder 3$\frac{7}{10}$ in. 5,700 lbs. (total)
1 Cannon—18 Pounder 5½ in. 2,800 lbs.
1 Cannon—24 Pounder 5$\frac{11}{12}$ in. 4,500 lbs.

IRON
Weight 1 Mortar—6½ in. 1,000 lbs.
1 Mortar—10 in. 1,500 lbs.
1 Mortar—10¼ in. 1,500 lbs.
3 Mortar—13 in. 10,500 lbs. (total)
1 Howitzer—8 in. 4,200 lbs.
1 Howitzer—8½ in. 4,400 lbs.
6 Cannon—6 Pounder 3$\frac{7}{10}$ in. 14,400 lbs. (total)
4 Cannon—9 Pounder 4$\frac{6}{10}$ in. 8,400 lbs. (total)
10 Cannon—12 Pounder 4¾ in. 42,000 lbs. (total)
7 Double Fortification Cannon—18 Pounder 5½ in 28,700 lbs. (total)
5 Cannon—18 Pounder 5½ in 14,300 (total)[6]

Campeau makes his case this way: "Knox makes no mention of the actual weight of any of the 59 cannons he procures. The weight listed is what was found based off similar guns. The weight estimates are to assist the reader in seeing just how heavy these cannons were. All weight estimates obtained from Gunther Rothenberg, *The Age of Warfare in the Age of Napoleon*."[7]

It is possible that Knox hauled more weight than he knew. But for our purposes, adding some weight for barrels of flints, sixty tons seems to be the most accepted estimate of the weight of the cannons that Knox transported during the winter of 1775 from Fort Ticonderoga. Knox would haul the fifty-nine cannons weighing 120,000 pounds—for modern comparison purposes, the same weight as twenty-eight SUVs—across a frozen lake, then through forests, mountains, and rivers using no mechanical power beyond the teamsters' pulley and rope systems. This would be accomplished entirely by brute strength, oxen, boats, sleds, horses, wagons, and heart. Little wonder the soldiers stared at Knox and his men incredulously.

But first Knox had to get the cannons out of the fort and down to the boats by the landing. Here Knox shines again, converting the men in the frozen fort to his cause and inspiring them to assist him. Initially reluctant, they listened to the red-faced man with the colorful scarf on his left hand, wildly gesturing with his arms in the air, exhorting the nobility of his mission and the importance of getting the cannon to Boston. Surely Knox's oratory was part history lesson, part news, part inspirational. Whatever it was, the men agreed to help.

Along with the cannons were barrels of high-quality flint and twenty-three boxes of lead. The river leading to the fort and the main road both would be used to transport the cannons to Lake George. Knox later wrote in his diary, "Employed in getting the cannon from the fort on board a Gundaloe [gondola] in order to get them to the bridge. Employed in getting the cannon from the bridge to the landing at Lake George."[8] Knox had some of the cannons lowered over the walls of the fort, then "used the hired civilian boatmen to assist him in both loading the boats and transporting them down the waterway. The cannons were brought down to the boats from Fort Ticonderoga by a team of animals already present at the fort. They were separated from their carriages once they were loaded onto the boats to distribute the weight evenly."[9]

The method of transporting the cannons and supplies from Fort Ticonderoga to the boats has been a point of debate, but ultimately Knox would do whatever was easiest and fastest.

> If lowering any or all the guns were easier you can bet, he did it. . . . The chances are that Knox used both a water route and an overland route getting the guns to Lake George. While they moved some of the heavier ones to the Gundalow, the carts were hauling the other supplies such as flints and shot as well as some of the small guns up the road. . . . To Knox time was all important. He was not only anxious to get his cargo to Cambridge, but he was in fear that a heavy spell of bad weather and a severe freeze at this moment would have trapped him at Ticonderoga until springtime.[10]

This is where Knox excelled: improvising and using the best means available to transport the sixty tons of cannons down to the lake. Knox used oxen or cattle to pull the cannons down the road to the landing as well as the boats on the river portage. He recorded in his diary, "paid Lieut. Brown for Capt. Johnson which repaid the carriers for the use of their cattle in crossing the cannon from Ticonderoga to the north landing of lake George, 26 dollars."[11] Included was a receipt signed by Lieutenant Brown: "Recd of Henry Knox twenty-six dollars which Capt. John Johnson paid to different carters of the use of their cattle in dragging cannon from the Fort of Ticonderoga to the North Landing of Lake George."[12] Clearly, oxen were used here to get the cannons to the waiting boats.

Knox carefully supervised the loading of the separated cannons into the forty-five boats of his fleet of gondolas, bateaux, and piraguas. Careful weight distribution would be key in avoiding becoming swamped in the choppy, freezing lake waters. The fifty-five-foot gondolas could hold 2,300 to 3,000 pounds. Sixty- to seventy-five-foot bateaux could carry 5,500 to 6,000 pounds. Thirty- to forty-foot piraguas could hold 1,200 to 2,000 pounds. The three cannons that weighed 5,000 pounds were on the bateaux, as these were the only boats capable of carrying these massive cannons. The other artillery pieces required a symphony of men, iron, and brass balanced perfectly to execute the hazardous thirty-eight-mile journey back to Fort George.

On the afternoon of December 6, 1775, the last boats were loaded, and Knox was ready. He stopped and wrote hurriedly into his journal, "Employed in loading the scow. Piragua and a Bateaux. At 3 o'clock in the afternoon set sail to go down the lake in the piraguas."[13]

The wind was already beginning to blow from the south and snow wisped the air. Whitecaps kicked up in the narrow passage on the lake. Knox looked up into the darkening snow-swollen sky. The return trip across the lake would not be the same as the trip north. The boats sunk low, moving slowly in the syrupy, almost frozen water. Knox stared at the water spraying on the black iron of the cannon next to him. Frost already ringed the barrels, but Henry Knox now had the cannons from Fort Ticonderoga in his possession. The victory was that the cannons had proved to be real, and the three large five-thousand-pound cannons were powerful enough to threaten the British in Boston and the fleet in the bay. The temperature was dropping quickly and ice had spread out farther from the shores as they sailed the long narrow channel that one good freeze could obliterate.

Early winter darkness crept across the lake and the wind picked up steadily. Snow filled the air. They entered the lake where it widened, and the headwind immediately precluded the use of sails. Fort Ticonderoga was no longer visible as Knox looked up at the darkened mountains. It was hard to believe that less than six months before he was a bookseller worried about the shipping costs and the best way to entice customers. Now he was the man who would deliver desperately needed cannons to George Washington that would be used to dislodge the British from his beloved city in the winter of 1775.

Knox crossed his arms against the cold as the men around him started to row against the wind. The boats moved slowly in the slushy water. If Lake George froze overnight, they would be stranded with no way to transport the cannons across the ice. Knox hoped that George Palmer or General Schuyler and John Becker would come through with the much-needed oxen and sleds. Knox watched the water spray over the low boats and felt icy drops claw at his beard. Above all else, they must get across before the lake froze. Nothing less than the future of the American Revolution hung in the balance.

13

THE HELL OF
LAKE GEORGE

December 9, 1775

Knox stared into the blinding snow that blended the water and sky together. His frozen hands could barely grip the paddle. His face was numb with the wind that turned his nose and ears blue. Knox turned his piragua into the open lane of water. Snow blinded him so that he couldn't tell where the lake ended and land began. He paddled in the ice-laden water back toward Fort Ticonderoga. His arms ached and his hands no longer closed around the oars. Knox kept his head down against the snow, and when he looked up, he saw men waving to him through the blizzard on the ice.

Knox had been at the lead of his armada of loaded-down boats. The wind that had carried them so swiftly up the lake was not a friend going down the lake toward Fort George. "The movement on the boats was very difficult due to the howling winds produced from the lakes blowing against the heavy weight of the cargo laden vessels. Since there were so many smaller vessels, there was no way Knox could be everywhere at once. William remained in the tail end of the movement with visibility of any stragglers."[1]

The problem was the gondolas, bateaux, and piraguas were not aquatically swift vessels, and without a trailing wind they became low-riding sleds. The first day out the wind died and the rowing began. Progress was slow. "The boats Knox used tended to be awkward unless they had a fair or following wind, and most of the time the wind was against them. This forced them to depend on muscle power or oarsmen, and it was no easy task."[2] Some of the boatmen found that rowing was problematic, as well, and after stowing the sails, they resorted to using poles. The howling wind only increased.

Knox had been having a good run of luck up until this point. He had moved swiftly and coordinated the logistics along the way and reached Fort Ticonderoga and then turned around the cannons in a matter of days. But now the endurance began. Lake George was a meandering horseshoe of islands and ice-covered shoals that threatened to freeze entirely. The waterline was inches away from the gunnels of some of the boats as the men pushed or rowed furiously, moving thousands of pounds of iron just a few feet with every stroke. It was like rowing a loaded truck through choppy, frozen water. The men were soon exhausted, and Henry moved around the various boats in the lighter piragua, keeping track of their movements, along with his brother William. Along with the cannons, one barrel of flints had been packed, which Washington had explicitly requested, along with Indian arrowheads and twenty-three boxes of lead.

Knox rowed ahead to see if the ice was closing farther along the lake. The trouble began when a scow hit a rock. William oversaw the scow, and the crew navigated to shallower water before the boat sank entirely. The boat and the cannons were still visible, and William quickly organized the men to recover the cannons and make the necessary repairs. This would take hours of painstaking effort in freezing water, ice, and snow. But this also showed that Henry Knox was unwilling to leave any cannons behind. He knew that every cannon would be needed by Washington to use against the British and even the loss of one might be a deciding factor.

A five-thousand-pound cannon along with others was now partially submerged in the icy water. The only means of extracting it was with men, ropes, makeshift pulleys, and boats. It is remarkable that the cannons were not abandoned, but more men came from Fort Ticonderoga to help. Henry wrote in his diary and recorded the day's events: "The scow coming after us run aground we being about a mile ahead with a fair wind to down but unfair to help with the scow, the wind dying away with the utmost difficulty reached Sabbath Day Point around 9 o'clock in the evening."[3]

Darkness fell early on December 9, and they stayed the first night on Sabbath Island, an island a third of the way down the lake. A large fire was built, and it was there that Knox learned about the scow that had sunk with the cannons. Knox's diary entry tells the story:

> We had been there when of the Battoes [bateaux] which had set out nearly the same time we had, allured by the view of the fire likewise came on shore, the crew of which informed that the Scow had run on a sunken rock but not in such

a manner as to be irretrievable; that they had broken all ropes which they had in endeavoring to rouse her off—but was ineffectual that they had sent up to the Fort for more ropes and hands and intended to make another trial and doubted not but that they should succeed.[4]

The men could go no farther that night, and Knox's diary entry shows the fleet had spread so far apart that many had no idea that the scow had sunk until that evening. The boatmen discovered an Indian village on Sabbath Point where the Indians gave them food and allowed them to bed in their huts. Knox recorded in his diary, "went ashore and warmed us by an exceedingly good fire in a hut made by some civil Indians who were with their ladies abed—they gave us some venison, roasted after their manner which was very relishing."[5] With plunging temperatures and without shelter, this was a fortuitous turn of events for the men who had fought their way to the island.

That the Indians had been friendly to the invading force of white men in boats was just luck. Henry Knox's expedition could well have been attacked as they came ashore. Indeed, his brother's account is not as warm and welcoming as Knox recalls in his diary. "Soon Algonquin Indians appeared and surrounded the camp. William ran for his knife and alerted others to do the same. As it turned out the Indians were just curious as to why there was such a large fire in an unpopulated area of the lake."[6]

The most populous of the Native American Indians, Algonquin tribes were those who spoke the Algonquin languages. Dialects were shared by hundreds of tribes that lived across eastern North America stretching from the Rocky Mountains to the Atlantic Ocean and up to northern Canada. Before the Europeans arrived, the Algonquins subsisted by gathering nuts, roots, wild rice, fruits, and berries along with hunting and trapping. Some Algonquin tribes cultivated tobacco along with corn, beans, and squash. These Indians were nomadic and followed the weather, moving their families from place to place. The Indians whom Knox encountered on the island traveled by canoes made of birchbark and wore snowshoes and often used toboggans in deep snow. When the Europeans arrived, the Algonquins occupied Canada east of the Rockies and down through the East Coast.

The Indians initially struck alliances with the French, who cultivated the Algonquin ways of travel, using their canoes to trade furs with the French. The English quickly became involved in wars with the tribes dating back to the massacre of 1622, which occurred in the colony of Virginia on March 22. It involved John Smith and more famously Pocahontas. According to Smith, the Indians "came unarmed into our houses with deer, turkey, fish, fruits and other provisions to sell us."[7] The Indians then used the colonists' tools and weapons to massacre men, women, and children. Eventually 347 colonists would die.

The roots of the massacre, like many other Indian massacres, were the taking of their lands by the Europeans for crop cultivation. The English retaliated by "the use of force, surprise attacks, famine resulting from the burning of their corn, destroying their boats [and] canoes, breaking their fishing wares . . . pursuing them with horses and using bloodhounds to find them and mastiffs to seize them, driving them to flee . . . [and] abetting their enemies against them."[8]

The French and Indian War would lead to the Battle of Sabbath Day Point. In March 1757, Fort William Henry was attacked by the French, who were unable to take the fort. The British claimed victory, and Lieutenant Colonel George Monroe sent out a reconnaissance force to assess French and Indian movements. Colonel Parker led 350 men in boats to Sabbath Day Point. The French discovered the lead boats, and a force of 450 French soldiers, supported by Algonquin Indians, left Fort Carillon to attack the British. Parker's men sailed to the island unaware of the trap awaiting them. Once the British came ashore, they were met with a volley of musket fire from the French soldiers. The Indians then attacked from the water, sailing around the point in canoes. The Englishmen were drowned, speared, or shot. Less than one hundred of Parker's men survived, who then were taken prisoner. Knox's night of venison and warm fires could have turned out very differently given the history of the Europeans and the Indians during the last hundred years.

The warm fire was just a memory by December 10, which ushered in a howling, freezing wind from the south. The sails were useless as the men left Sabbath Island and rowed into the teeth of the wind, moving ever slower with their dangerously overloaded boats. Knox had been at the front of the boats in his Pettigrew, "a double ended boat, based on a dug-out design, but most notable for a double mast rigging, the forward mast being canted forward, while the aft mast as canted astern. . . . It is said that the configuration gave the effect of a gaff rigged jib sail."[9]

Knox's Pettigrew was best with the wind behind it, but now he was facing a dead-on wind that required everyone to row. Add to this the weight of thousands of pounds of iron and brass in each boat along with the whitecaps that whipped from the south wind, and progress had all but slowed to a crawl on Lake George. Knox now hitched a ride with the men who told him the scow had sunk.

The crew of the Battoe having sufficiently refreshed themselves told me that as they were not very deeply loaded that they intended to push for Fort George. I jumped into the boat and ordered my man [Miller] to bring my baggage and we would go with them—accordingly we set out it being eleven o'clock with a light breeze ahead the men rowed briskly but we had not been out above an hour when the wind sprung up very fresh and directly against us.[10]

Knox wanted to get to Fort George as quickly as possible to organize the oxen and sleds. The men fought the wind for five hours and at that point were frozen and exhausted. The entire trip down to Fort George depended on muscle power. There were more close calls with boats nearly capsizing and "the boatmen having to rearrange the cargo of the boats several times to stop them from sinking. Sometimes cargo had to even be cross loaded to the larger bateaux boats. William and Henry had to ensure each boat stayed in contact with the other boats to prevent accidents or loss of cargo."[11]

The temperatures continued to drop on the lake. Wind chills plunged below zero as the men kept their heads down and rowed against the icy wind. Knox hurriedly recorded snippets in his diary at night during their stops, writing under harsh conditions of wind and snow. He later wrote about that day:

> The men after rowing exceedingly hard for above four hours seemed desirous of going ashore to make a fire to warm themselves. I readily consented knowing them to be exceedingly weary they made an Excessive fire having perhaps one or two cords of wood at a time there being very large quantities of dry wood ready cut—we warmed ourselves sufficiently and took a comfortable nap—laying with our feet to the fire.[12]

Cleary the men and Knox were frozen. Their feet were wet and frostbite had taken hold. Warming their feet closest to an "excessive" fire shows that they could lose no time in trying to save their extremities. The best guess where Knox and his men stayed the second night is "at the tip of Tongue Mountain or on the opposite shore now sometimes called Shelving Rock. There are some islands in this area that could have been used instead, but this is the part of the lake known as 'the narrows' where it would have been more logical for the boats to cross to the eastern shore."[13] The next morning Henry forged ahead to try and reach the fort and ensure there would be oxen and sleds waiting for the cannons. "About half an hour before daybreak that is about a quarter after six, we set out and in six hours and a quarter of excessive hard pulling against a fresh head breeze we reached Fort George on Monday December 11."[14]

Knox lost no time in sending out "his man" Miller on an express, which was essentially a hand-carried message. "I sent an express to Squire Palmer of Stillwater to prepare a number of sleds and oxen to drag the cannon presuming that we should get there."[15] This brings up the first big mistake that Knox would make. His inexperience in transporting 120,000 pounds of artillery three hundred miles would manifest itself in different ways, but his ability to procure a good deal was even more lacking. The messenger, who had to go all the way back to Stillwater, held a message from Knox about a deal he had made with a man, Palmer, he knew not at all.

Fort George December 12, 1775
Capt. Palmer,
Sir

In consequence of the intimation given to you by me some time since that I should want your assistance I now write you.—I must beg that you would purchase or get made immediately 40 good strong sleds that will each be able to carry a long cannon clear from dragging on the ground and which will weigh 5,400 pounds each and likewise that you procure oxen or horses as you shall judge most proper to drag them. You will also be the best judge of the number which will be wanting—I think that you may be able to purchase sleds that are ready made which by strengthening might do—the sleds that they are first put upon are to go to camp near Boston—the cattle as far as Albany or Kinderhook where we must get fresh ones—I most earnestly beg of you to spare no trouble or necessary expense in getting these things—from the character universally given to you and from your known attachment to the cause of your country I promise myself the completest assistance in your power—whatever expense you are at I shall pay you immediately. I send this by an express by who I wish you to send me answer directly.

By the interim
I am Sir Your Most Humble Servant
Henry Knox[16]

Knox was desperate. He had men waiting to load the cannons onto the sleds, which begs the question, where were Schuyler and Becker's promised sleds and oxen? Knox still was dealing with procurement on his own, and we can surmise there had been some sort of disconnect among the men involved. Knox anxiously awaited the arrival of the other boats from Ticonderoga. He had gone ahead, but the straggling boats stretched all the way back to Sabbath Island. Because of weight variance, some boats moved exceedingly slowly, and some of course foundered and had to be pulled from the water as best they could. But the letter Knox sent to George Palmer showed a naivete in dealing in a world with which he was not familiar. His letter "was all but a blank check issued to a man who was virtually a stranger to Knox, and which called upon a rumored reputation for honesty plus a supposed patriotic fervor."[17]

Knox was now waiting for his cannons, his sleds, his oxen, and more than all that, snow. Schuyler and Becker were in the process of rounding up the sleds and oxen, but Knox had no way of knowing this. There is the impetuosity if not impatience of youth in Knox and a reluctance to relinquish control of his expedition. Schuyler may have promised the oxen, but Knox must have felt he had to take matters into his own hands and hire Palmer. The tone of Knox's letter suggests that Palmer was promising a quick turnaround.

But still there was the weather to contend with. If there was no snow, it wouldn't matter how many sled or oxen he had; the cannons were simply too heavy to be pulled along the roads and trails Knox would have to follow. He could only wait and hope that George Palmer could deliver, that it would snow, and that George Washington and the Continental Army were faring better than he was at this point.

There was confusion now. Sinking boats plagued his flotilla. Temperatures continued to fall as the heavily laden boats inched from Ticonderoga. Knox had no idea if anyone was procuring his sleds and oxen. He had no idea what was happening in Concord or if George Washington had managed to hang on. All he could do was stare northward, waiting for his boats, which contained the salvation of the American Revolution. Then an arriving boat reported that a scow with all its cannons had sunk off Sabbath Point.

THE MAN WHO STARTED THE FRENCH AND INDIAN WAR

1755

The man who sent Henry Knox on the seemingly impossible task of trans-porting artillery three hundred miles did not expect any less from Knox than he did himself. On one hand, George Washington was a supremely regulated man who never wasted a moment. His punctuality was part of his preoccupation with time. A sundial was front and center at Mount Vernon, and Washington checked it every day when he returned from his rides. He was a man of routine who never deviated. He rose before dawn and padded around in his dressing gown and slippers, working and reading in his library, then ate the same breakfast of corncakes, tea, and honey.

Washington dressed and rode off to his five farms, and as one amazed visitor observed, "often works with his men himself, strips off his coat and labors like a common man."[1] He was a man with slavish devotion to detail and often quoted the Scottish idiom, "many mickle make a muckle"—that is, "tiny things add up."[2] He always returned for dinner at 2:45 p.m. He liked to eat fish from the Potomac, he usually drank three glasses of Madeira, then he retired to his library before a final supper. He could not tolerate shoddiness in work or in a person. "I shall begrudge no reasonable expense that will contribute to the improve-ment and neatness of my farms, for nothing pleases me better than to see them in good order and everything trim, handsome and thriving."[3]

On the other hand, he was a wild man, a man who did not sit. He was the man of the bold stroke, the man who did not exercise prudence, the man who courted disaster by charging into the face of the enemy. He was the man responsible for starting the French and Indian War.

George Washington expected great things from Henry Knox, and Washington was four years younger when he himself charged into the wilderness under the charge of Lieutenant Governor Dinwiddie to give the French an ultimatum to vacate land claimed by England. He was twenty years old, and thirty years later he recalled the amazing circumstances "that so young and inexperienced a person should have been employed on a negotiation with which subjects of the greatest importance were involved."[4]

Like Henry Knox, Washington had seen an opportunity and had ridden to Williamsburg to offer his services. He probably had learned of the envoy position from Colonel William Fairfax and presented himself to Governor Dinwiddie much the way Knox presented himself to George Washington on the road outside of the Roxbury fortifications. Like Washington, Knox knew the best way to advance was to prove oneself in battle or to accomplish some feat that forced the powers that be to recognize talent. Washington had qualities that would later be ascribed to Henry Knox. He had a "robust constitution to survive the winter woods, was mostly unflappable, had a mature appearance and sound judgement."[5] Although Knox knew nothing of the country outside of Boston, he was hearty, steady in his outlook for his years, and projected a can-do attitude that immediately instilled a sense of confidence in his abilities.

Washington enlisted Christopher Gist as a guide and Jacob Van Bramm, a French interpreter, along with two Indian traders. He then galloped into the forests of the Ohio with an edict in his saddlebag signed by none other than King George II. "We do hereby strictly charge and command you to drive them off by force of arms."[6] With four other men from the backwoods and two Indian traders, Washington embarked on a grueling 250-mile journey through the wilderness, reaching to "within 15 miles of Lake Erie in the depth of winter, when the whole face of the earth was covered with snow and the waters covered with ice."[7]

This was eerily similar to the conditions that Henry Knox would find on his own expedition. It took Washington a week to cross the Allegheny Mountains on a wilderness trail turned muddy and slippery from "excessive rains and vast quantities of snow."[8] After a tortuous week, they stayed in the cabin of an Indian trader, John Fraser, then pushed on to the Forks of the ice-laden Ohio. The other men did not want to cross, but Washington plunged in with his horse. Sitting upright, he glided across while the others took a canoe.

One of Washington's mandates was to establish contact with the Indians and get intelligence on French designs regarding forts and troop strength. On

November 22, he met with Chief Shingas of the Delaware tribe. He found the Indians "mercenary—every service of theirs must be purchased—and they are easily offended, being thoroughly sensible of their own importance."[9] Washington set off on a five-day journey through unrelenting rain to the trading post of Venago, where he met a French officer, Captain Philippe Thomas de Joncaire, who became drunk and bragged about the French's "absolute design to take possession of the Ohio."[10] Washington then pushed into Fort Le Beouf, reaching it after dark on December 11, and presented his communiqué to Captain Jacques Legardeur de St. Pierre. "As to the summons you send me to retire," he told Washington. "I do not think myself obliged to obey it."[11]

So much for telling the French to leave. On December 14, the captain gave Washington a sealed message for Governor Dinwiddie then stocked Washington's canoe with supplies and sent him on his way. The young Washington then discovered that his Indian guards had been bribed to stay with the French, leaving Washington and Gist on their own. Their horses quickly tired, and Washington donned moccasins and leather leggings as they hiked with backpacks. They picked up some Indian guides and trudged for miles. Washington was so exhausted he allowed one of the Indians to carry his backpack. Gist was suspicious of the Indians, who turned against them when approaching a meadow, "the Indian hustled out into the clearing without warning, spun around and fired at them point blank from fifteen paces."[12] Gist jumped on the Indian and was about to execute him when Washington pleaded for his life. They tied him up and then released him after dark with Gist telling Washington, "We must get away and then we must travel all night."[13]

They pushed on without rest and reached an icy river, spending the day hacking out a crude raft. In the middle of the river, they became trapped against an ice floe so Washington tried to push them off with a pole. "I put out my setting pole to try to stop the raft that the ice might pass by, when the rapidity of the stream threw it with so much violence against the pole that it jerked me into ten feet of water."[14] Washington grabbed a log on the raft and pulled himself back on. They spent the night on an island where Gist developed frostbite, but Washington seemed impervious to his dunk in the freezing river. By morning the river had frozen and they crossed to safety, eventually making it back to Williamsburg.

A man of a lesser constitution would have perished but Washington was already becoming known for his strength and endurance. He wrote a seven-thousand-word report on his journey that would eventually be published as *The Journal of Major George Washington*. In an ode to the power of the written word that a bookseller like Henry Knox would understand, "this slim volume helped kindle a spark that eventually led to the conflagration of the French and Indian War."[15] The journal put Washington on the map. Now a commissioned lieutenant colonel, the twenty-two-year-old was authorized to train a one-hundred-man militia.

In shades of what was to come, Washington found the new soldiers wanting and complained to Dinwiddie that many were "loose, idle persons that are quite destitute of house and home and I may truly say many of them of clothes."[16] He was once again sent into the wilderness by Governor Dinwiddie to intercept a French raiding party on the banks of the Ohio. He then authorized Washington to use deadly force, telling him, "you are to restrain all such offenders and in case of resistance to make prisoners of or kill and destroy them."[17] Lieutenant Colonel Washington now had 160 new recruits with him.

Their convoy moved slowly and "three weeks later at the junction of Wills Creek and the Potomac" he received news that the French had attacked the British at the forks while building a fort and renamed it Fort Duquesne.[18] The British had been reinforced by the Indian Chief Half King and his warriors who joined Washington. The British regulars had only thirty-four soldiers against one thousand French along with eighteen artillery pieces. Washington sent for reinforcements then received the news that a French detachment had crossed the Youghiogheny River just eighteen miles away. Washington established a defensive position in a place called Great Meadows and wrote to Dinwiddie: "We have with nature's assistance made a good entrenchment and by clearing the bushes out of these meadows prepared a charming field for an encounter."[19]

Washington's sentries heard movement in the woods that night and fired on the unseen soldiers. The lieutenant colonel kept his men by their guns until daybreak, when news came that the French were a mere seven miles away and had set up camp. Washington decided to strike and had his men march "in a night as dark as pitch" through torrential rain in a single-file line on a narrow path.[20] The men kept bumping into each other, and seven soldiers were lost in the black woods. On the morning of May 28, Washington and Chief Half King attacked the encamped 324 Frenchmen. Washington rode at the front with the Indians circling behind, cutting off any escape. Ten French soldiers were killed and twenty-one captured to Washington's loss of one man and three wounded. What happened next is legendary.

Ensign Coulon de Villiers Sieur de Jumonville had an important diplomatic message for the British and began to read the scroll demanding that they leave the Ohio country. As Jumonville read, Chief Half King stepped forward and split his skull open with a hatchet and then "dipped his hands into the skull, rinsed them with the victim's brains, and scalped him."[21] The rest of the Indian warriors then swooped down and scalped the hapless wounded. It was an Indian massacre that Washington now presided over.

The French army nearby heard of the atrocities and pinned down Washington and his men in a hastily constructed fort dubbed Fort Necessity. The French attacked in three columns and "bullets rained down from everywhere. French and Indian soldiers advanced with shouts and dismal Indian yells to our entrenchments," Washington recalled.[22] The fort was surrendered to the French that night and Washington and his men were released with the understanding they would return home and not fight the French anymore.

History did not treat Washington well at this point "for advancing when he should have retreated; for fighting without sufficient reinforcements; for picking an indefensible spot [Fort Necessity]; for the slapdash construction of the fort; for alienating his Indian allies and for shocking hubris in thinking he could defeat an imposing French force."[23] But Washington learned from his mistake, noting the Indians fought by "a mobile style of warfare that relied on ambushing, sniping from trees, and vanishing into the forest."[24] The European style of warfare of massing troops simply didn't work against a stealthier foe. He also learned the value of surprise.

For Washington, his humiliation was complete when the French published his journal, which had fallen into their hands, that recorded the earlier massacre of the unarmed Frenchmen. "In this manner they cast the British as the first belligerents in the French and Indian War."[25] The Fort Necessity defeat was blamed on Washington and "the Jumonville incident was recognized as the opening shot that precipitated the French and Indian War. . . . In the words of Sir Horace Walpole in London, 'The volley fired by a young Virginian in the backwoods of America set the world on fire.'"[26]

This was the man who, twenty years later, had sent Henry Knox into the frozen wilderness in the winter of 1775. He expected Knox to succeed because Washington himself had faced the hardships and trials of war and wilderness survival. Knox's personality was not that different from the young George Washington who had charged into the wilderness and into harm's way. It was the spirit of embracing adventure, one that assumed success over any obstacles, no matter how daunting. Knox and Washington were both men of destiny. George Washington had started the French and Indian War, and now Henry Knox would save the American Revolution.

15

A NOBLE TRAIN

December 13, 1775

It had taken a little less than a week for Henry to return from Fort Ticonderoga. Now Knox was still at Fort George waiting for his nineteen-year-old brother William. George Palmer had returned with Knox's messenger to Fort George. "On Wednesday the 13th he [Palmer] came up and agreed to provide the necessary number of sleds and oxen and they to be ready by the first snow."[1] This raises some questions. Why did Palmer come all the way up from Stillwater when he could have sent a message back with Knox's messenger? Perhaps to ensure Knox was serious or to take payment for the oxen and sleds. A more experienced negotiator might have smelled something sour at this point.

By now, Knox was imagining catastrophe. "On the 13th being very uneasy at not hearing of our little fleet we dispatched an express boat—about 2 o'clock but in the afternoon we received advice that on the morning of the 10th the scow had gotten off the rock on which she had run and with great difficulty had reached Sabbath Day Point on the same night the wind being exceedingly high the sea had beat her in such a manner that she had sunk."[2]

We can take several things from this diary entry. The boats were spread out widely with Knox far in the lead and others just making it off Sabbath Island. This news was brought to Knox by men who pulled in on another boat. His "express boat" returned with a letter from his brother William on December 14:

North Landing Dec 14, 1775 at Sabbath Day Point

Dear Brother,

    Last evening the boat arrived which you sent with the letters and provisions we got off the scow Sabbath day morning and immediately set off for Sabbath Day Point where we arrived in the evening beating all the way against the wind. Monday morning our scow sunk but luckily so near the shore that when she sunk her gunnel was above water so that shortly we were able to bail her out and tow her to the leeward shore of the point where we took out the three mortars and by shifting the cannon aft bottomed her and now she stands ready for sail the first fair wind—Capt. Johnson arrived at Sabbath Day Point about the time your boat did and this morning I set out with him in your boat for the landing when we arrived we sent off the new [boat] with the 2 18-pounders and with the 4 12-pounders as far as she could get for the ice for it is frozen a mile which they will have to cut through—but I expect she will be at Lake George by the time the scow does I intend coming in her because I think it is necessary that one of us should see that they do their duty faithfully—Capt. Johnson paid 20 dollars for carting which if you have opportunity to send him before the Lieut. arrives you had better. God send us a fair wind.[3]

This letter is illuminating. It shows William had to orchestrate the rescue of the scow along with the mortars and cannons while also supervising Captain Jack and his men, who had been hired to transport the cannons safely to Fort George. It also revealed that the lake had frozen solid in parts and the boats had to cut their way through. The fleet had essentially become separate, isolated boats trying to make it to Fort George the best they could. At Sabbath Island we get from Knox's diary a feeling of cohesion among the boats, but now it is evident the unity has turned into a desperate, solitary struggle to cross the frozen thirty-eight-mile lake.

As if things were not bad enough, Knox had to turn to the next crisis at hand, the procurement of sleds and oxen. Palmer had promised to return with the first snow, but by December 14 there was none, despite William's report of plummeting temperatures and the advancing ice on the lake. Knox used the following three days to orchestrate the next phase of preparation as the boats continued to drift in one by one. He first wrote instructions for his brother about the loading of the cannons into the sleds.

Endeavor that the heavy cannon and mortars go off first. Let the touch holes and vents of all mortars and cannon be turned downwards. The lead and flints are to come up as far as Albany which will serve to make up a load. Observe that 2 pair of horses be to deliver two or three thousand weight and 3 or 4 oxen for the 4,000 weights and 4 spans for those of 5,000 weight but Mr. Schuyler the DIG will see more particular to this affair. The one span will take about 1,000 weight they are to receive seven pounds and ten for every 62 miles or 12 per day for each span of horses.[4]

In this detail Knox was delegating the off-loading of the cannons from the boats and the arrangement of the oxen, horses, and sleds into groups that resembled their arrangement during the journey across Lake George. He was also instructing William how much to pay the teamsters on the way, along with specific instructions about positioning the cannons to keep snow and rain from getting into the barrels and the number of oxen and horses required for the four- and five-thousand-pound cannons. He said Schuyler would oversee the oxen and the horses but at this point there is no Schuyler. Knox again took the role of an advance man anticipating the next problem for the train—and there were many.

Knox then sent off a letter to Colonel McDougal requesting the shells for his new cannons. This was hubris, as he was 250 miles away from his destination, but it also showed the confidence Knox had in completing his mission.

Sir,
When I was in New York, I did not know of any 13 inch mortar among munitions of which I found at Ticonderoga—I must beg you sir that you would use your influence that there is sent immediately to camp at Cambridge the following number of shells. You are too well acquainted with the importance of this equipment to want the urging of an additional motive for this utmost expedition. The business upon which I came up here has succeeded very well.
500 13-inch shells
200 5¾-inch shells
400 4½ inch shells[5]

Knox had established a list of shells needed for the cannons. Knox wanted to be ready for action with his new artillery when he reached Concord. Henry then paid off the boatmen on December 15: "Paid the Battoe men for going up to Ticonderoga and bringing . . . the cannon."[6] This meant that the majority of the boats bearing the cannons had arrived, so it was now a matter of getting the sleds and oxen. One of the great problems of his expedition had been solved: moving the cannons from Fort Ticonderoga across the ice-laden Lake George. Sinking boats, freezing temperatures, no wind at all then a punishing headwind, along with Indians, submerged cannons in icy shallows, separation, and hellish rowing all had been part of the trial by fire that Henry Knox had endured.

This twenty-five-year-old former bookseller had no experience moving anything, yet he had moved one hundred and twenty thousand pounds of cannons in 1775 across a frozen lake to Fort George. There in Fort George on a cold Sunday, December 17, 1775, Knox sat by candlelight and allowed himself to return to the world that had nothing to do with "the glorious cause" or the titanic task ahead of him. For a moment in the bitter night, awash in the yellow glow of the candle, he could write to the woman who had given up everything to be with the man who was now the hope of the American Revolution. Alone, pregnant, and living with strangers, Lucy Knox was undergoing her own test of faith for the cause.

Fort George, Dec. 17, 1775
My dearest companion,
    It is now twelve days since I've had the least opportunity of writing to her who I value more than life itself. How does my charmer? Is she in health and spirits? I trust in God she is—My last letter mentioned that I was just going over Lake George about 38 miles in length—We had a tedious time of it altho the passage was fine—in coming back it was exceedingly disagreeable but all danger of the principal difficulty is now past and by next Thursday I hope we shall be able to set out from hence on our journey home—with our very valuable and precious convoy—if we have the good fortune to have snow I hope to have the pleasure to see my dearest in three weeks from this date—don't grieve my dear at its length. I wish to heaven it was in my power to shorten the time—a time already elapsed far beyond the bearence of an eager expectation to see you—We shall cut no small figure in going through the country with our cannon mortars drawn by eighty yoke oxen—I have not had an unwell hour since I left you. My brother William is also exceedingly well and has been the utmost service to me. I most fervently wish that my dear Lucy might have been equally happy with respect to her health—had I the power to transport myself to you—how eagerly rapid would be my flight—it makes me smile to think how I should look—like a tennis ball bowled down the steep. Give my love to my friend Harry I certainly should have written him before but every minute of my time is taken up in forwarding the important business I'm upon—My compliments to Mr. Pelham and family—I have had the pleasure of seeing a considerable number of our enemies prisoners to the Bravery of America—Enemies who would not before this allow the Americans a spark of military virtue—their note is now changed—some are to be much pitied—others are not so much—all in a degree of their infatuation is surprising but I trust will have its end—May he who holds the hearts of all flesh in his hands incline America to put their sole confidence in him and then he will still continue to be their leader and may he condescend to take particular care and give special directions to your Guardian Angel Conserving you—
    Adieu my only love
    For the present adieu[7]

This letter reveals Knox's guilt, his love, and his uncertainty about when he would return. As of December 17, there was still no snow for the sleds, and Knox fully anticipated the full accompaniment—eighty oxen to pull at least forty sleds—to be delivered in four days, the next Thursday, by George Palmer. Also, Knox had seen a good number of British soldiers heading south, and like many Americans was still smarting under the British assumption that the colonial army was a rabble that didn't know how to fight. This was disproven at Bunker Hill and by the capture of Fort Ticonderoga, and, Knox hoped, it soon would be disproven at Boston as well. Knox's letter also shows that his belief in the American cause of liberty and freedom was encompassed in his belief in God: the Revolution was a holy cause and procuring the cannon to defeat the British was now a holy quest.

This letter also communicates how frantic Knox was to reassure his young wife that everything would work out. He was keenly aware of what he has done to Lucy Flucker's life. She was cut off from her family and the world she knew with a husband who was largely absent. She was supportive, but in a letter less than two years later, she revealed the extent of her sacrifice for Henry Knox and the realization that she would never see her family again.

> I am sick at heart, low spirited and almost indifferent whether I live or die. Had I no friends I suppose I should not take it so hard, but when I reflect that I have a father and a mother, sisters, and brothers, and yet am this poor neglected thing, I cannot bear it. . . . I underwent almost every distress for the sake of being yours, and you forsake me. My poor dear father I must never see again. When I reflect upon his excessive tenderness for me when a child, upon the thousand times he has helped me and prayed God to make me the comfort of his age, I am half distressed and yet believe me, dear Harry, I cheerfully remained the best of partners and would do it again and again to live to be with you. But this you refuse me, I have been confined to my room almost a week, have been alone most of the time, and have given myself up to the horror of my situation.[8]

Zealotry is a lonely business for the spouse of the zealot. Lucy, like many during the American Revolution, found herself torn away from friends and family as sides were chosen in the deepening war. But Lucy was married to Henry Knox, who was flying on the wings of destiny. Although most of her letters were supportive, she was human and she excoriates Henry Knox for what he had done to her. For Lucy, the bitterness over never seeing her family again was compounded by the fact that she would rarely see her husband during the American Revolution. Knox's expedition north to retrieve artillery was just the beginning.

Finally, Knox wrote to George Washington. This was his triumph. The Boston bookseller, who had built efficient fortifications but not much else, had taken on a task that Washington's inner circle said could not be done. Henry Knox now could point to a real success at last, something that would justify the colonelship he wanted. This was his boot camp for service in the military, and failure surely would muster him out of George Washington's inner circle of confidence. But now he could lay it on.

On December 17, 1775, he wrote:

> Fort George
> May it please your Excellency,
>   I returned to this place and brought with me the cannon. It being the time I conjectured it would take us to transport them to here. It is not easy to conceive the difficulties we have had getting them over the lake owing to the advanced sea- son of the year and contrary winds, but the danger is now past and three days ago it was uncertain whether we could have gotten them until next spring.

Knox admitted here that the lake could have frozen completely, which would have prevented transport until spring thaw. "But now please God they must go—I have had made forty-two exceedingly strong sleds and have provided 80 yoke of oxen to drag them as far as Springfield where I shall get fresh cattle to carry them to camp—the route will be from here to Kinderhook from thence into Great Barrington Massachusetts Bay and down to Springfield."[9]

Knox accomplished several things in this letter. He laid out his plan to Wash- ington for getting the cannons from Fort George to Concord, and he implied that he had forty-two "exceedingly strong sleds" and "provided 80 yokes of oxen to drag them as far as Springfield."[10] Then he planned to swap out the oxen at Springfield for the rest of the journey. Simple. Washington, in reading his letter, could envision Knox with his sleds and waiting oxen lined up and ready to go. In truth, this hinged on George Palmer's promise.

Knox misled Washington, intimating either that he already had the oxen and sleds or that they were to be delivered at any moment. Knox seemed to be working surreptitiously with Palmer, and as events progressed, it would become clear the young bookseller had made an almost fatal error for the ex- pedition. Knox was simply too trusting and assuming in his letter to Palmer that "from the character universally given to you and from your known attachment to the cause of your country I promise myself the completest assistance in your power—whatever expense you are at I shall pay you im- mediately."[11] This is a blank check to a man Knox didn't know at all. In his letter to Washington, Knox described how he expected the expedition to proceed with the cannons and indicated that he anticipated sufficient snow to get to Saratoga.

> There will scarcely be any possibility of carrying them from here to Albany or Kinderhook but on sleds the roads being very much gullied—at present the sledding is tolerable to Saratoga, about 26 miles; beyond that there is none—I have sent for sleds and teams to come here and expect to begin to move them to Saratoga on Wednesday or Thursday next trusting that between this and then we shall have a fine fall of snow which will enable us to proceed further and make the carriage easy—if that should be the case I hope in 16 or 17 days' time to be able to present your Excellency *a noble train of artillery* the inventory of which I have enclosed.[12]

A noble train of artillery. From Knox's letter, it would seem there was snow or that he was confident there would be, but of course there were no sleds. Knox calling his cannons "a noble train of artillery" lifted his mission to biblical proportions and was in line with Washington's view of the Revolution as "the glorious cause." Knox lifted their desperate gamble to a Holy Grail. It was divinely inspired, and this appealed to Washington who saw his calling as one of divine inspiration as well. He left Mount Vernon because he was called to the honorable cause of the Revolution, and Knox applied this to his herculean struggle to move cannon three hundred miles across frozen lakes, rivers, and mountains. It was a quest. Only God could move one hundred and twenty thousand pounds of cannons in the dead of winter because God believes *in the nobility of their cause* to create a nation based on liberty and freedom and the credo that all men are created equal.

"The Noble Train" would be used to fight a holy war. A war in which oppression would be lifted, Gideon's trumpet would blow from on high, and Washington and now Knox would be divinely protected. There was certainly more than a hint of the divine surrounding Washington and his ability to achieve the near-impossible, leading men into battle on a large, white horse and returning every time unscathed. And now Henry Knox was invoking the divine and anointing his train of artillery with nobility, which would enable it to reach Concord and change the course of the war. It was really a brilliant piece of phrasing that justified all the sacrifice that he, Washington, and the men and women of the Revolution were making.

One of Knox's strengths was unbridled optimism in the face of crushing adversity, resilience he must have developed at a very young age following his father's abandonment and subsequent extreme poverty. He found that in running a bookstore, the smiling confident proprietor was apt to sell more books than the gloomy recalcitrant owner. So to tell Washington he could arrive in little more than two weeks fits his enthusiastic approach to the problems of life. He could own his own bookstore in Boston, and he could marry a desirable girl from a well-respected Tory family, and he could retrieve cannons from three hundred miles away and deliver them in record time.

Knox's journey was just beginning: it would take him forty days to reach Concord. He closed his letter to Washington by updating him on the supplies he requested.

> I also send a list of these stores which I desired Col. McDougal to send from New York. I did not know then of any 13-inch mortars which was the reason of my ordering but few shells of that size. I now wrote to him for 500 13 inch and also 200 5¾ and 400 4½ inches for the cannons if these sizes would be had there as I think they can I imagine it would save time and expense to get them from thence rather than cost them.[13]

The new commander of the artillery was playing the role and explaining to Washington his decisions regarding the amount and type of shells. Knox then wrote to the committee of safety in the towns along the way, requesting food and shelter for his men as well as possible horses and sleds. Knox erroneously told Washington that "I have very little doubt that General Montgomery has Quebec in his possession." Knox had no way of knowing of the American defeat, which shows how long it took news to travel at that time. He told Washington that he had heard "that General Montgomery had gone to join him [Benedict Arnold] with a considerable body of men and a good train of artillery."[14]

Why shouldn't there have been victory at Quebec? Knox was doing the impossible, surely other men could as well. The man who was about to deliver a "noble train of artillery" to George Washington to defeat the British saw only the bright lights of victory, not the agonizing days of toil that lay ahead. Knox dispatched his three letters, not knowing when they would be delivered, and turned to the immediate problem at hand. Where were his sleds and oxen?

George Palmer had appeared on December 13, and it would seem Knox received a subsequent message that the sleds and oxen would arrive Tuesday or Wednesday, December 19 or 20. Apparently General Schuyler had also been working on procuring sleds after meeting with Knox. Here the newly commissioned colonel of the army's artillery branch experienced his first serious stumble. "He expected by Wednesday to have 42 strong sleds and more than 160 oxen and 500 fathoms of sturdy three inch rope to haul the 43 cannons and 16 mortars as far as Springfield, Massachusetts, where he planned to get fresh animals for the final leg of the journey."[15] But the best-laid plans go astray. Knox would have been happy with half that number of oxen and any sleds at all, but a letter from General Schuyler changed everything. At best, Henry Knox was making a deal any way that he could in order to have sleds and oxen ready when the cannons arrived from Ticonderoga. At worst, he was being taken advantage of by unscrupulous characters who Knox assumed had his commitment to the "cause" and who therefore would act honorably. Capitalism and patriotism rarely go hand in hand. Knox wrote to General Schuyler on December 17 from Fort George.

> Sir, We have been so fortunate as to get the mortars and cannon safely over the lake to this place—I arranged with Captain Palmer of Stillwater to get proper conveyances for them from here to Springfield—we are apprehensive of a difficulty necessary carrying over at Albany for want of a proper scow. I am not well enough acquainted with the road after we cross at the half moon to know whether it be practical to keep on the east side of the river entirely to Kinderhook—I expect Capt. Palmer up with the teams on Tuesday or Wednesday and I expect on Thursday to move as far as Saratoga if the sledding continues as at present—from thence we must wait for snow—I had heard sir that you were gone to Philadelphia in consequence of which I wrote to Mr. Livingstone at Albany for 500 fathoms 3 inch rope to fasten the cannons on the sleds—it has not yet arrived. I beg sir that you will please give the order for it being forwarded with the upmost expedition and sir I take the liberty of requesting the favor of you to forward the enclosed letters by the speediest conveyance.[16]

This letter revealed "that enough snow has fallen at Lake George for Knox to plan to move his sleds at this time."[17] When Palmer had arrived on December 13, his reported promise "to have sleds ready for the first snow indicated there had been none up to then."[18] That Knox says the sleds can go as far as Saratoga until there is more snow "implies that he has received a message from Palmer to this effect, probably at the same time that he advised that the teams would be brought up about Tuesday or Wednesday, the 19th or 20th of December."[19]

Knox divulged that he was unsure of his route and whether he should stay on the east side of the Hudson or cross the river at Half Moon, as "I am not well acquainted enough with the road."[20] He also desperately needed "500 fathoms of 3 inch" rope to fasten the cannons onto the sleds.[21] Knox tried to plan for the next phase of his journey, but he was dependent on the promises of others. General Schuyler fired off a letter on December 18 to Knox, essentially halting his arrangements with George Palmer:

Sir,

I am happy to hear that all the military stores you had in charge to bring from Fort Ticonderoga are arrived at Fort George. I have taken measures to forward them to Boston as soon as we shall be favored with a fall of snows. But I am informed that you have applied to Mr. Palmer to construct carriages for this purpose. This is very unnecessary and expensive as there are a sufficiency of carriages available for the purpose in this country to carry ten times the quantity; you will therefore countermand any directions you may give Mr. Palmer in this.[22]

Reprimanded for his decision to employ Palmer by a high-ranking general, Knox has no choice but to follow orders. Obviously, Schuyler was annoyed that Knox had contracted with Palmer and felt that Knox was being taken advantage of and had overstepped his authority by paying for oxen and carriages when Schuyler felt capable of providing what was needed. Schuyler might have had inside knowledge on Palmer, as well. How Knox responded to this is not clear, "but it is quite clear that something was done. Either he communicated with Palmer indicating that he felt compelled to follow the explicit instructions of such high-ranking officer and thus had to cancel his earlier liberal agreement or Schuyler himself took the initiative to send a directive to Palmer to desist from any further construction."[23]

Henry Knox was in a panic. He could no longer use the man he had been depending on to deliver sleds and oxen to Fort George. Yet the boats and the cannons had arrived from Lake George with men awaiting the sleds and oxen. Knox had to do something, and he was not about to get derailed by logistical snafus. Clearly Schuyler knew something about Palmer he didn't, but at this point it didn't matter. Knox needed to get his oxen and sleds to Fort George, and if they wouldn't come to him, he would go to them.

16

THE BEST LAID PLANS

December 24, 1775

The narrative of Henry Knox's life is much like the genesis of America at this point: a series of starts and stops, maneuvers, serendipity, surprises, and unforeseen problems—with much depending on luck. Knox was an inexperienced man attempting impossible tasks while hoping for the best. Henry Knox was not a good administrator. He was a zealot who led by momentum. He was a man of action who had undertaken George Washington's bold attempt to dislodge the British from Boston by doing the unexpected while the British army languished in winter quarters. But no blueprint for pulling this off existed. He had been chastised by his commanding general and denied his supplier of oxen and sleds despite the daily arrival of more cannons from Lake George. It was time for action, and Knox was not a man to sit idly by.

George Palmer acted as a contractor, fanning Knox's urgent request for oxen, horses, and sleds among the populace of Albany. Before Knox can shut him down, Knox received a message from a man who promised horses and sleds on December 18.

Sir,

The bearer can procure four pairs of horses to carry one of the longest cannons but would rather go with two sleighs and two pair of horses to each. I believe there will be enough engaged by evening to carry the lightest cannon. If you can persuade him to go with four horses, he will take an order for one of the longest.[1]

The procurement of the sleds and livestock was becoming a major problem. On December 24, Knox took matters into his own hands. He and his party of militiamen headed to Albany in a blinding snowstorm in order to see George Palmer and General Schuyler himself. In a frantic run from Fort George to Albany, Knox and the militiamen retraced their steps on the trading path. It was Christmas Eve 1775 and snow had begun to fall. Knox plowed ahead "on foot about six miles in the midst of an exceeding fine snow—when Judge Dewer procured me a sled to go to Stillwater."[2] Judge Dewer apparently lived near the small village of Fort Miller along the Hudson River. His assistance in helping Knox clearly put him in the category of Whig patriot, although his associates, Pat Smyth of "Fort Edward along with Gil Harris of Hudson Falls, incited violent Tory activity during the later days of Revolution."[3] This reveals the sharp divisions that tore families apart in the early days of the Revolution.

After Knox and his men borrowed this sled, they "proceeded on to Saratoga in Yuletide style."[4] It is worth noting that if Knox had his sleds and oxen at this point, he would have been sleighing along with cannons in tow. Knox recorded in his diary, "After crossing the ferry we got with considerable difficulty to Arch McNeil's Saratoga where we dined."[5] Roads during this time were so bad that travelers had to rest every few miles, and taverns or inns like McNeil's provided necessary shelter and food. "Prior to the construction of actual hostelries, almost every farmer along the highway offered shelter, food, and refreshments for which they received much of the little cash money that they had for their transactions."[6]

Arch McNeil's was one of the first of these inns. Locals later told stories about turning over the wide floorboards after the inn had been used as a British hospital during the battle of Saratoga, "because of the blood which had penetrated too deep to be washed or sanded away."[7] McNeil's was undoubtedly a relief to the numb and weary travelers far from their families during Christmas. Knox, a habitual early riser, was up the next morning and they resumed their journey, sleighing toward Stillwater.

The snow was becoming a problem. It had been snowing for several days, and after a brief rest they "set off about 3 o'clock it still snowing exceedingly fast and it being very deep after the utmost efforts of the horses we reached Ensigns Dec 26 about eight miles beyond Saratoga where we lodged."[8] Inns like Arch McNeil's appeared on early maps as a tavern and then a farm; many times the two were much the same. It snowed all night and "in the morning the snow being nearly two feet deep we with great trouble reached about two miles we then procured saddles and went to Stillwater where we got a sleigh to go to Albany but the roads not being broken prevented our getting further than New City about 9 miles above Albany—where we lodged."[9]

Knox picked up a sleigh in Stillwater without seeing George Palmer and continued to New City, now known as Lasingburg, nine miles from Albany. Knox had to cross the Hudson and Mohawk Rivers in his journey several times as 'the customary route in the 1770s was to cross at Lansing's Ferry by the old Half Moon Fort, travel south through New City and what became Troy but was often called Stone Arabia . . . and then back across the Hudson at Schuyler Flatts and on down to Albany."[10]

One could make a case this was a dry run for bringing down his cannons, but this last-minute expedition was more desperate. Knox's expedition was at a standstill, his men and cannons stuck at the south end of Lake George. He risked his life by traveling in a snowstorm and now that storm was becoming dire, and the brutal wilderness conditions endangered Knox and his men. "In the morning we set out and got about 2 miles when our horses tired and refused to go any further."[11] Knox's horses had given out, leaving the commander of the American artillery on foot in the wilderness. Henry Knox wrote in the singular, and it would seem that he alone decided to push on through the snowy woods: "I was then very obliged to undertake a fatiguing march of about 2 miles in three feet deep through the woods there being no beaten path."[12] Knox was not a thin man, and he huffed and puffed his way through heavy snow. It was an astonishing sight, this bearded, heavyset man on whom George Washington had pinned his hopes and the hopes of the American Revolution plunging through snow up to his knees in the woods in order to bring back the cannons to defeat the British. Disorientation along with the real prospect of freezing to death could not have been far from Knox's thoughts as he struggled through deep drifts, stopped, caught his breath, and then plowed on. The temperature was near zero, and the wind-whipped snow stung his face and numbed his hands.

Those who become lost in the woods must fight a sense of panic. In snowstorms, disorientation turns people around, and they find themselves going in circles, struggling for hours through a forest only to find themselves back where they began. This desperate mission was putting the American Revolution in jeopardy. If Knox failed, so might Washington. Thinking he was heading south, Knox groped though the woods in the blinding white snow until he finally saw a cabin. He later wrote in his journal that he "got to Squire Fisher's who politely gave me a fine breakfast and provided me with horses which carried me as far as Colonel Shuyler's where I got a sleigh to carry me to Albany which I reached about two o'clock, *almost perished with the cold.*"[13]

Almost perished with the cold. Henry Knox nearly froze to death. Many did in these snowstorms where lodging was few and far between. Knox was not a man who would prepare for the possibility of a brutal snowstorm. Winter gear consisted of layering coats and scarfs and wrapping oneself against the cold. Clearly Knox and his party had nearly perished on his mission to reach General Schuyler and ascertain what was going on with his sleds and oxen.

Schuyler was the man who could answer all his questions, and Knox "in the afternoon waited on General Schuyler and spent the evening with him."[14] Schuyler informed Knox that he had "received word from Washington that good reports had come regarding the progress of Knox and his train."[15] Knox and Schuyler immediately sent off for Mr. Palmer to come immediately down to Albany on December 27. Knox recorded what happened when Palmer met with him and Schuyler:

> Dec 28 Mr. Palmer came down and after a considerable degree of conversation between him and General Schuyler about the price, the General offering 18 p [pounds for the oxen and sled] and Palmer asking 24/ p [pounds per day] for 2 yoke of oxen, the treaty broke off abruptly and Mr. Palmer was dismissed and by reports from all parts the snow was too deep for the cannon to set out even if the sleds were ready.[16]

General Schuyler's suspicion that Palmer was taking advantage of the young bookseller seems warranted here. "That the rate was totally unacceptable is well established by the fact that men with sleds and teams have responded at a price even less than the best Schuyler would offer Palmer."[17] Palmer was finally out of the picture. The reality is that Schuyler saved Knox from being taken advantage of financially by Palmer. More importantly, Palmer probably could not have produced the sleds and oxen needed (he seemed to be more intent on getting paid), which would have stopped the Noble Train on the shores of Lake George, unable to proceed. Knox was lucky to have Schuyler step in when he did.

As snow continued to fall, making the roads impassable, Schuyler swung into action. It was now up to Schuyler and teamster John Becker to round up the necessary oxen and sleds. Feeling that the young Colonel Knox needed all the help and guidance he could give, Schuyler might have wanted to control as much of Knox's expedition as he could. In all probability, Schuyler had already put out word himself and did not want to disappoint his contractors, either. Knox's harrowing journey into the snowy wilderness ultimately proved to be essential to straightening out the confusion regarding procurement of the oxen and sleds. Communications were poor, one-sided, and took days if not weeks or months to reach correspondents. There was no time to lose, and on December 29, Knox wrote:

General Schuyler sent out his wagon master and other people to all parts of the county to immediately send up their sleighs with horses suitable he allowing them 12/p [pounds per day] for each pair of horses or 7 p ton for 62 miles. . . . The 31st December the wagon master returned the names of [those] who [had] gone up to the lake with their horses in the whole amounting to 124 pairs with sleighs which I'm afraid are not strong enough for the heavy cannon if I can judge from the sample shown me by General Schuyler.[18]

So the word went out and no less than "124 pairs with sleighs" were headed up to the lake.[19] Most likely, the 248 animals supplied were a combination of oxen and horses. Many accounts of Knox's journey had him waiting for snow, but in truth the storm had provided too much snow and there were no sleds ready to go until January 1. Knox worried that the sleds might not be strong enough, but there was little Knox could do about it now.

His advance run let Knox know the condition of the roads and the rivers he would have to cross. During the first four days of January, he wrote that he was "employed in getting holes cut in the different crossing places in the river to strengthen the ice."[20] This is a method of thickening ice, in which water is forced through the cut holes and then refreezes. Obviously, Knox also was worried that the ice might not be strong enough to bear the weight of the cannons. At this point, the Hudson and Mohawk Rivers—which are one and the same when they join above Albany—are frozen solid. This reassured Knox that he could transport the artillery across the ice, though the real test would be the three five-thousand-pound "Big Bertha" cannons.

Knox returned to Lake George to oversee the loading of the sleds and livestock as they arrived. This is in line with the account by John Becker Jr., the son of the teamster, regarding how the sleds and oxen were procured and then taken to Fort George:

The cannon captured from the enemy were next to be brought down from the north, and as many as one hundred and twenty, besides howitzers and swivels, had fallen into our hands with the two fortresses before mentioned. They had been in part removed to the head of Lake George and thither we directed to proceed for them. Col. Knox afterwards the able chief of our artillery, undertook to superintend their removal in person. He had very heavy sleds prepared for the occasion and a numerous train set out from our neighborhood.[21]

Clearly Becker Sr. had rounded up the sleds, oxen, and horses from "our neighborhood" and sent them northward to the lake. Knox then received a letter from George Palmer to Colonel Henry Knox, Esquire, of the Train Artillery at Albany. Palmer was not happy with the turn of events:

> Since your departure from here I have an opportunity with many of the inhabitants with whom I have contracted for the removal of the artillery and stores I find all determined to a man to fulfill on their part and that I shall on mine be able to do. Depend sir the people and not only those employed in service but others general are not indifferent, they are sensible of the importance of the grand cause they are sensible to the minutest degree of the insult offered in counteracting your measures. I take this earliest opportunity to inform you of the disposition of the people among whom I live with whom I am concerned particularly in this affair your penetration will easily discern the consequences that will follow disappointing such a number of people so resolutely determined as you may depend and hope are with regard to what you mentioned at our carrying the heavy pieces they are determined since there is such an attempt made to supplant them to fulfill the whole contract.[22]

Palmer was mad and not above veiled threats. He had contracted out the building of sleds and procuring of oxen and now that Knox was backing out, these people might resort to taking revenge against the train. Knox seemed somewhat oblivious to the real danger posed by those who were sympathetic to Britain and would sabotage his efforts. Historian Paul Rayno points out that the "divided feelings of the colonists were marked in the upper Hudson Valley by strong pockets of Tory sentiment in the vicinity of present-day Hudson Falls and Fort Edward. Such centers must have had adherents in most of the communities along the river in that region, just as some of those who were such violent Loyalists also found close blood relatives were of quite opposing views as Whig Patriots."[23]

Besides a general danger from Indians allied with the British, an equal if not more dangerous threat stemmed from these pockets of Tories who would sabotage Washington's artillery-train Hail Mary. To secure the sleds and oxen, George Palmer surely had spread word far and wide, leaving a sour taste with friend and foe. The fact the British believed it impossible to bring the cannons from Ticonderoga to Boston was one of the reasons they didn't send a force to intercept Knox, but that did not mean that local Tories would not take matters into their own hands.

Despite invoking the "grand cause" as a motivating factor, Palmer's prime motivation was surely money, and the loss of the money, not patriotic involvement, prompted his letter. After the deal with Palmer fell through, some of Palmer's contractors contacted Knox on their own. Knox didn't act on these offers since the procurement of the sleds and oxen was out of his hands. Knox must have been relieved to relinquish control as General Schuyler and wagon master Becker took over and the sleds and oxen began to arrive at Fort George. Knox and his brother William could now concentrate on the composition of the artillery train. Like the crossing of Lake George, the cannons would be divided into groups that would travel together but could spread out as required by the difficulties in moving the heavier cannon versus the lighter ones. It is logical that John Becker Sr. was now also part of the organization of the train, as his son, John Becker Jr., began his account of events. "I served in the unpretending but not useless character of a wagoner in the quartermaster's department, at one time actively employed in forwarding cannon."[24]

Young John Becker Jr. gives insight into why his father was chosen to head the teamsters: "My father having a good share of the patronage, as well as the confidence of the leading men in our neighborhood, with a snug property of his own and good number of horses, was very much in demand when any urgent and rapid stores of supplies were to be effected. The cannon captured from the enemy were next to be brought down from the north and as many as one hundred and twenty, besides howitzers and swivels. . . . They had been in part removed to the head of Lake George, and then we were directed to proceed for them."[25]

To John Becker Jr., it was logical that his father should be chosen to bring down the cannon. Freighting is his business, and artillery is just another type of freight. Becker Jr. began his journal as he and his father made their way to Fort George with a team of horses and men. The Beckers dealt with more oxen than horses, but many of Knox's teamsters used horses. "The New Yorkers have been always noted for the prevailing use of horses and the assertion may be hazarded, that in that day, as well as now, they possessed a greater number of these animals than any other state."[26] Knox would use whatever draft animal provided him, be it oxen or horses.

The young boy's account of the journey to the fort offers some idea of what it was like to travel with teamsters in 1775:

> Long before daylight we were on the move. I had trouble of managing an extra pair of horses. We had taken on many more than the usual number in consequence of the service in which we were engaged. My father was some distance in the rear, while by accident I was considerably in advance of him. The road was dreary, the darkness great, and I anything but comfortable during the morning drive. We were approaching the bloody pond, and the scene of terrible slaughters.[27]

This was a reference to a battle fought in 1755 around Lake George in which French soldiers were ambushed by the British and their bodies tossed into a shallow pool, forever after referred to as the bloody pond.

My imagination peopled every bush with ghosts. In this pond hundreds of those slain in the battles between Sir William Johnson and the French Baron Dieskau were carelessly thrown, the hurry and distress of the hour permitting no other receptacle for the dead. My nervous excitement increased every instant. I anxiously turned my ear to listen to the sounds of the voices behind me, which came along in melancholy intervals, and would then be lost for apparently an interminable period.[28]

John Becker Junior led his own team of horses but became separated from his father and succumbed to the darkness, the hour, and the eeriness of passing through woods where vicious battles had been fought. His fears, albeit those of a boy, show the loneliness of passing through a wilderness that few had traveled and the long hours of monotony that was travel in the eighteenth century punctuated by the terror of the unexpected:

While I was thus in spite of myself giving way to the most unpleasant feelings, my leading horses, which had been jogging along on a pace quite inconsistent with my views of propriety, made a sudden halt and fell back upon the pair next to the sled. This sudden stop only increased my confusion. I could not help thinking that the animals saw something I could not. I remembered an old superstition that dogs can see ghosts and I now fancied that horses might have the same facility. I did not however forget myself. I made a most rapid and liberal use of my whip, when, with first a recoil, then a plunge, and a desperate scramble, the horses leaped over something which seemed to be in their way and went on at a full gallop for some distance. I at length succeeded in arresting their flight and began to bawl lustily to those who were far away in the rear. . . . My father came swiftly up, when I informed him of what had occurred. A diligent search was then made along the road by persons in our company. What should the cause of my anxiety prove to be but a drunken soldier, who had, in some unaccountable way, fallen asleep on the road, overcome by fatigue and exhaustion.[29]

As the sleds and oxen arrived, they were separated into five separate serials. Henry Knox, the self-taught military engineer, emerged here as he orchestrated the progression of the train. In this moment, we can assume it was Knox calling the shots to get the cannons to Boston, and this is no ordinary movement of freight by teamsters. Nothing short of the Revolution was riding on safe transport of the artillery. Major Thomas Campeau, in his master's thesis, *The Noble Train of Artillery*, reconstructed the five groups the teamsters, sleds, oxen, and militiamen formed:

Five separate serials made up the movement, with no serial carrying more than 17 cannons. Each piece had remained with its broken-down carriage as it crossed the lakes. Each gun and its carriage were loaded onto sleds and tied down with ropes. Great care was taken not to separate a cannon from its carriage as there were multiple versions present. There was a total of thirteen 18 and 24 pounders, which comprised the heaviest version of guns present. Henry had the 13 heavy guns comprise the first serial to set the pace of the movement. These 13 cannons were to be drawn by two yoke of oxen each. This configuration required every 18 pounder to have four oxen, plus a team of teamsters and soldiers accompanying the gun.[30]

The heavy guns would be challenging for the men and the oxen as they moved across rivers and into the mountains, and John Becker felt it was better to have the most experienced teamsters dealing with these cannons. His son later wrote that he and his father supervised the lead sled. "Both he and his father rode horseback constantly observing their assigned yoke. One teamster could control no more than two yoke of oxen."[31] And each yoke required two oxen to pull the sled.

The militiamen were dispersed among the five groups. When all the sleds were loaded and the oxen in place, the composition of Knox's Noble Train was established by using "the mathematical determination that 1 ox can carry 700 lbs. Using that formula all the weights for all the cannons were computed and it was determined what that serial would look like inside the larger movement."[32] Knox rode the length of the convoy at times but primarily stayed with the second group to "set the pace and avoid bunching up with the slower moving first serial."[33]

Serial 1
12 soldiers
7 iron 18 pounders, 7 sleds, 14 yoke, 7 teamsters (Becker Sr. and Jr. included)
4 iron 24 pounders, 4 sleds, 8 yoke, 4 teamsters
1 brass 18 pounder, 1 sled, 2 yoke, 1 teamster
1 brass 24 pounder, 1 sled, 2 yoke, 1 teamster
Serial total: 12 soldiers, 13 cannons, 13 sleds, 26 yoke, 13 teamsters

Serial 2
8 soldiers
Henry Knox
1 mortar, 3 Cohorns, 1 sled, 1 yoke, 1 teamster
3 Cohorns, 1 sled, 1 yoke, 1 teamster
2 9 pounders, 1 sled, 1 yoke, 1 teamster
2 9 pounders, 1 sled, 1 yoke, 1 teamster
Serial total: 8 soldiers, Henry Knox, 11 cannons, 4 sleds, 4 yoke, 4 teamsters

Serial 3
7 soldiers
3 6 pounders, 1 sled, 1 yoke, 1 teamster
4 3 pounders, 1 sled, 1 yoke, 1 teamster
4 3 pounders, 1 sled, 1 yoke, 1 teamster
Serial total: 7 soldiers, 11 cannons, 3 sleds, 3 yoke, 3 teamsters

Serial 4
7 soldiers
3 mortars, 1 sled, 1 yoke, 1 teamster
2 howitzers, 1 sled, 1 yoke, 1 teamster
10 12 pounders, 12 sleds, 22 yoke, 12 teamsters
Supplies, 2 sleds, 2 yoke, 2 teamsters
Extra yoke, 0 sleds, 4 yoke, 0 teamsters
Serial total: 7 soldiers, 15 cannons, 16 sleds, 31 yoke, 16 teamsters

Serial 5
8 soldiers
William Knox
3 mortars, 1 sled, 1 yoke, 1 teamster
3 6 pounders, 1 sled, 1 yoke, 1 teamster
3 6 pounders, 1 sled, 1 yoke, 1 teamster
Supplies, 2 sleds, 2 yoke, 2 teamsters
Supplies, 1 sled horse drawn, 0 teamsters
Extra yoke, 0 sleds, 4 yoke, 0 teamsters
Serial total: 8 soldiers, William Knox, 9 cannons, 6 sleds, 9 yoke, 5 teamsters[34]

These groups were not set in stone, and as the expedition progressed the groups bunched up and spread out and horses were swapped for oxen and vice versa. The Noble Train moved as a stretched-out caterpillar with conditions determining the pace.

Becker only reported going from Fort George to Glen Falls in the first day's run—a distance short enough to represent only a part of a day of actual travel. There seems to be a clear indication that each sled left as soon as it was loaded, and the train was spread out along the road accordingly until weak ice at river crossings and breakdowns forced groups to gather and eventually stay together for mutual aid.[35]

The snafu regarding who would supply the oxen and sleds slowed the progress of the expedition, but sometime during the first four days of the new year, the sleds departed Fort George for the run to Glens Falls, 9.1 miles away. The fact that Knox got the oxen and sleds in place so quickly shows that Schuyler had made advance arrangements to procure them, which shows why he was flabbergasted when Knox contracted with George Palmer. The Noble Train had to set out, but the snow had dissipated by the New Year and a thaw had set in. The bitter cold that almost killed Knox abated, but the milder temperatures created soggy conditions that necessitated cutting more holes in the four crossings of the Hudson River to thicken the ice. Time had been lost in the drama of getting the sleds, oxen, and horses; now rain or shine or snow or sleet be damned.

They had to start.

THE BAD GENERAL

January 1, 1776

The British officer walked toward the American lines under a white flag. It had been a busy fifteen months for both sides, particularly for the British, who had built fortifications to the furthest point of the Neck. Earthen walls were backed up by floating artillery in Back Bay with tree trunks and sharpened branches in front of the fortifications to stop any approaching soldiers. Then a moat had been dug across the Neck, severing the connection to the mainland and turning Boston into an island. Through this no-man's-land, a British officer advanced, accompanied by several soldiers.

Both sides had settled into an uncomfortable stalemate. General Howe was satisfied with his mistress, Elizabeth Lloyd Loring, the wife of a prominent Loyalist, Joshua Loring, and going to the theater, fully convinced he was in control. After all, it was winter, and it was understood that no one fought in winter. But Howe could let the rebels know what they were up against, so he sent an officer carrying a copy of the king's October 27 speech to Parliament. It was a threat that Howe thought might bring the errant colonists to their senses when they realized what they were up against. The king had declared:

> America was in open revolt. . . . They have raised troops and are collecting a naval force. They have seized the public revenue, and assumed to themselves legislative, executive, and judicial powers, which they already exercise in the most arbitrary manner . . . and although many of these unhappy people may still retain

their loyalty . . . the torrent of violence has been strong enough to compel their acquiescence until a sufficient force shall appear to support them.[1]

The king recognized the true intent behind the rebellion: "The rebellious war . . . is manifestly carried on for the purpose of establishing an independent empire."[2] Then came the threat that Howe thought might bring about mass desertions from the rebel army; King George III affirmed that he was committing land and sea forces and entertaining "friendly offers of foreign assistance."[3] Which translated into augmenting the British army with brutal Hessian troops. After delivering copies of the speech, the officer and his men picked their way back through the marshland and returned to the British fortifications.

George Washington was no doubt aware of the king's speech and the clumsy attempts by the British to frighten Americans. Washington was a frustrated man. He had been told by the Continental Congress that he would be leading an army of twenty thousand men, but what he found was a disintegrating army of "undisciplined militiamen . . . puritanical savages that included seventeen actual Indians from the Massachusetts town of Stockbridge."[4] Worse than that, Washington came to doubt the caliber of New England soldiers in general.

He wrote his cousin, saying New Englanders were "an exceedingly dirty and nasty people"[5] and that he thought most of them had "an unaccountable kind of stupidity in the lower class of these people, which believe me prevails but too generally among the officers of the Massachusetts part of the army, who are nearly of the same kidney with the privates."[6] This was a patrician planter who found himself interacting with people unfamiliar with the caste system of the South. Washington doubted the very fabric of his own officers and found them wanting. A revolution begun by yeoman farmers at Lexington now was being led by a man with more in common with British lifestyle and culture rather than that of the average patriot. Washington was in fact comparing his citizen soldiers to the British soldiers.

However, General Charles Lee, a former British officer with more military experience than Washington, thought the militia model of the army could be harnessed for the type of war facing the Americans. "These farmers might lack the rigid training of British regulars, but they knew how to fight."[7] Horatio Gates, another former British officer, was quoted as saying, "he never desired to see better soldiers than the New England men made."[8] By judging the men under him so harshly, Washington was on thin ice with an army he desperately needed.

The first problem Washington identified was how the officers were chosen. Many of the officers of the New England army were selected by the number of men from their hometowns who could be convinced to serve under them. This was based on popularity rather than leadership ability, and if the men decided they didn't like the officer, they simply refused to reenlist and left the army. This also proved to be a problem for Washington's position as the supreme leader of the army: the men's allegiance was to their hometown officers and not to the new leader selected by the Continental Congress. Moreover, each company was loyal to its town of origin; a national sense of allegiance to the new country had yet to take hold.

Add to all of this that George Washington had no experience laying siege to a city to expel an occupying army. Siege warfare dated back to 3000 BC in the Middle East, where settlement inhabitants built large stone walls, ditches, and towers to protect themselves from attack. The Chinese, Romans, and Greeks of the Middle Ages perfected siege techniques, which led to castles and then to the creation of heavy artillery to conquer these fortifications. The seventeenth and eighteenth centuries saw advances in fortifications and artillery, one outpacing the other through the years. By 1775 the techniques for laying siege to a city were much the same: "through intimidation, attrition, and if necessary, force."[9]

Through the fall, Washington had his men construct "a line of contravallation," which were rings of earthworks that encircled Boston. The problem was that the British warships could keep the harbor open, so there was no starving the British. All that left was an all-out attack. In short, Washington "had inherited an army that had a fighting reputation, a reputation, he was convinced, it did not deserve. And yet so far he had done nothing that could compare to the achievement of Bunker Hill and Lexington and Concord."[10]

The man from Mount Vernon had taken over the army in July with the expectation he would go on the offensive, but he had been denied permission to attack the British by his war council and had to settle for harassing the occupying force any way he could. He had been as bold as he dared, constructing fortifications closer and closer to the British and building a "bomb battery" on Lechmere's Point, and he was mystified the British allowed them to complete the work unmolested. He wrote that he was "unable upon any principal whatever to account for their silence, unless it be to lull us into a fatal security, to favor some attempt they may have in view about the time the great change they expect will take place the last of this month."[11]

Washington was certain an attack was coming and determined to stop the British any way he could through fortifications and batteries. He planned to move three hundred troops under General Putnam over the causeway to Lechmere's Point, but this time the British woke up. "The morning was foggy and the party at work was not discovered until about noon when the ship began to cannonade with round and grapeshot and a battery at Barton's Point with twenty-four pounders and mortars. A soldier was wounded, and the party was driven from the works."[12] The next morning the Americans began to fire upon the ship, forcing it to hoist anchor and move away.

These low-level skirmishes between the two armies went on throughout the winter. It was meant to harass, and the Americans became used to the cannonballs lobbed by the men-of-war. Many times, the work on fortifications continued while the cannonballs rained down. "Shells fell, burst and covered the party with dirt and one broke in the air about seventy feet above it. The men in the works were ordered, when sentinels cried, 'A shot' to settle down and not leave their places."[13] Such was life under the stalled siege of Boston.

Washington knew that the British could wait in Boston while his army slowly fell apart. He even considered destroying Boston in an all-out attack and wrote to Congress for permission. "The general wishes to know how it may be deemed proper and advisable to avail himself of the season to destroy the troops who propose to winter in Boston by a bombardment, when the harbor is blocked up, or in other words whether the loss of the town and the property therein are to be considered."[14]

This included burning Boston to the ground to force the British out. Benjamin Franklin replied that his committee must "refer it to the Honorable Congress."[15] Meanwhile General Artemas Ward had his eyes on Dorchester Heights and as early as August had written, "We . . . ought carefully to consider what steps may be taken, consistent with prudence and safety should an enemy in part gain such an ascendency. . . . I beg your Excellency to give me some instructions relative to my duty in that case."[16]

The British—looking to strike back at the rebels, who had been disrupting British shipping with their whaleboats—ordered towns "up and down the New England coast to the torch as a demonstration of the fearsome might of the British navy."[17] The Burning of Falmouth, an attack on what is now Portland, Maine, served to make an example of the town. Gloucester escaped such a fate after the British determined that the houses there were too far apart. Two fourteen-gun British warships opened fire on the town, and the inhabitants began to flee in panic. By 6:00 p.m., the town was ablaze. From the water, the town looked like one long flame. When Washington received this news, he was overcome with impotent fury.

A revolution depends on momentum, which was slowly draining away in the winter of 1775 while Henry Knox trekked through the wilderness to retrieve the cannons that were hoped would change the course of the war. Washington fumed while his army withered away, and many blamed him for the stalemate. It would seem George Washington had a public relations problem. Nathaniel Greene, a friend of Henry Knox, placed some of the blame on his commanding general as he watched the Connecticut soldiers march home after their enlistments expired. "His excellency had been taught to believe the people here a superior race of mortals and finding them of the same temper and disposition . . . of the common people of other governments, they sink in his esteem. . . . You cannot expect to make veterans from a raw militia after only a few months service."[18]

The former commander in chief, Artemas Ward, had heard of Washington's disparagement of the troops under him. He criticized the commander's discipline of the troops and his obvious low opinion of the New England soldiers in general. The former commander wrote that his

> great concern about the raising of the new army, for the genius of this people is different from those Southward. Our people are jealous and are not inclinable to act upon implicit faith; they choose to see and judge for themselves. They remember what was said of them by some from the Southward last summer, which makes them backward in enlisting or manifesting a willingness to enlist. . . . Some have said hard things of the officers belonging to his colony and despised them, but I think as mean as they have represented them to be, there has been no one action with the enemy, which has not been conducted by an officer of this colony.[19]

Ward fairly roasted Washington. Putting aside their natural antipathy—Washington did take Ward's command—Washington's comments filtered back to the men, especially the officers. Washington's adjutant Joseph Reed reported that his remarks about the army had reached as far as Congress and caused some rumblings by the delegates. The prevailing view was Washington had been handed an army that had neatly bottled up the British in Boston, an army that had punished the British at Bunker Hill. The people were waiting for an early victory, and Washington knew it.

Always an astute judge of character and where he stood with people, Washington immediately began to adjust. "I am much obliged to you for the hints," he wrote back to Reed. "I will endeavor a reformation, as I can assure you my dear Reed that I wish to walk in such a line as will give most general satisfaction."[20] Washington realized that he had made a real error in ostracizing the men in his creation of a new army, not a colonial army, but an American army. He wrote again to Reed, "I can bear to hear of imputed or real errors. . . . The man who wishes to stand well in the opinion of others must do this, because he is thereby enabled to correct his faults . . . for as I have but one capital object in view, I could wish to make my conduct coincide with the wishes of mankind as far as I can consistently."[21]

A young George Washington, about the same age as Henry Knox when he headed off into the wilderness.

Twenty-five-year-old Henry Knox.

The Noble Train going through the Berkshire mountains.

Lake George that Knox had to sail up and down again with the sixty tons of artillery.

Fort Ticonderoga on Lake George, where sixty tons of artillery were waiting for Henry Knox.

George Washington greeting the Knox Expedition.

Henry Knox's cannons dragged through the snows of 1775.

The Knox train in the Adirondacks.

The Heights of Dorchester from where Washington launched his attack with artillery.

Like Henry Knox, George Washington was engaged in on-the-job training. The American Revolution was an experiment held together by the glue of the "glorious cause," but no one, including George Washington, had any experience in their positions. Washington had never created an army out of a ragged colonial militia under a young democratic system, nor did he have any experience in siege warfare. This would seem to be the reason he resorted to attacking the British outright. It was the maneuver with which he *did* have experience, but the army's perpetual lack of gunpowder, men, and the war council's lack of confidence in Washington's plans precluded attacking the British.

To Ward, George Washington may have seemed a bad general. Washington was struggling for respect from Congress, the American people, his army, and even the British. Before he was replaced by Howe, General Gage had sent Washington a condescending letter about the mistreatment of American prisoners. "I recognize no rank among American prisoners for I acknowledge no rank that is not derived from the King,"—that is to say, Gage pointedly disavowed Washington's rank, as well. Then he lectured the new general on etiquette: "Be temperate in political disquisition, give free operation to truth, and punish those who deceive and misrepresent and not only the effects, but the causes of this unhappy conflict will be removed."[22]

Even George Washington's mother gave him little respect. Mary Ball Washington had a cold relationship with her son, and George returned the favor. When he had resigned from the army after the French and Indian War, she said, "There had been no end to my trouble while George was in the army, but he has now given it up."[23] Washington was a dutiful son, but it was an unemotional duty, and he frequently gave her money, which she never repaid. She never recognized her son's accomplishments and felt he had chosen the wrong side of the Revolution. Later, some would accuse her of being a Tory.

Once, when her famous son was to be honored at a ball in Fredericksburg, she was told that "his excellency" was on his way. Mary Ball Washington snapped, "His excellency! What nonsense!"[24]

Frustrated, Washington attempted to harass the British. On January 8 he sent General Thomas Knowlton with his Connecticut regiment to probe the British forces. That very evening, British General Howe attended a farce titled *The Blockade at Faneuil Hall in Boston*, which portrayed George Washington in an oversized wig, dragging a rusty sword. When Knowlton attacked Charlestown and the British guns roared in reply, the audience assumed it was part of the show until a Yankee sergeant dressed as a farmer ran onstage, proclaiming the rebels were "at it tooth and nail over in Charlestown."[25]

The audience laughed and clapped, but General Howe and others realized something else was happening. General Howe sounded the alarm, shouting "Turn out! Turn out!" The British soldiers "soon finding their mistake, a general scene of confusion ensued. They immediately hurried out of the house to their alarm posts, some skipping over the orchestra, trampling on the fiddles, and, in short, everyone making this most speedy retreat, the actors [who were all officers] calling out for water to get the paint and smut off their faces, women fainting."[26]

Knowlton's men retreated under the barrage. These probing attacks on both sides broke out sporadically, setting nerves on edge and reminding Washington that he was powerless to do anything but wait. His excellency could find no release as a long hard winter settled in. George Washington needed something to break the logjam. He needed the fifty-nine cannons that were now loaded onto sleds and about to head south under Henry Knox.

18

HEADING BACK DOWN

January 2, 1776

Henry Knox learned all he knew about military matters from books and from drilling with the local Boston militia. He learned all he knew of cannons and artillery from books and from a local unit of artillery that he joined while still a bookseller. He learned about fortifications, at which he proved to be adept from inception to execution, from books as well. But he had no idea how to move thousands of pounds of cannons lashed to sleds and pulled by oxen and horses on slushy, muddy roads.

Knox would rely on John Becker and his teamsters and the oxen that dragged the heavy wooden sleds on a trading trail in the foothills of the Adirondacks. The snow had melted, spelling disaster for the Knox expedition. The teamsters were learning as they progressed, and they were progressing slowly. The oxen on each sled had to navigate a steep, narrow trail, their hooves slipping and sliding in the mud.

Horses were present along with oxen, but for the Knox expedition, oxen were the logical choice. Oxen were castrated adult male cattle, castration making them easier to control. In 1775 they were used for plowing, pulling carts or wagons, and sometimes riding. Often used for threshing, powering machines grinding hay, and hauling logs by lumber companies, the oxen were the heavy trucks of their time. They were usually yoked together; heavy loads might require eight pair.

Oxen were taught to respond to commands, usually a combination of body language and specific words: *back* for "back up," *gee* for "turn right," *get up* or *giddy up* for "go," *haw* for "turn left," and *whoa* for "stop." Whips and long poles also were used to guide them. Oxen were preferable to horses on Knox's expedition because they can pull heavier loads for longer periods and are far less excitable than horses. This would be particularly important when crossing frozen rivers or traversing mountains where accidents were more likely. In pulling of thousands of pounds of iron, the oxen had a better chance of getting the job done.

Knox did not simply plunge into the wilderness with a compass. There was a customary route of travel often used by the military that he would follow. The first run extended nine miles from Fort George to Glens Falls, a small town on the Hudson. From there they would travel to Saratoga, another twenty-two miles. They would then proceed to the town of Halfmoon located at the convergence of the Mohawk and Hudson Rivers, another sixteen miles. "Halfmoon was a waterway trading center. . . . The convoy had to cross the Mohawk River to reach Albany."[1] After crossing the Mohawk, it was another seven miles to Albany. Then the train would cross the Hudson River. The rivers being sufficiently frozen was critical to these crossings.

They would slog another twenty-two miles to the town of Kinderhook, at the foot of the Berkshire mountains. This was the most difficult passage: twenty-three miles of treacherous paths winding through steep mountains and valleys would have to be traversed before passing through the town of Hillsdale. The great climb of the Berkshires would continue through Great Barrington, Otis, Bluford, Westfield, then Springfield, another fifty-nine miles.

From Springfield it would be a relatively straight run to Worchester, where Lucy was staying, then Farmington, and finally, Cambridge, another ninety-one miles. That is, assuming that the rivers were frozen, that there would be no breakdowns of man or beast, that there would be enough snow for the sleds—and that they would be able to pass through the Berkshire mountains. The amazing component of Knox's route was that it would require his train of cannons to cross the frozen Hudson River no less than four times, each crossing more hazardous than the last.

From Fort George, the sleds would move along the old military road to what was then the inhabited center of Queensbury . . . which would one day become the city of Glen Falls. From there they would pass along the military road to Fort Edward and then along the east side of the river to the village opposite Fort Miller and on to the ford or ferry near Fort Hardy a bit north of present-day Schuylerville . . . then called Saratoga."[2]

This would be the first crossing of the Hudson River. Once across, the expedition would travel south across "low rolling hills and along the edge of the river on the plain, through Stillwater and onto the usual crossing place at old Fort Half Moon, called the half-moon crossing by Knox but also known as Lansing's Ferry."[3] Here Knox would cross the Hudson a second time, then move south through Lansingburg, then cross a third time at Schuyler Flatts, and finally crossing the fourth time at Albany or South Ferry. Knox would follow the Old Post Road to Kinderhook, then Claverknack, entering the Berkshire Mountains and passing through the Green Woods, then the town of Great Barrington, coming out of the Berkshires on the western side into Massachusetts, where he would follow rural roads to Westfield, Springfield, Worcester, Framingham, and into Concord. Much of the route would be improvised as conditions dictated.

But this was all in the future. Knox's train began slowly. John Becker Jr. recorded the progress of the train in his journal.

> Our business as I have already mentioned was to transport the captured artillery. It was a seasonable supply and we felt an unusual degree of interest in fulfilling out contracts. The pieces were apportioned to our respective companies. My father took in charge a heavy iron 24 pounder (5,000 pounds), which required the exertions of at least eight horses. We had altogether about forty or fifty pieces to transport, and our cavalcade was quite imposing.[4]

John Becker Jr. mentioned using horses, and the benefit of oxen is clear: it took eight horses to do what two oxen could accomplish. John Becker Sr. and his son rode between the groups to ensure that all the animals were pulling. The militiamen walked on the outside with muskets at the ready should Indians, Tories, or British soldiers appear. No one knew if the British would try to interfere or stop the train. The horses whined, the oxen huffed, blowing out steam, the teamsters fought to keep the oxen in the center of the trail, calling out to each other and to the animals. The whips snapped, men swore, the oxen moaned, then a rollover.

The teamsters were not used to the physics of the sleds, and the trail going through the foothills had steep sides. The caravan stopped with a call of *whoa!* The teamsters unhooked the yokes of the oxen from the overturned sled and used rope pulleys wrapped around trees for leverage, along with the oxen, to right the sled. This was the first time the rope pulleys were used, which would be instrumental in hauling the sleds up steep, uneven terrain. "This was difficult work and required a very skilled crew."[5] The first few times that rollovers occurred, Knox had the serials ahead keep moving. When he realized the groups were getting too far ahead, he halted the train whenever a sled turned over.

Knox learned as he traveled along. The young commander had done all the planning he could. "He has checked his route. He has had guns go over it, including some of the heaviest. He has not relished the risks he foresaw but has faced them as unavoidable. His only serious planning error, other than misjudging Palmer, has been to neglect that standard of military philosophy which says, 'If anything can go wrong, it will.'"[6]

Knox was now riding herd with his scarf trailing, his wrapped left hand in a colorful bright handkerchief, his long hair flowing behind him, managing one crisis after another. The physics of the extreme weight, the hastily constructed sleds that were probably off-balance to begin with, and the half-frozen terrain conspired to turn over the sleds. The oxen were slipping on the muddy trail along with the swearing men. Moving a five-thousand-pound cannon would be comparable to moving several trucks by oxen on a muddy, narrow trail—almost impossible.

A different man might have waited for snow, but Knox had promised George Washington he would get the cannons in little more than two weeks, though this would prove to be woefully overconfident. Knox could travel only so far without snow, but he could not wait for the weather to change. So they trudged on, men fighting the cold and the terrain as they bedded down at night with tents and warmed themselves by fires, drinking whiskey and smoking pipes. There were no good roads to follow in 1775. The early roads were so bad that travelers had to pause every mile or so to rest, and inns were usually just a few miles apart. The old military road, or footrail as some historians called it, had no inns, so the men and oxen slept in the cold until finally reaching Glens Falls.

John Becker Jr. made note of the Glens Falls townspeople who emerged from their homes and stared at the cannons in fascination. This was virtually all of the American Continental Army's artillery, and news of Knox's expedition preceded him. Knox led the procession into town and rode back and forth along the trail to ensure that all was well while shouting orders to the teamsters. John Becker Jr. was glad to have arrived in Glens Falls. He was at the front of the train and his father further back. Near Lake George, "The road was dreary, the darkness great, and I anything but comfortable during the morning drive."[7] The men bedded down for the night at an inn while Henry made plans to ride ahead and inspect the Hudson River for crossing. He had soldiers pour water on the ice to thicken it and cut more holes to allow the water to flow over the top. Henry Knox was trying to create an ice road for his cannons, oxen, horses, and men. The temperatures were still dangerously warm, which could spell disaster for the heavier cannons.

Knox would have to check every mile of ice they had to cross. In time the Noble Train would spread out over five miles with Knox doing advance work, drilling holes, supervising the men, and procuring more oxen, horses, and teamsters. For all his careful planning, Knox now would have to cross the Hudson River, and if it wasn't frozen solid, his Noble Train could go no further.

CROSSING THE ICE

January 3, 1776

Ice, of course, is frozen water. A water molecule is composed of one oxygen atom bonded to two hydrogen atoms. In its liquid state, in which the temperature ranges from 32 to 212 degrees Fahrenheit, the hydrogen atoms slide around, making and breaking bonds with oxygen atoms. But at 32 degrees and below, the hydrogen atoms lock together in a set pattern that creates crystals. These crystals require more space than the sliding water molecules and are less dense, which is why ice cubes float.

Henry Knox would have to depend on these locked-down hydrogen molecules to support his sixty tons of artillery as he crossed the Hudson River. Knox wrote to George Washington on January 4, 1776, "The want of snow detained me some days and now a cruel thaw hinders us from crossing the Hudson River which we are obliged to do four times from Lake George to this town. . . . These inevitable delays pain me exceedingly as my mind is fully sensible of the greatest expedition in this case."[1] This had been Knox's problem with the rising temperatures. He had gone down to the banks of the Hudson at Glens Falls and stared at the blue ice under the moon. To lose his cannons to the river would be disastrous. General Schuyler supported Knox, writing Washington as well and explaining "the uncommon mildness of the weather for several days past. One frosty night if not deferred too long, however, will put everything in order."[2]

Henry Knox and his train of artillery would cross the Hudson in varying states of frozen and thawing ice. He alternately traveled with the train and then led the way with advance parties. Knox was now fulfilling the role of a commander, being everywhere at once—delegating to his brother and the teamsters; obtaining more horses, oxen, and sleds; and ensuring that food and provisions were available as they progressed southward. He had his eye on the date and felt the pressure to deliver the cannons to Washington as quickly as possible. This meant that the train must keep moving. He had holes cut in the ice and had soldiers throw buckets of water on the ice in order to thicken the ice road where the expedition would cross.

The convoy started out at Glens Falls and headed for Saratoga twenty-two miles away. The first real test would be crossing with their five-thousand-pound sleds. The Mohawk River is a tributary that flows into the Hudson ten miles above Albany. The Hudson then flows south and eventually drains into the Atlantic Ocean. It is the political boundary between New York and New Jersey. Named after Henry Hudson, who explored it in 1609, its strategic importance as the gateway to the American interior led to years of competition between the English and the Dutch over control of the river and colony. During the eighteenth century, the river valley and its inhabitants were the subject of and inspiration for Washington Irving, the first internationally acclaimed American author. In the nineteenth century, the area inspired the Hudson River School of painting, an American pastoral style. The eastern outlet for the Erie Canal empties in the river as well, an important transportation vein for the early-nineteenth-century United States.

After a hearty breakfast at Glens Falls, the men got the oxen moving, the sleds grooving snow that had fallen overnight. It would take two days to reach Saratoga. William had galloped ahead and reported back to Knox that the Hudson was frozen. Henry had already scouted out the river himself on his advance ride to see General Schuyler. He had ordered the ice thickened at key points, "getting holes cut in the different crossing places in order to strengthen the ice."[3] Henry had learned this method of strengthening ice from his reading. Knox instructed his men to cut holes in the four locations where the train would most likely cross the ice.

Upon reaching the river, Knox directed the sleds to spread out with the first heavy cannon in the lead. If the five-thousand-pound sleds could make it across, then so could the lighter ones. The ice had to be seven inches thick to hold the combined weight of the brass twenty-four pounder (five thousand pounds in weight), the men, the oxen, and the sled. No one knew how thick the ice was, and temperatures had varied widely during the last two weeks. Their only option was to cross the river and see if the ice would hold the cannons.

Knox stared across the white frozen expanse and heard the wind whistling through the far trees. He clucked his horse onto the ice, riding ahead with John

Becker, who walked beside the first sled with an axe ready to cut the ropes from the oxen if the cannon broke through the ice. John Becker Jr. gives some insight as to how his father handled the heavier cannons on a different crossing with horses:

> My father took in charge a heavy nine pounder [2,800 pounds], which required the united efforts of four horses to drag it along. Others had the heavy resistance of 18s and 24s (5,000 pounds) to overcome which required the exertions of at least eight horses . . . as the ice was not uncommonly strong, so precautions were taken to get along to safety. The method adopted was this; a rope forty feet long was fastened to the tongue of the sleigh and the other end was attached to the horses. The first gun was started across in this way and my father walked alongside the horses with a sharp hatchet in his hand, to cut the rope, if the cannon and sled should break through.[4]

They began slowly, hearing long groans punctuated by cracks in the ice. John Becker Sr. didn't want to lose the oxen and kept his eyes on the thick corded rope that he would slash with the axe. He would have only seconds to separate the yoke of oxen from the heavy weight of a sinking cannon. The worst scenario was that the cannon would plunge through, cracks rippling outward, sending men, sleds, and animals under. The best case should the ice break was that they would lose only the cannon. Extra ropes had been tied around the neck of the cannon with an eye toward retrieval.

The wind blasted across the desolate river with the far pines frosted white. The oxen made their way, hooves clicking on the ice. Becker pulled back, calling out *whoa!* to the oxen, slowing them further. Knox had dismounted and guided his horse, staring ahead and then behind. The other men stood by their sleds on the near side of the river, watching to see if disaster would strike and their expedition would fall into the icy water below. Along with the Indians, the Tories, and the British, the ice was another foe that could obliterate the entire train.

Silent now in the middle of the frozen river. The creak of the ropes, the slide of shoes on thin snow. The grunt of heavy animals. Knox felt his heartbeat with every step. The far side of the Hudson drew closer and Knox turned, staring at the light grooves the sled left in the ice. Seven inches of ice must be beneath the oxen and the rails of the sled; other than a groan and an occasional heart-stopping rifle crack of shifting ice, the river seemed to be holding their weight. Knox felt the stiff wind pick at his scarf. His eyes watered. He led his horse off the ice and watched the oxen find their footing in the snow with the teamster following.

Knox breathed out in relief. The worst had not happened. John Becker had not been forced to swing his axe to free the oxen from the sinking cannon.

The reality was they couldn't afford to lose a single cannon, especially the big twenty-four pounders that Washington needed to shell the British in Boston and the ships in the harbor. Knox had to deliver all the cannons he had picked up to Ticonderoga; if they fell through the ice, then every effort must be made to retrieve them. Knox turned around and waved to William on the far shore. The others could now proceed but must remain spaced out to avoid stressing the ice. An hour later, the five groups had crossed the Hudson River and were headed south to Albany.

The terrain leveled out and the sleds moved along steadily in the snow. Knox could not help but take pride as his train moved along with the men, oxen, and cannon. "Gazing upon his noble train, Knox wrote how the white snow as a background made the images of the people appear crisp and sharp. The blue uniforms of the militiamen stuck out along with the brown wooden sleds all along the convoy."[5] He had commanded men in groups before and he knew teamwork was essential. To fire a cannon, it took a team of men in which each man performed his specific job. He knew that the same type of dedication that ensured accurate cannon fire would ensure the transportation of the Ticonderoga artillery.

Indeed, firing an eighteenth-century cannon required many hands, perfect timing, and some degree of luck. If one man did not do his job, then the whole team suffered. Knox had seen men maimed badly because one man had shirked his responsibility. Cannons were unforgiving that way. If the barrel was not cleaned properly, a cannonball could seize in the barrel with its exploding charge ignited, blowing the cannon apart and killing or maiming the men. Firing the cannon was a choreography of moving parts that, when done properly, resulted in an amazing feat. A foe could be vanquished from a mile away. A ship could be sunk from high atop a hillside. An army could be eradicated from a bluff. Or an occupying army could be forced to retreat, abandoning his beloved town of Boston. To Knox, the cannons were nothing less than a liberating force that would vanquish the tyranny that had forced him to flee his bookstore under the cover of night. He knew of no greater motivation.

Knox and his men spent the night in Saratoga before pushing on the next morning. Eight miles south of the town the weather changed. A blizzard descended and men could not see three feet ahead. "Men started freezing in the plummeting temperatures and the animals had a very difficult time crossing the snow drifts. Soon 18 inches of snow had fallen, and the expedition could not go any further."[6] Henry ordered a halt in the late afternoon among a clearing of pine trees that offered some shelter and met with William and Becker to decide what to do. Henry would ride ahead to Albany to get "supplies and fresh animals from General Schuyler."⁷ William would stay behind and manage the best he could until his brother returned.

Knox and his men were not arctic explorers. They were men with a set mission to pull cannons through lakes, rivers, and wilderness and to deliver the artillery to George Washington. But they were not protected from the elements and would endure several winter storms without clothing suited for long periods exposed to winter weather. "They wore homespun coats and shirts, those often in tatters from constant wear, britches of every color and condition, cowhide shoes and moccasins, and on their heads old broad brimmed felt hats, weathered and sweat stained, beaver hats, farmer's straw hats, or bandannas tied sailor fashion."⁸ A sudden drop in temperatures or a blizzard could be their undoing.

William ordered the animals unyoked and circled them together for protection. Finding a protected spot among the pine trees, the men set up camp with a roaring fire. Some were already suffering from frostbite and "starting to lose feeling in their extremities."⁹ The horses and oxen were unable to move in the deep snow. All they could do was wait for Knox's return.

Henry reached Albany the next day as the snowstorm subsided. Schuyler once again provided him with men, wagons, and supplies. Knox returned a day later with the fresh animals and wagons, allowing some of the severely frostbitten men to ride in the wagons as they headed south once again toward the city of Half Moon, a waterway trading center where the Mohawk and Hudson Rivers converged. Once again, the convoy faced a treacherous ice crossing, but in a cruel reversal, the blizzard stopped and temperatures rose quickly. A thaw set in and Knox had to determine the best way to cross the river again.

Knox allowed the train to rest up in Half Moon while he and William scouted the condition of the Hudson, which they had to cross in order to reach Albany. There was a bridge, but it was woefully inadequate for men, horses, cannons, sleighs, and oxen. The ice had turned cloudy with the thaw, which was not a good sign. Knox knew that clear ice was the strongest. He had some of the teamsters drill holes in the ice in the hopes that it might freeze overnight and thicken. The temperature was just above freezing, and Knox wasn't sure his trick of drilled holes would work this time. He stared across the river glowing eerily in the darkness and felt an unseasonably warm wind blow across the frozen expanse of deliverance. Knox could only hope that overnight the temperature would fall.

20

THE LIFE AND TIMES
OF A TEAMSTER

The men who moved Henry Knox's cannons are a story in themselves. The life and times of John Becker Sr. and his scribe, twelve-year-old John Becker Jr., give a rare glimpse into the hidden world of this group of men who literally did the heavy lifting for the American Revolution. The country and the economy were evolving at a rapid pace, but the entrepreneurial ethos was predominant from farmers to blacksmiths. Everyone had to figure out how to make a buck, and the Beckers were a perfect example during a time when the country was in its infancy.

"Newspapers we had none and the simplest complications of grammar and arithmetic were scarce and unobtainable,"[1] John Becker Jr. wrote almost sixty years later, lamenting the lack of education when he was a child. "I feel at what a vast disadvantage the young men of my time were from such enviable disadvantages. The whole country was disturbed and continue so until after the revolution."[2]

John Jr.'s father fell into "wagoneering" the way many men found vocations: through a combination of accident and circumstance. His father was pressed into the service of the British in 1755 when "my father's farm equipage engaged the attention of a wagon master who without any ceremony pressed him into service."[3] The young farmer was directed to take "a load" up north, where the goods were placed in a warehouse. John Jr. asserted that "a large number of persons was engaged in the same business; most of them against their wishes and interests."[4] His father wanted to witness the British attack on French Fort Ticonderoga and dressed up as an Indian after being told the British wanted no more soldiers.

After the battle of Lexington, the Beckers were in high demand. The freighting of the cannons from Fort Ticonderoga was just one of their many trips north to bring down war material needed by the Americans. John Jr. wrote of their situation two years into the war. "Early in the year 1777 my father and I were again in active employment. Large quantities of provisions had been accumulating at Bennington for the use of our Northern armies and the New England people had been quite industrious in furnishing their quota of supplies. It was their fashion in those days to use oxen almost entirely for draught, and horses were scarcely seen among them."[5] This would seem to settle the issue of whether oxen or horses were used on the Knox expedition, which puzzles many historians.

That the Beckers were patriots is a given, as John Jr. writes, "The bloodshed in the neighborhood of Boston, which in those days seemed to be the center of motion and conferred its name on everything connected with our colonial resistance, gave a new impulse to our cause."[6] John Sr. was picked in Albany to be a captain of the local militia. He declined, citing his lack of experience, and continued his wagoneering. The Beckers, like many, distilled the concerns that forced the Americans to break with Britain as "the colonies were taxed as well beyond the necessity of the times, as their ability to pay, and the belief that individuals might be carried to England to be tried for criminal offences."[7]

This made the Beckers ideal for the task Henry Knox and General Schuyler presented to them. They had already performed similar operations to Ticonderoga and Crown Point and many others after their contract to transport Knox's artillery was finished. On a return trip afterward to Ticonderoga, "sixty-two sleighs on this occasion were under the care of my father," John Jr. wrote.[8] This trip was a version of the Knox expedition, and he wrote about what camp life was like on such trips:

> Our sleighs were all driven together in a row. Our horses were rubbed, fed, and blanketed and tied to the sleighs. We were divided into messes of six men each and went to work quite systematically to secure ourselves a comfortable night, notwithstanding the snow was three and a half feet deep. We dug it away in different places in the manner of the Esquimos and in our frozen apartments we likened ourselves to lodgers in a lower story.[9]

The Beckers often found themselves between the British and American armies, with each side using them for their benefit—and sometimes against their will. When an American Colonel Hay demanded that the Beckers assist in the building of a bridge, John Sr. protested, citing a previous obligation to deliver a load for which he had not fulfilled his contract. Hay insisted and the wagoneer negotiated, offering to deliver his load and then to work on the bridge. He then whispered to his son to follow him in a sleigh. An officer jumped into John Jr.'s sleigh to ensure they returned, and his father took off in the opposite direction.

"Where are you going to?" the officer demanded of the twelve-year-old whipping the horses in front of the sleigh.[10] John Jr. took a fast turn and left him "stuck upright in the snow."[11] When John Jr. caught up with his father, they were stopped by a sentinel, where once again the Beckers flew away in a flurry of snow, whips, and galloping horses. The sentry fired upon some other teamsters who wanted passage as well, and "the ball struck the nearest sleigh, passed between the legs of the driver, between the horses in front, and struck the next sleigh, where it lodged."[12]

But John Becker Sr. did return the next day to Colonel Hay after he had delivered his load.

"Well, here we are again, Colonel Hay," he said.[13]

Colonel Hay nodded. "Yes. So, I perceive . . . and the public interests have suffered severely by your late conduct. I must hold you responsible for the consequences."[14]

"I have no objections to be held responsible, my urgent business is now finished. My word is kept, my contract finished," John Becker Sr. replied.

Upon his promise to stay for a few days and use his sleighs to help in building the bridge, all was forgiven. The British and the Americans both needed what the Beckers had to offer: men who kept their word and made sure the goods were always delivered. While working on the bridge, John Jr. and his father "were served with the same food which was dealt out to the garrison"[15]

John Jr. did not take well to soldiers' rations. "My organs of digestion were not quite equal to the task imposed upon them by our new diet. I became most deplorably sick and often wished myself home that I might share in the daily comforts of a well-stocked larder. . . . I really thought my last hour was come. Brandy and burnt sugar were scarcely a palliative."[16]

When the contracts for loads dried up, the Beckers returned to Albany, where farming became their vocation again. But the war would not give them peace, and the Indians who had aligned themselves with the British became a danger to the lone families. During one of their many journeys transporting war supplies, John Jr. was exposed to the horrors of war when they met a procession of the wounded returning from a battle. "A great many were carried on litters, which were blankets fastened to a frame of four poles. . . . The sight of these wretched people, pale and lifeless, with countenances of an expression peculiar to gunshot wounds, as the surgeon informed us, and the sound of groaning voices, as each motion of the litter renewed the anguish of their wounds, filled me with horror and sickness of heart."[17]

The war then came to the Becker farm. After dinner one evening the Beckers were warned that Burgoyne's army was advancing, and John Sr. went to his brother's house to warn him. The Beckers would have to abandon their home as advancing Indians were attacking the lone settlements. "I can never forget, and I feel it now impossible, with sufficient force to describe the distress of our family at this moment of peril and alarm. The wagon was soon at the door and as my father came up, he directed us to carry a few loads down to the river,"[18] John Jr. later wrote.

The family transported what they could with the knowledge that the Indians would try to kill them, not sparing women or children. The danger was so intense that "a gun was loaded and placed in my hands and I patrolled about the house with a feeling of some responsibility."[19] This was not an idle threat. The atrocities were numerous, and John Jr. wrote about a neighboring family who had fallen victim to the British-aligned Indians.

Upon seeing some Indians approaching, a man "by the name of Ephraim ran into his house to get his gun and powder horn, determined to sell his life as dearly as he could; but as he was in the act of taking them from the wall where they hung, he was clenched by a savage who followed him in and was made prisoner."[20] His wife then ran and was "shot dead ere she reached the road. . . . A daughter whom she fondly loved, of the age of eleven years, had hold of her clothes and ran with her. An Indian came up to them, and observing the child lying close to her mother, as if seeking her protection, he snatched up a stone from the ground and dashed out her brains."[21]

In the evening the Beckers crossed the river and joined other families who had fled. "I and one of the blacks [slaves] were put into a small canoe and we proceeded down the stream as fast as we could play our paddles."[22] The refugee families escaped, "A long cavalcade of wagons from other farms filled with all kinds of furniture not often selected by the owners with reference to their use or value on occasions of alarm, stretched along the road."[23] Later John Becker Sr. returned to their farm to see if he could salvage any of their cattle or pigs and drive them toward the woods, where he could corral them, leaving John Jr. in charge.

His father "committed to me the care of his wagon and horses and the safe conduct of my mother and the family."[24] John Jr. found that he couldn't handle some of the "spirited" horses that "were continually attempting to run past the wagons ahead of me." He could no longer hold on to the reins and his mother, while nursing an infant in her arms, tried to assist. "In this dilemma, with tears in her eyes, and despair in her looks, she got out of the wagon, and picking up a stout club in the road, walked on for many miles at the head of the unruly animals, and with her infant on one arm, actually kept them back and restrained from breaking the line by striking them over the heads with the stick she held in the other."[25]

A mother with a suckling babe smacking a horse in the head with a club while Indians and the British were in hot pursuit sums up the incredible fortitude, courage, and sheer will of Revolutionary War–era families. The Beckers would endure many hardships throughout the war with Becker Sr. and Jr. transporting load after load across the battle lines. It is hard to imagine the times in which Henry and Lucy Knox and the Beckers lived in which life itself was a daily struggle, the revolution uprooting families and separating loved ones for long periods of time. "The men of this generation can never know what were the sorrows of those fathers that saw their children exposed to dangers and to death, and what the agonies of those mothers who pressed their offspring to their bosom, in the constant apprehension of seeing them torn from their embraces to become the victims of savage cruelty."[26]

General Schuyler had chosen well in his selection of the Beckers to transport the artillery from Fort Ticonderoga. The quiet fortitude of John Becker Sr. and his son would be tested many times, but along with running from bloodthirsty Indians, hauling the Ticonderoga cannons through the Berkshire Mountains would be one of their biggest challenges.

21

CANNON DOWN, HALF MOON

January 4, 1776

Henry Knox, a colonel in the Continental Army, was beginning to explore the meaning of that position. General Schuyler probably informed him about his commission, and Knox now was supervising all aspects of Washington's "Noble Train": logistical, physical, and, to some degree, public relations. Knox, after overseeing the drilling of the ice on the river once again, returned to Half Moon to confer with General Schuyler and arrange for more men, oxen, and horses. The animals were weary from their constant labor, and fresh oxen and horses were required. The composition of the serials changed as they progressed.

And so, on the morning of January 4, 1776, another laborious crossing occurred over the ice with John Becker Sr. holding the axe ready to cut the horses free if the ice didn't hold. The temperatures had risen, and the ice was not as hard on the Hudson now. Apparently General Schuyler was now supervising the crossing as well, and Knox returned to Half Moon for dinner. A five-thousand-pound cannon—six thousand pounds with oxen or horses—was making the crossing. Rain began to fall, an ominous sign that the temperature had shot up well above freezing. John Becker Jr. recorded the moment of disaster: "We had altogether about forty or fifty pieces to transport and our cavalcade was quite imposing. We traveled back towards Albany without incident until we reached Lansing's Ferry on the Hudson."[1] The men and the oxen proceeded cautiously in the airy silence. They had reached the middle of the river when a crack echoed across the wide river. Another crack echoed like a shot and the ice split under the cannon. John Jr. wrote, "In the center of the river the ice gave way as had been feared and a noble 18 [cannon] sank with a crackling noise and then a heavy plunge to the bottom of the stream."[2]

Men and the animals scrambled away as cracks rippled out in all directions, one fissure leading to another, endangering the entire train. It was the nightmare that had haunted Henry Knox: his precious cannon plunging through the ice to the bottom of the river, lost forever. In seconds, John Becker Sr. swung his axe furiously and slashed the ropes as the cannon plunged into the water with a loud gulp and settled to the floor of the Hudson. But Becker didn't cut the animals—horses this time—free entirely, making one last-ditch effort: "With a desperate hope of overcoming its downward tendency and just as the cracking of the ice gave the alarm, the horses were whipped up into a full jump, but to no purpose."[3] Becker tried to stem the fall of the cannon by lashing the horses to lunge ahead. He clearly risked the team of animals, but apparently the teamster knew that Knox could not afford to lose any cannon.

John Becker Jr. wrote, "The gun sank unfortunately, not in very deep water. The horses kept their feet and the rope was used to secure a buoy over the place where the cannon was lying and afterwards materially aided its recovery."[4] The horses were cut loose, but luck had smiled once again on Henry Knox. John Becker's quick thinking had allowed them to keep a line attached to the cannon, and the river was shallow where it had broken through. If the ropes had been slashed entirely and the river deep, there would have been little possibility of retrieving the cannon.

John Becker Jr. revealed that no cannons could cross, and the party would have to find an alternative route. "In this dilemma we had no alternative but to abandon the idea of getting on the east side of the river. It began to rain, the weather was changing, and we were forced to retrace our steps in some measure and seek a passage across the Mohawk [further up on the Hudson]."[5]

Knox was in Half Moon having dinner when he found out that the cannon had broken through the ice:

> In the afternoon much alarmed by hearing that one of the heaviest cannon had fallen into the river at Half Moon ferry General Schuyler came and informed me just as I was going to sit down to dinner. . . . I immediately set out to Allen's [a nearby farm] and went up to the Half Moon ferry where I reached at dusk and not hearing of the others and I caring that they would meet the same fate I sent of an express to Claus ferry about seven miles distant.[6]

Knox was beside himself. He found the hole in the ice and his artillery train gone. He discovered that the teamsters decided to cross at another point on the river. Afraid that cannons will break through the ice again, he sent a message to the teamsters to take extreme "precautions which by his instructions he was bound to have done and by no means to attempt crossing where he was until I came."[7]

Knox was livid and blamed the men, not the weakened ice, for the accident. He clearly believed that if he had been there, it wouldn't have happened. He was frantic that the train might attempt to cross again without waiting until he could personally supervise the crossing. Knox promised the cannons to George Washington, and he was in agony that all might be lost. Knox was heading for the second crossing point when the messenger returned. "The express returned and informed me that they had all got safely over. . . . I then sent another express to Mr. Schwartz [another teamster] to cross at Sloss as the ice was so much stronger there than at Half Moon, the usual place of crossing."[8]

Knox breathed a sigh of relief. John Becker Jr. later wrote in his diary, "We reached the ferry . . . [and] crossed in safety."[9] Disaster narrowly had been averted. Knox let the others in the train know that there were better places to cross than Sloss's, changing his mind again. Knox was paranoid now that the ice was not safe for crossing. John Becker Sr. retrieved the cannon that sunk using oxen and horses on shore pulling long lines attached to the cannon. The oxen and horses hoisted the cannon back to the surface of the ice, dragging it the remaining distance across the ice to the shore. Becker could not have salvaged the cannon if the Hudson had been deep or if he had slashed the lines when it sunk. On this day, all of Knox's cannons were accounted for.

The train made its way to Albany on January 5, and here Knox wrote several letters. The first one was to George Washington, in which he explained the delay from his earlier sanguine prediction that he would see Washington in two weeks:

> I did myself the honor to address your Excellency from Fort George on the 17th. I was in hopes that we should have been able to have had the cannon at Cambridge by this time. The want of snow detained us some days and now a cruel thaw hinders from crossing Hudson River which we are obliged to do four times from Lake George to this town—the first severe night will make the ice on the river sufficiently strong till that happens the cannons and mortars must remain where they are—most of them will have different crossing places and some few here—the inevitable delays pain me exceedingly as my mind is fully sensible to the importance of the greatest expedition in the case—they will be at Springfield from which place we can get them easily transported although there should be no

snow—but to that city, roads are so excessively bad [that] city roads will be necessary—we got over 4 more 18 pounders after my last to your excellency—I send a duplicate of the list for fear of miscarriage at the pier. General Schuyler has been exceedingly assiduous in this matter. As to myself my utmost endeavors have been and still shall be used to forward them with the utmost dispatch.[10]

The letter told a story of hardship, of waiting for snow and for freezing temperatures, and the problems of crossing the ice. The thaw along with the rain and the cannon breaking through the ice convinced Knox that he must wait for temperatures to drop. He might have written this letter to Washington before the Half Moon crossing, but most likely it was written in parts and finished in Albany afterward, when he realized that the train's progress was contingent on the variations in temperature. Knox said nothing of the difficulties in procuring the sleds, which made the lack of snow a moot point. His sleds would arrive *after* the early snow at Christmas. The slow movement of the train for lack of snow occurs on January 1, when he set out in the slushy muddy conditions of a thaw.

His tone differed significantly from the letter sent from Fort George, in which he promised to have the cannons in Cambridge in a matter of weeks. After crossing the frozen rivers and experiencing firsthand the brutality of the icy wilderness, Knox knew what he would be facing. He knew it would be a struggle to get the cannons to Washington, and his early hubris had worn off. He was a man who had a job to do and who recognized the difficulties confronting him.

His train of artillery had spread out widely, some of the sleds still en route to Albany. The transportation of heavy cannons through wilderness in the winter of 1776 was neither uniform nor pretty. It was a patchwork of individual efforts by men and animals to move their loads as best they could with little communication between each serial. It is conceivable that any one of the five groups—if they even held together in their groups—could simply veer off track and disappear. This strenuous, difficult, nerve-racking transport of heavy iron and brass under brutal conditions of snow and ice slowed down man and beast. The teamsters as well as the animals had a limit, and Albany would be a welcome respite.

With his letter, Knox sent along a second inventory of the cannons. Washington could compare the lists to ensure all was accounted for. If Knox did lose a cannon, Washington would know: "Having sent these two inventories, he had to deliver or offer a darn good reason why a piece should go missing."[11] This was Henry Knox's first test as commander of the artillery; more than that, it was his first test to show George Washington that he was a man capable of delivering on his promises. Knox already felt as if he had let down Washington by adjusting his timetable; losing cannons on top of that was unthinkable.

He then wrote Captain Baylen about a horse he had borrowed:

Dear Sir,

I wrote to you from New York apologizing for taking your horse which my brother had in charge—I think the leaving of him on the road would be hazardous—his getting to you uncertain and his keeping expensive—I have left him since I first came to this town where he has not been rode any and has been well kept—had I thought I should have been obliged to stay so long I believe I should not have taken him—but I must appeal to your good nature as an excuse.[12]

This letter shows the piecemeal nature of the expedition in which Knox borrowed horses, oxen, sleds, and men in order to keep the train moving at all costs. In this case, he was trying to return a horse he has procured, which he intends to leave in Albany for the captain.

The next letter Knox wrote was to Lucy:

My dear and lovely friend,

Those people who love you as I do ought never to part. It is with the greatest anxiety that I am forced to date my letter this distance from my love at a time when I thought to have been happily back home. I feel for you my Lucy I feel for myself as the seeing her without whom life is a blank must in the course of events be protracted for a week or two longer I am resolved to write her a long letter—a man whom General Washington has sent express to General Schuyler has promised me to deliver it with his own hands to you.[13]

Mail was uncertain and many times never reached its destination, and Knox made use of "expresses" to communicate up and down the line of his expedition and with others. Here he caught Washington's messenger on his return trip, "for which you will give something with what rapture should I receive a letter from my angel's hands I should think it one of the best boons of heaven—I would kiss and would put in my bosom and wear it there till no part remained." Henry Knox had been away from his wife for more than fifty days and must have felt extreme guilt for leaving her for such extended periods of time despite being in service of the "glorious cause."[14] He was also in extreme peril, not only from the elements and the accompanying dangers of dying from exposure or falling into a frozen river, but he was also now a colonel in an army waging war on the British. He was guilty of treason; and until the British recognized the American army as representing a new nation, Knox, Washington, and all the others dedicated to the Revolution could be executed. All he could do for his pregnant wife, destined never to see her parents again, was to express his undying love and devotion:

My Lucy is perpetually in my mind constantly in my heart. It wishes my interest was as sure in heaven as it is in my Lucy. I would pray without ceasing for her happiness. May that being who blesses the universe with the ray of his benign providence bless you with a Happy New Year and give you every joy and every wish necessary to your felicity—I am exceedingly concerned for fear my love should repine at not being able to come at the time expected do not I beseech you consider and keep in mind the happy day and happy meeting we shall have after two months of very strained absence.[15]

Knox attempted to break the news that he won't be returning anytime soon gently. His dedication to the Revolution was sanctioned by God as was his love for his wife, but even in his loving prose the guilt over inflicting disappointment once again was obvious. The cold wilderness must have seemed very lonely to Henry Knox at times, so far away from his wife and unborn child, unsure about when he would be able to spend time with his family now that he was a colonel in the American army. At this point, Lucy knew nothing of his recent promotion; if she had, she might have been crushed with the realization that she had lost her husband for years.

If my dear thinks of it as being the expectation I do as I believe she does it will go a great way in soothing the present in expectation of the future—I don't know what kind of reasoning that is but I know it certainly is so tho I know I've not clearly expressed it. . . . This is only the fourth letter that I have had an opportunity to write to you, one of them being a very little sneaking one indeed which was owing to it being written before day in the most rushing hurry as General Schuyler had just arrived from Ticonderoga over Lake George and was going to set out immediately for Albany.[16]

This bit of information also shows how Schuyler was orchestrating all parts of the train as well. "There was little or no snow then on Christmas Eve there was a plentiful fall with exceedingly cold weather as I ever knew,"[17] Knox wrote about his advance traveling to Albany, where he almost froze to death, to see about the sleds and oxen. "The weather for three or four days has been intolerably warm considering my wishes—the thaw has been so warm I have trembled for the consequences for without snow my important charge cannot get along. . . . I came from Lake George some days ago in the severely cold weather and suffered by it considerably . . . excepting which although I cannot say much for the pleasantry of the journey yet it has been tolerable."[18] Knox was the master of understatement here; when he and his men were forced to leave their horses to reach Albany and march through the snow, he nearly froze to death.

My brother is now at Lake George busily engaged in loading sleds as they come in and there are a considerable number employed in getting them down to this place where if the weather should come cold which I hope for—they will all be on next Tuesday or Wednesday at the next at Springfield and four or five days after at Cambridge . . . after I shall see them all set off from Springfield I shall leave them and push on, on the wings of expectations and love.[19]

Knox wrote these letters in parts, and obviously this passage was written closer to the first of the New Year. Knox then mentioned the treatment of American officers at the hands of the British, citing a controversy that was raging at the time: "If there was such a thing as discrimination, they must see the infinite difference with which they are treated to which our officers are who are so unfortunate as to fall into their hands."[20] The British had yet to recognize the Americans as fighting for a legitimate country and had not accorded them the same respect given to other foreign officers. "Seventeen of them set out from this for Pennsylvania yesterday among whom was General Prescott who by all accounts behaved exceedingly ill in putting Colonel Allen of ours who was taken at Montreal. General Schuyler favored me with the sight of a letter which George Washington sent to General Howe in Boston and Mr. Howe's answer."[21]

The treatment of Colonel Allen by the British had become a point of contention for Washington, who wrote General Howe protesting the treatment of American officers in general. This is the letter Schuyler showed to Knox wherein George Washington promised revenge on the British General Prescott. "General Washington tells General Howe as soon as he gets answers to certain questions of Prescott's treatment of Allen—that Prescott shall be served in the same manner."[22] The British threatened to hang American officers; Washington likewise threatened to do the same with Prescott. The war evolved on its own course as Knox's expedition made its way through the wilderness. It was telling that Schuyler showed Henry Knox Washington's confidential correspondence, reinforcing Knox's importance as colonel of the artillery. Including information quoted from Washington's letter also showed Knox's naïveté in trusting the mail, which was frequently intercepted by the British or those loyal to the crown.

Knox then wrote about British prisoners he saw being brought down from Canada. "About 60 commissioned officers—no tool of security for the British folk . . . about twenty of the Canadian notables who appear as if nothing happened—one or two of the officers I pitied the others seemed concerned but humbled—the women and children suffer amazingly as this advanced season of the year for being transported in so frozen a climate."[23] This party would have been British prisoners from one of the forts along with the women and children Knox saw passing through Fort George or at one of the landings.

Knox's letter was long, and it speaks to the fact he wasn't sleeping in a tent or on the ground but in an inn in Albany. "It is now past twelve o'clock therefore my Lucy I wish you a good night and will mention you in my prayers. . . . Adieu for tonight, adieu."[24]

Again, Knox was overly optimistic in telling his wife he would see her within a few weeks. He still had miles to go, and his biggest test—which would stress his men, the animals, and the will to persevere—was yet to come. The Berkshire mountains are a hell of sheer cliffs and frozen passes. Pulling 120,000 pounds of cannons along its ice-laden trails is almost impossible to conceive. Henry Knox had no idea what was facing him.

22

THE THIRD COLUMN

January 7, 1775

George Washington was not a gifted speaker. When he joined the Continental Congress in 1774, he left Mount Vernon with a pamphlet written by Jefferson, *A Summary View of the Rights of British America*. Jefferson warned George III about his view that America existed to serve the British. "Kings are the servants, not the proprietors of the people."[1] When Washington arrived, Silas Deane of Connecticut observed that Washington had a "hard countenance" and was a "tolerable speaker . . . who speaks very modestly in a cool but determined accent."[2]

His taciturn manner won him converts in the Continental Congress, where "every man in it is a great man—an orator, a critic, a statesman and therefore every man upon every question must show his oratory."[3] As the subject of independence from Britain was debated, Washington's calm, cool style and quiet manner of speaking carried much more weight than the bloviators. When Congress adjourned, Washington had supported the move to "wholly discontinue the slave trade."[4] He returned to Mount Vernon and oversaw the sale of ninety slaves. "The Negroes, horses, and stock have all sold exceedingly high," he wrote later; in February 1775 he paid £52 "for the value of a negro boy, Tom."[5] The two paradoxical sides of Washington are on display here: the man of the "glorious cause" who favors abolition of the slave trade and the practical man who runs a plantation that is dependent on slave labor.

By late November 1775 Washington realized the folly of his decision to become commander in chief of an army that was slowly melting away, vanishing before his eyes, with no means of waging war. His pilgrimage to his headquarters to meet with his war council always resulted in the same wait-and-see admonishment while the British remained ensconced in Boston with the assumption that the winter precluded warfare, so they ought to make the best of it while the Continental Army froze in their tents and flimsy wooden barracks. "No man I believe ever had a greater choice of difficulties and less means to extricate himself from them," he wrote to his brother Jack.[6]

Now Washington considered doing the unthinkable: arming free blacks for enlistment in the Continental Army. Like many in the South, George Washington, a large slaveholder, had a recurring nightmare that the slaves might one day arm themselves and undertake a rape and murder spree. There was no social component to Washington's consideration of "negros" for soldiers; rather, it was his dire need for troops. The soldiers of Concord and Lexington had fought side by side with African Americans and did not hold the hard-and-fast prejudice of the southerners. General John Thomas of Massachusetts told John Adams, "We have some Negroes, but I look upon them in general as equally serviceable with other men. . . . Many of them have proved themselves brave."[7]

When Washington took over as commander in chief in the summer, he had forbidden free blacks to enlist in the army, prohibiting "any deserter from the ministerial army no stroller negro or vagabond."[8] But the men who had fought the British at Concord, Lexington, and Bunker Hill had seen the worth of black soldiers in combat. Peter Salem was a black man who fought heroically at Bunker Hill and was brought to Washington's attention as an example of what the black soldier could do if given a chance.

Still, during the October war council, Washington and his generals voted "to reject all slaves and by a great majority to reject Negroes altogether."[9] Then a month later Washington clearly delineated his personal policy on the issue of negro enlistment: "Neither Negroes, boys unable to bear arms, nor old men unfit to endure the fatigues of the campaign are to be enlisted."[10]

Washington's policy put blacks in the same camp as old men and boys with the assumption they were just as unfit for service. The British stoked the fire with a proclamation on November 7 by Lord Dunmore that would open a third column against the Americans. Dunmore announced "that slaves or indentured servants who had fled from their rebel masters could soon join his Royal Ethiopian Regiment and win their freedom."[11] This was a dagger to the southern heart of George Washington: the British were inviting slaves to run off and offering to arm and train the new recruits to fight against their former masters. Eight hundred slaves escaped to British freedom and were soon clad in uniforms with "Liberty to Slaves" emblazoned on the front.

Freedom proved elusive to many of the new soldiers as smallpox and other diseases decimated the American soldiers. Freed and newly uniformed slaves cruised up and down the Potomac in British ships, giving rise to fears of wholesale insurrection. Indeed, George Washington feared his own slaves at Mount Vernon might run off to join the British, though his brother Lund Washington wrote that he did not think the commander in chief's slaves would take the British offer. This hit Washington where it hurt, putting his own personal property and by extension his personal fortune at risk. Washington would later write about Dunmore that it would be a good thing if "one of our bullets aimed for him, the world would be happily rid of a monster."[12]

George Washington, while risking all for the "glorious cause," was keenly aware of the Achilles' heel that slaves represented to the Americans. He was a slaveowner with those inherent prejudices who at the same time broke ranks with his own generals by writing a letter to John Hancock in late December 1775 that reversed his previous proclamations: "It has been represented to me that the free Negroes who have served in this army are very much dissatisfied at being discarded. As it is to be apprehended that they may seek employ in the ministerial army, I have presumed to depart from the resolution respecting them and have given license for their being enlisted."[13] Congress approved this amazing decision two weeks later, and the first step toward black empowerment in the new country of America had been taken.

Washington was the meticulous, plodding planner who appreciated the bold stroke in all areas of life. He desperately needed troops for his army but at the same time it also shows that he could rethink his own assumptions and recognize the worth of free black men as soldiers. How much the fear of slaves defecting to the British played a part we will never know, but it was "a watershed moment in American history, freeing the way for approximately five thousand blacks to serve in the Continental Army, making it the most integrated fighting force before the Vietnam War."[14]

Ultimately 6 to 12 percent of Washington's army would be black soldiers fighting side by side with white men for freedom and liberty and to form a new country founded on the ideal that all men are created equal. It would take another one hundred years and a brutal civil war for this creed to play out, but the first step was taken here, by a slaveowner risking all in a fight for an ideal of a country of free men.

It was no coincidence that the first antislavery society was formed in Philadelphia that winter. The American Revolution was a petri dish of experimentation that pushed against the entrenched system of slavery, but George Washington's back was against the wall, and he was using every advantage at his disposal to fight an enemy that could decimate his weakened army at any point and abort the infant Revolution. Arming former slaves and sending a bookseller to retrieve cannons three hundred miles away were both bold, risky, brilliant moves by a man whose neck was literally on the line.

23

THE ALBANY

January 5, 1776

General Schuyler greeted the tired men and animals in Albany on January 5. Once again, the townspeople turned out to see the big guns and the train of men, horses, and oxen that would soon be crossing the Hudson. John Becker Jr. wrote in his journal, "The next day we entered Albany. Our appearance excited the attention of the burghers. They were accustomed it is true, to seeing fine artillery, as some well-appointed armies had been encamped within this city. But this was the first artillery which congress had been able to call their own and it led to reflections not in the least injurious to our cause."[1]

General Schuyler wrote a quick note to Washington: "This morning I had the satisfaction to see the first division of sleds cross the river. Should there be snow all the way to Cambridge, they will probably arrive there about this day next week."[2] This was very good news for Washington to hear: a third party confirming that the cannons were drawing closer. In the shifting equation of Washington's daily strategizing against the British, the cannons could now be factored in.

But, of course, the train had spread out, and Schuyler speculated about the arrival of the first cannon. The Noble Train was a fluid creature that wiggled and snaked its way along, spreading out further and further as it progressed, bunching up at the various crossings and towns for rest and replenishment of supplies. Also, there was always the unexpected, the accidents that would plague Knox the entire expedition. John Becker Jr. recorded one such incident after crossing the Mohawk River, which we can assume was one of many such accidents along the way: "The weather became colder and we crossed at South ferry, without difficulty or even apprehension. . . . We received for drawing such one and four pence a mile and when we were detained by breakages or accident and laid by for repair, we received 15 shillings a day."[3] Henry Knox was desperate to keep the train moving since he had to pay his men for each additional day.

> As we reached the shore at Greenbush, a tongue of one of the sleds, which was loaded with a smaller gun, struck and perforated the side of a very handsome pleasure boat and made a breach in it of rather a ruinous nature. The driver seemed to have no alternative but to keep moving; he drove fairly over it, and the boat was made a complete wreck. The idea that congress would pay all the damages was the only sympathy that we then had time to bestow on the owner.[4]

This was not a smooth, trouble-free operation, and there were many such casualties of unintentional damage along the way to the towns, homes, and roads, as well as the punishing grind on the animals who pulled day after day. Surely some died en route from exposure and exertion. It was small consolation to the men who owned the animals—or the owner of the boat—that the Congress of a country very much in doubt would pick up the cost. Schuyler and Knox would do their best to obtain fresh animals and supplies required for the looming mountain crossing.

Knox explored the Mohawk River on January 5, "about seven miles and there crossed over on very weak ice for the horses and run down alongside the river until we came to the falls, so famous in this part of the continent and known by the name of the Cohoos Falls."[5] Knox was looking for safe passage across the river and had stumbled on the falls. As a man who had never ventured out of Boston until this trip north to retrieve the cannons, he recorded the wonder he felt at the winter spectacle. It is difficult to imagine the sights that greeted the young man in 1776 as he came to appreciate the country for which he was risking everything:

> Those stupendous falls inferior to none save the grand one of Niagara are formed by the whole body of the Mohawk River falling at one pitch form the perpendicular of eighty feet—it is the most superb and affecting sight I ever saw—the river is about 4[00] or 500 yards wide, at the time I saw it was about nine o'clock in the morning when the beams of the sun reflected on the whole icy scene around—vast icicles of twenty feet long and three or four feet thick hanging pendent from the neighboring rocks—which were formed from the rain and melted snow falling from the neighboring heights and very severe frost coming up which arrested the

water in its fall—this ornamented the scene in a very particular manner—the water falling from such a height gave the water the look of milk. It looked like one vast torrent of milk pouring from a stupendous height.[6]

This is a very descriptive passage from Knox's diary, which primarily contains random thoughts, impressions, payments, and problems encountered. This was the only interlude wherein Knox turned from the mission at hand to contemplate the natural wonders of the American continent.

"In its fall occasioned a very thick mist to arise, which looked like a shower of rain and I was told that in summer time a perpetual rainbow was be seen here after having gazed and wondered for a long time I returned to the Albany about 12 miles from my admiring the stupendous works or nature and not a little humbled by thoughts of my own insignificancy."[7]

The wonder of the young nation impressed upon Knox an intense sense of the majesty of the continent. He was a man who saw God's hand all around him in nature, and as he traveled, he surely saw his quest as fighting for an Eden on earth.

The men and animals now having rested in Albany went down to the banks of the Hudson River for the next crossing on the morning of January 7:

> Along the shores inhabitants and soldiers watched throughout the day, many holding their breath as each team inched across the precarious bridge of ice. Teamsters walked the animals slowly to prevent the hammering of hooves on the fragile ice, but they will be needed to move with enough celerity and momentum to tow the weighty cargo. The teams had to work hard against the slippery surface. At the completion of each successful crossing to the east side of the Hudson, onlookers cheered, and heads shook in almost disbelief.[8]

This was an amazing moment for the citizens of Albany: the guns intended for George Washington to fight the British—the guns that could deliver the independence of their country—were going through their town. The townspeople cheered for the men risking life and limb as they crossed the ice. The teamsters proceeded carefully but steadily; they had to keep the sleds moving or they would dig down and groove the ice. And yet the cannons made it across, one at a time, and each citizen saw victory over the British one step closer with each successful crossing. Finally, it was time for the cannon that had broken through before. The five-thousand-pound cannon started across the ice, but John Becker was not accompanying it this time, having gone ahead with cannons that had already crossed. The teamsters walked alongside the cannon with axes at the ready, breathing the heavy cold air. They were nearing the far side and the frosted pines were large. The sleds had been spaced out on the ice and this was the last one. Big Bertha was always the test, and the ice creaked with the cannon's weight, the men fearfully watching. Knox described what happened next.

"The cannon which came the night before last over at Sloss ferry . . . fell into the river and notwithstanding the precautions we took and in its fall broke all the ice for 14 feet around it."[9] One of the teamsters slashed the ropes before the cannon pulled oxen and horses into the Hudson River. This time, the ice had collapsed around the cannon, creating a fourteen-foot hole. This was disastrous; Knox could not afford to leave it behind. Knox continued, "This was a misfortune as it retarded the dispatch which I wished to use in this business we pushed the 10 sleds on which we got over safe and then I went to getting the drowned cannon out which we faintly effected but by seven of the night's coming could not do it entirely."[10]

Knox and his men could not pull the cannon out of the Hudson this time. The fourteen-foot hole in the ice surely hampered their rescue effort. Assuming there was a rope tied to the sled and the cannon, it became a matter of how much pulling power they possessed. After sending the other ten sleds on their way, Knox turned back to the sunken cannon but simply didn't have the man or animal power to extract it from the frozen river. The one thing Knox had in his favor was a cold front that had come through, making the ice harder every day. On the morning of January 8, Knox was back down by the river, supervising the other sleds while contemplating what to do about the sunken cannon.

This is where the glorious cause, the national will, the people of the new country gathered together and came from Albany to assist Knox and his men. "Went on the ice about 8 o'clock in the morning and proceeded so cautiously that before night we got three sleds and were so lucky as to get the cannon out of the river owing to the assistance of the good people of the city of Albany."[11] How many oxen or horses it took is anyone's guess. The teamsters used pulleys and ropes wrapped around trees to increase the pulling power of the animals. "Some of the citizens were so anxious to participate that they even paid certain of the hired haulers to allow them to ferry the guns across."[12] The cannon submerged in the fourteen-foot opening in the ice slowly surfaced and was dragged to the shore by the combined citizenry of Albany. "Even though Knox and his men and a number of Albany people were at the task early in the morning, all day was required in raising the huge cannon [5,000 pounds] and ferrying it across the river."[13]

As a gesture to the townspeople who had assisted him, Knox "in return . . . christened her 'the Albany.'"[14] Knox was slowly coming into his own as a commander of men and a man who understood the power of symbolic gestures. He continued conveying the remaining sleds across, and on January 9 he "got several sleighs also some spare strings of horses in case of any accident."[15] The ubiquitous General Schuyler made sure Knox's party was well provisioned for the next leg of the journey, as "the expedition was resupplied with food and stocked with proper ropes and pulleys."[16]

On January 9, Knox and his train headed out on Amherst Road. "After taking my leave of General Schuyler and some of my friends in Albany I set out from thence about twelve o'clock."[17] Knox had made many friends in Albany; he needed all the horses, supplies, and oxen he could muster, to say nothing of the assistance given to him to rescue his cannon from the Hudson. But now he faced the seemingly impossible task of transporting sixty tons of artillery through mountains in winter. He was headed for the Berkshires.

24

ALL THE KINGDOMS
OF THE EARTH

January 10, 1776

Like the soldiers who would stare at the wide beaches of Normandy a century and half later and wonder how they would get across, Henry Knox stared at the snow-crusted Berkshire mountains running into the distance where streaked clouds hovered halfway up. A hawk soared down into valleys then rose over the far peaks. It was snowing and the flakes withered into the blue mountains, disappearing against the peaks that no man toting five thousand pounds of iron could ascend. For the first time, Knox had real doubts about being able to deliver his Noble Train of Artillery to George Washington.

His men were exhausted, the oxen and horses were played out, and there were rumblings among the teamsters of turning back home and leaving the cannons where they were. Knox couldn't feel his hands or feet anymore and he was sure his nose was frostbitten. He stared at the mountains again. The Berkshires stood there in their frozen indifference as immovable as the British army in Boston and as implacable as the beaches on D-Day.

Knox and his men had followed the Old Post Road to the town of Kinderhook and then "went as far as Claverack about 9 miles beyond Kinderhook."[1] Kinderhook was the door to the Berkshire mountains, and Knox felt renewed after Schuyler informed Washington that the cannons were on the way. All five serials were together now. There had been an immediate breakdown of a sleigh when they reached Claverack, which stopped the entire train. As John Becker Jr. recorded, "We made the best of our way to Claverack and there the breaking down of a sleigh detained us two whole days. The dependence we were under to each other for assistance, in case of accident, made it necessary for us to move in a body."[2] The train moved in groups, the largest being fourteen sleds. Knox now kept the groups together for mutual aid as they entered the mountains.

Knox was in a hurry not only to get the cannons to George Washington, but also to see Lucy. Since their marriage in May, the young couple had not spent a full two weeks together. Their escape from Boston led directly to Knox joining the rebel army and then becoming Washington's choice to head up a new artillery unit. Even with his return, there was no guarantee he could see his wife, as he would be responsible for overseeing the artillery and its placement for Washington to lay siege to Boston. Henry would finish several letters to Lucy with the closing "kiss your heavenly babe and bless it for me."[3] At a time when infant mortality was high, there was a good chance Knox would never see his new baby.

The Berkshire mountains brought with them the problems of hauling thousands of pounds of iron and brass up steep cliffs, down precipices, and across gorges. The mountains were the southern end of the Green Mountains of Vermont and separated New York from Massachusetts, extending from the Housatonic River in Massachusetts to the Connecticut River valley and to the Westfield River valley in Massachusetts. The mountains were marked by hills and high peaks and cut by several river valleys that carved deep gorges across the mountains. It was no place for men, oxen, horses, and thousands of pounds of artillery on sleds in the middle of a brutal winter.

Knox was anxious to get going and he set out on a mountain trail from Claverack. He rode to the top of one of the snow-peaked mountains, recording his first impressions of the Berkshire mountains on January 10: "After having climbed mountains from which we might almost have seen all the Kingdoms of the Earth."[4] This might have been the Great Barrington peak Knox ascended, where he looked across the peaks and valleys below. The Berkshires were formidable, and the cliffs and valleys would test the endurance of the most hardened teamsters.

Not only was pulling a five-thousand-pound cannon up a mountain with oxen extremely difficult but coming down could be very dangerous. The winds cutting through the mountain passes penetrated the coats and scarves of the teamsters and froze the breath of the oxen. The oxen struggled, breathing steam in the cold air as they lost their footing and struggled up toward the higher latitudes. The men breathed heavily climbing the steep path where a thousand pounds became two thousand and five thousand became ten thousand pounds. Many times, the sleds got ahead of the oxen and the teamsters had to devise new ways of hauling their freight up and down. A modern equivalent of what the

Knox artillery train was attempting would be pulling twenty-eight loaded trucks through the Adirondack Mountains without roads or mechanical conveyances. This was the test then. This was where Knox climbed and, looking across the misted snowy peaks, wrote that it was "almost a miracle that people with heavy loads should be able to get up and down such hills as are here with anything of heavy loads."[5]

It would take a miracle for the cannons to come through the mountains. The New York teamsters, along with John Becker and his son, were at the breaking point. This was beyond the call of duty for many, and Henry Knox would use all his powers of persuasion to keep his expedition intact. There were no advance parties now. Everyone depended on each other for safety and mutual assistance in moving the cannons. Knox didn't mention the breakdown of the sleigh in his diary, but we can assume such things happened often when the train moved as independent units.

On January 11, Knox noted in his journal that the expedition "went 12 miles through the Green Woods to Blanchrod."[6] The Green Woods was a dense and forbidding evergreen forest, now covered in snow and ice. They were entering the heart of the Berkshires. "From these woods to East Otis, the slender cortege of cannon bearing sleds, their drivers shouting at the oxen and horses and cracking whips, passed between the two Spectacle Ponds and then through a mountain pass where today there is no road whatever."[7]

The mountain trail was very different from the military roads and trading paths the train had followed before and much harder to follow than the roads around Lake George. This trail might have been acceptable for foot traffic and small wagons drawn by horses, but for oxen hauling cannons, it was almost impossible to navigate. The snow itself was problematic as the oxen lost their footing on steep grades and slipped down inclines. The Noble Train began to break down. Men and beast were giving out in the thin air and plummeting temperatures. "The greatest challenge travelling uphill was it quickly tired the animals. When the animals reached exhaustion, they had to be disconnected from the sleds to rest. Soon the movement slowed to a crawl, and the teamsters became very discouraged at their slow progress. The wagoneers had to cut down smaller trees out of their way to make the movement easier for the heavy cannons."[8] The Berkshires were becoming almost impassable when the train came to a pass where "it would be utterly impossible for a road ever to have been in such an ominous confusion of mountains, precipices, chasms, and deep valleys, which were interspersed with rivers, lakes, and dank swamps."[9]

The snow was becoming thinner and the sleds digging into the rutted trail. Although the Berkshires were only four thousand feet above sea level, the effect of climbing the mountains wore the men down. Mountain climber Eric Shipton wrote about the psychological impact of mountains on the human psyche: "Smoking is impossible, eating tends to make one vomit, the necessity of reducing weight to a bare minimum forbids the importation of literature beyond that supplied by the labels on tins of food; sardine oil, condensed milk and treacle spill themselves all over the place; except for the briefest moments, during which one is not usually in a mood for aesthetic enjoyment, there is nothing to look at but the bleak confusion inside the tent and the scaly bearded countenance of one's companion."[10]

A new method of moving the cannons would have to be adopted or the artillery would be abandoned in the Berkshire mountains. Henry Knox, for all his bravado and can-do aplomb, was no match for the natural barriers of ice, snow, and mountainous rock that now faced him. There were places where sheer cliffs plunged 214 feet. Cannons had to be lowered by block and tackle at some places, but simply moving the artillery up and down the mountainside was becoming impossible. The teamsters adopted a different strategy of moving the cannons a few miles into the mountains:

> Instead of having the oxen drag the sleds up normally; the teamsters unhooked the animals and brought them up the hill separately. Then they attached the sled at the bottom of the hill with ropes and pulleys and attached it to the free yoked oxen. The pulley system multiplied the strength of the oxen and allowed them to achieve this difficult task. It also required the teamster crews from three separate sled teams to move one sled up a hill based on this new configuration.[11]

The pulley system worked, but it was very dangerous. A mortar broke loose from the ropes and almost crushed some men at the bottom of the hill. John Becker Jr. had to jump out of the way when a runaway cannon crashed down a steep incline. This slowed the movement of the cannons through the mountains even more. The grumbling that developed into a slower pace and then a mutiny among the teamsters who refused to go any further was not surprising.

Knox described what happened in his journal: "At Blandford we overtook the first division who had tarried here until we came up and refused going any further on account there was no snow beyond five or six miles further in which space there was the tremendous Glasgow or Westfield mountain to go down."[12]

The teamsters had simply had enough. They were on a narrow, ice-laden path on the side of the mountain. The oxen were too tired, the snow had become too thin, the elevation too steep, the cannons too heavy, and the men were a long way from home. They were making no headway and the mountain peaks in front of them were all too daunting. Although this was not Everest, the reflections of mountain climber Reinhold Meisner have relevance here:

> Not only during the ascent but also during the descent my will power is dulled. The longer I climb the less important the goal seems to me, the more indifferent I become to myself. My attention has diminished, my memory is weakened. My mental fatigue is now greater than the bodily. It is so pleasant to sit and do nothing and therefore so dangerous. Death through exhaustion is—like death through freezing—a pleasant one.[13]

Henry Knox's Noble Train was now off the tracks, and the teamsters were ready to abandon the cannons of the Continental Army in the Berkshire mountains. Knox was facing a disaster of unbelievable proportions. He had pushed the men as hard as he dared and now his precious cannons were stuck in the frozen mountains, no less than the lifeblood of the American Revolution. Knox faced the men who would either destroy him or save him. Night was coming, and Knox could identify with the men who had become stranded on mountains before, questioning how they had arrived at that moment. He had left everything to go on this noble errand. Leaving his wife and his unborn child, he was now on an icy precipice. As Thomas Horbein wrote in *Everest: The West Ridge*, "I felt sinkingly as if my whole life lay behind me. At times I wondered if I had not really come a long way to find that what I really sought was something I had left behind."[14]

25

COMMON SENSE

January 10, 1776

It was brutally cold in Cambridge with a foot of snow on the ground. The cold was so extreme that sentries had to be replaced every hour or risk freezing to death. George Washington, who loved spring in Mount Vernon with the blossoming cherry trees and the sunny Potomac rippling by, found himself staring at the horror of a gray, frozen landscape stripped of trees for firewood as far as the eye could see. Worse than the dystopic countryside was his army's situation. Many of his soldiers had to use spears because of the shortage of gunpowder; many had gone home; those who had reenlisted were trying to survive a winter outside of Boston with no real way to dislodge the British.

Washington tried to appeal to the sense of honor among the men leaving, whereas General Charles Lee, the older, crankier general with a hair-trigger temper, took a different tack. One soldier recorded in his diary, "We was ordered to form a hollow square and General Lee came in and the first words was 'Men, I do not know what to call you, you are the worst of all creatures' and he flung and cursed and swore at us."[1] General Lee recorded the scene between the soldiers who remained and those who left: "Some of the Connecticutians who were homesick could not be preserved on to tarry, which means in the New England dialect to serve any longer. They accordingly marched off bag and baggage, but in passing through the lines of regiments, they were so horribly hissed, groaned at, and pelted that I believe they wished their aunts, grandmothers, and even sweethearts, to whom the days before they were so attached, were at the devil's own palace."[2]

Knox's old friend from Boston, Nathaniel Greene, now a general on Washington's council of war, wrote to Congressman Samuel Ward about the dire situation facing the army in the New Year. "We have suffered prodigiously for want of wood. Many regiments have obliged to eat their provisions for want of firing to cook, and withstanding we have burned up all the fences and cut down all the trees for a mile around the camp, our suffering has been inconceivable. . . . We have never been so weak as we shall be tomorrow."[3]

Greene anticipated even more expiring troop enlistment and the further dissolution of the American army. But the New Year had brought a message from General Schuyler that the cannons were on the way from Ticonderoga, though Washington was unsure when they would arrive.

As of January 10, 1776, one-third of the colonists still believed reconciliation with Britain was desirable. Thoughts of complete independence were the backwater of a movement focused on fighting for colonial rights. But after King George's proclamation and the increasingly protracted Siege of Boston, the time was right for the next evolution. Washington himself had written to his adjutant Joseph Reed after reading the king's proclamation that the rebellion must be crushed. If nothing else could "satisfy a tyrant and his diabolical ministry . . . we were determined to shake off all connections with a state so unjust and unnatural. This I would tell them in words as clear as the sun in its meridian brightness."[4]

Nathanael Greene went further in another letter to Samuel Ward in Philadelphia:

> Heaven hath decreed that tottering empire Britain to irretrievable ruin and thanks to God, since Providence hath so determined, America must raise an empire of permanent duration, supported upon the grand pillars of Truth, Freedom and Religion, encouraged by the smiles of Justice and defended by her patriotic sons. . . . Permit me then to recommend from the sincerity of my heart, ready at all times to bleed in country's cause, a Declaration of Independence, and call upon the world and the great God who governs it to witness the necessity, propriety and rectitude thereof.[5]

The time had come for a corset maker from England who had arrived in Philadelphia two years before to change the course of the war. Thomas Paine barely survived the harrowing three-month voyage to America and was too sick to disembark after typhoid fever had killed five of the passengers in the crossing. It took Paine six weeks to recover, but he became a citizen of Philadelphia and soon was the editor of the *Pennsylvania Magazine*. Embroiled in the politics of the rebellion against the British, he wrote many articles on the struggle for

American liberty. An article he began called "Common Sense" soon expanded, and he realized it would have to be published as a pamphlet.

The thirty-eight-year-old Paine did not hold much hope for sales of his pamphlet, which he signed "by an Englishman." While George Washington waited for Knox to return to Cambridge with the cannons, *Common Sense* was published on January 10, 1776, and became an immediate sensation, selling one hundred thousand copies in three months, despite a population of only two million people in the thirteen colonies. Eventually more than a half million copies of the pamphlet would be sold. Paine put the argument for independence from Britain front and center. "While many colonists clung to the fairy tale of George III as a benign father figure in thrall to a wicked ministry, Paine bluntly demolished these illusions, dubbing the King 'the Royal Brute of Great Britain.'"[6]

Paine's polemic was written in a conversational style that the average citizen could comprehend and was divided into four sections: "Of the Origin and Design of Government in General with Concise Remarks on the English Constitution," "Of Monarchy and Heredity Succession," "Thoughts on the Present State of American Affairs," "On the Present Ability of America with some Miscellaneous Reflections."[7]

In the first section, Paine proclaimed "government a necessary evil" and that society made people happy. He went on to point out two problems with the English Constitution, which he defined as monarchial and aristocratic tyranny. Paine stated that the king ruled by heredity and contributed nothing to the well-being of the people. "I challenge the warmest advocate for reconciliation to show a single advantage that this continent can reap by being connected with Great Britain. I repeat the challenge, not a single advantage is derived. Our corn will fetch its value] in any market in Europe, and our imported goods must be paid for by them where we will."[8]

In the second section, Paine smashed the idea of a divine king whose power comes from God and postulated that all men are created equal at birth from their creator. He then pointed out that the king had no real role in governing people and was overpaid to boot. "In England a king hath little more to do than to make war and give away places, which in plain terms, is to impoverish the nation and set it together by the ears. A pretty business indeed for a man to be allowed eight hundred thousand sterling a year for and worshiped into the bargain! Of more worth is one honest man to society and in sight of God, than all the crowned ruffians that ever lived."[9] Paine dismissed the idea of a constitutional monarchy, pointing out that the king would take the power away from the parliament every time.

The third section of *Common Sense* was the heart of Paine's argument and the one that would have the most impact on a populace perfectly positioned to entertain the idea of separation and independence from mother England. Paine argued the best course for America was total independence and proposed a Continental Charter, which would be the equivalent of an American Magna Carta. He then proposed a congress with each colony sending thirty delegates, with the total number of delegates to be at least 390, and that the congress would elect a president. *Common Sense* is an amazingly prescient document in terms of the eventual composition of American government.

The final section proclaimed America's nascent military might and pushed for an American navy. Paine realized the biggest impediment to American independence was fear of British military supremacy and made the argument that in time America would eclipse England in military force. This was just the tonic for Washington and the demoralized Continental Army, shivering from cold and inactivity outside of Boston. General Lee wrote Washington and pronounced the pamphlet "a masterly irresistible performance" and said he had become a "complete convert to independence."[10] Washington's brother-in-law, Fielding Lewis, wrote to Washington that talk of independence was growing and that "most of those who have read the pamphlet *Common Sense* say it's unanswerable."[11]

Washington saw the value of Paine's argument in framing exactly what he and the Continental Army were fighting for outside of Boston. As Paine finished up: "Everything that is right or reasonable pleads for separation. The blood of the slain, the weeping voice of nature cries, 'It's time to part!'"[12] This was the clarion call for separation from Great Britain, and it rang across the dawning republic. Washington and others felt that what had been brewing in the collective unconscious of the nation finally had been verbalized.

Citing British atrocities, Washington told his adjutant Joseph Reed, "A few more or such flaming arguments as were exhibited at Falmouth and Norfolk, added to the sound doctrine and unanswerable reasoning contained in the pamphlet *Common Sense* will not leave numbers at a loss to decide upon the propriety of a separation."[13] Paine's pamphlet ignited the fire of independence, which fanned out across the colonies and empowered the average citizen to believe that he had a role to play in the establishment of a new democracy. With its call to arms in pursuit of liberty and independence, *Common Sense* was the Pearl Harbor of its day. Washington's ongoing siege was now elevated to a crusade for the establishment of a new country. Although Washington and Knox firmly believed in the revolution which they were risking everything for, the average citizen had not yet made the psychological leap to American independence from England. As one Marylander wrote to the *Pennsylvania Evening Post*: "If you know the author of *Common Sense* tell him he has done wonders and worked miracles. His style is plain and nervous, his facts are true, his reasoning just and conclusive."[14] *Common Sense* was the burning fuse that eventually would trigger the American Declaration of Independence.

For George Washington, hacking it out with his army in the frozen hell around Boston, it provided a new argument for reenlistment: they were no longer just fighting the British; they were fighting for the establishment of a new country based on freedom and liberty. Paine would donate the money from his pamphlet to purchase wool mittens for the troops. In less than a year he became an aide-de-camp to General Nathanael Greene and friends with Washington. Paine never made any real money from the publication of *Common Sense*, and long after the war Washington asked of James Madison, "Can nothing be done in our assembly for poor Paine? Must the merits and services of *Common Sense* continue to glide down the stream of time, unrewarded by this country?"[15]

The nobility of Paine's pamphlet spurred the realization among Americans that independence from Britain was inevitable, but Washington still needed to defeat the British at Boston to legitimize their cause. The Americans needed a victory, and more personally, the new commander needed a win. Washington betrayed his own anxiety by writing to Colonel McDougall, "I am in daily expectation of Colonel Knox's arrival." Three days later he fired off another letter to General Schuyler: "I am in hopes that Colonel Knox will arrive with the artillery in a few days. It is much needed."[16]

For a man as understated as Washington, to admit the artillery was "much needed" showed that he had run out of options and his back was against the wall. He could not afford to let the British leave Boston on their own timetable. He had to show that he and the newly formed Continental Army could stand up against the formidable British empire and win. But, of course, Washington had no way of knowing that the very man upon whom he depended was far up in the icy Berkshire mountains, facing men ready to desert him and his cannons. Paine's *Common Sense* explained brilliantly what Henry Knox and his men were suffering for: nothing less than the creation of a new republic.

26

A SINISTER VIOLENCE OF INTENTION

January 12, 1776

"**P**assing through the towering ice pinnacles . . . we entered the rock-strewn valley floor at the bottom of the huge amphitheater. . . . Huge boulders lent an air of solidity to the place, but the rolling rubble underfoot corrected the misimpression. All that one could see and feel and hear—of icefall . . . was a world not intended for human habitation."[1] Thomas Horbein's recollection of climbing a mountain is an account of a man struggling with the elements. But he does not have with him oxen, horses, sleds, and thousands of pounds of iron to lug behind him.

Henry Knox listened to the wind whistling across the mountains, dusting a light snow on the cannons and oxen. The sky was low and the wind carried the icy breath of the subzero temperatures as the men, with numbed hands and faces, beards shaggy with ice, and bloodshot eyes, faced the heavyset young man who had grown a beard in the last month and still wore a dirty scarf wrapped around his left hand. The artillery of the "glorious cause" was not moving. The entire Noble Train had ground to halt "on account that there was no snow beyond five or six miles further in which space there was the tremendous Glasgow or Westerfield mountain to go down."[2]

This would be one of the last entries in Knox's diary as he stared down the barrel of defeat and, to some degree, disgrace. He had promised George Washington—he had promised his country—that he would get the cannons to Boston in order to defeat the British. To entertain failure now was almost unthinkable, but the black implacable stare of the men on the mountain inspired no confidence that this was not the case.

Knox would later write of "three-hour perseverance,"[3] which referred to three hours in which everything he had fought for and believed in was on the line. So Knox began to do one of things he did best: talk. He might have started with his childhood, when he began as a young apprentice for the booksellers in Boston, broke, abandoned by his father, his mother and brother just barely hanging on. That nine-year-old took on the duty of a man and received his education in the lively debates that swirled around the bookstore, learning about liberty and freedom and how the British took these things from the people.

Knox then may have reminded the men about the hated Stamp Acts, the Boston Tea Party, the Parliamentary Acts that slowly destroyed his own business, even as it became a place where Tories and patriots congregated to be in the company of the gregarious, witty young man with the twinkle in his eye. Perhaps he spoke of falling under the spell of John Adams, who believed that America should break from Britain and stand on her own as a country formed whole cloth on the precepts of liberty and the inalienable rights of man. He may have told of how, as a young man, he stumbled upon the Boston Massacre, and after that night there was no turning back and he became dedicated to an ideal that men should be able to labor and live under the free light of liberty.

And then he spoke of his wife, Lucy, who left everything she had ever known to marry him, who had risked being arrested, who had been cast out by friends and family for running off with a rebel bookseller not only because she believed in him but because she believed in the cause of the American Revolution. Knox explained how they escaped under the cover of night, leaving his business and the city he loved; he and his pregnant wife rowed out of Boston harbor with the knowledge that their lives would never be the same and if they were captured it could mean death. He spoke of how Lucy would never see her parents again and he would not be there when his baby come into the world. These were all things that Henry Knox could bring forth and point to the men and say they too were now caught up in something bigger than all of them.

He might have pointed out that George Washington had left his comfortable life at Mount Vernon and risked everything by taking over a young army and taking on a foe that ruled the world. Washington put his life on the line—it was a certainty he would be hung if caught—for an ideal personified in the struggle that began at Lexington and Concord, that began when a free slave, Crispus Atticus, became the first to die in the Boston Massacre. It was a mantle that he,

Henry Knox, had taken up when he said he would bring the cannons needed to defeat the British at Boston.

Now he told the men that if the cannons were left in the mountains, Washington would be at the mercy of the British who would eventually attack—if not Boston, then New York—and crush the new army, thereby crushing the ideals of all the people who assisted them in the towns they passed through, who offered their oxen and sleds, who helped them cross Lake George, who provided food and shelter along the way, and who cheered them on as they took the cannons to George Washington to fight for their country, which would stand as a beacon of liberty for the millions unborn. Could they really give up this charge of destiny toward their moment in history in the frozen, windblown mountains?

Knox put the cause of the American Revolution front and center for all the men to see. He had nothing to lose now. Why had they taken on the impossible task of bringing 120,000 pounds of brass and iron cannons all this way? If not for money, then what was it for? Because it had not been done. *No!* the former bookseller shouted into the frosted twilight. It was for the American ideal born this very moment on this frozen mountainside, which would be recounted through history a thousand times: these patriots, men of conscience, fought for the last best hope of free people everywhere. In the end, *it was* for the unborn millions. They could not fail now. They must not.

Knox was eloquent. He was well read. He was versed in the art of persuasion due to years of discourse in his Boston bookstore. He was a literate man. He understood the Lockean principles of his time and the outstanding men of intellect behind the "glorious cause," which compelled them to fight and die at Bunker Hill or to persevere in Boston without pay, trusting a new general yet unproven in the field of battle. He beseeched the drawn, haggard men who faced him now to carry on, pleading for nothing less than a willingness of the heart.

Knox was facing hardened men who were lugging the equivalent of twenty-eight heavy trucks up the side of an icy mountain, men whose lives were now on the line, too, halfway up the treacherous slopes of the Berkshire mountains. Joseph Conrad wrote of such men in *Lord Jim*: "There are many shades in the danger of adventure and gales, and it is only now and then that there appears on the face of facts a sinister violence of intention . . . with a strength beyond control, with an unbridled cruelty that means to tear out of him his hope and fear, the pain of his fatigue and the longing for rest."[4]

Although it is impossible to know exactly what Henry Knox said on that icy dark mountainside, he would later write in his journal, "after about three hour's perseverance and hiring two teams of oxen they agreed to go."[5] Three hours of perseverance: talking, arguing, pleading, and then Knox's promise of fresh oxen. But where to get these fresh oxen? Knox had a habit of procuring help from people at various points of his career. Solomon Brown was a soldier who had served in the South Militia of Hampshire County and lived in nearby Blandford. Knox asked him for his service and oxen. He was reluctant at first, according to Tim Abbot: "It required several hours of cajoling and subsequent engaging the services of one Solomon Brown of Blandford along with two additional teams of oxen to move the cannon eleven more miles though Russel to Westfield."[6] Brown worked for several days as a teamster and then returned home after reaching Westfield. Eventually he would serve in Captain William Knox's company in April 1776. A final entry in Knox's journal is for the oxen he bought, a receipt dated January 13, 1776, at Blandford: "Received of Henry Knox eighteen shillings blanket money for carrying a cannon weight 24.3 from this town to Westfield being 11 miles. . . . Solomon Brown."[7]

Once again Henry Knox had to depend on his oratorical gifts to keep his train of cannons moving. Challenges were still to come. Mountain climber Eric Shipton wrote in 1938, "It would seem almost as though there were a cordon drawn around the upper part of these great peaks beyond which no man may go. . . . We had forgotten that the mountain still holds the master card, that it will grant success only in its own good time."[8] Due to the fresh oxen, Solomon Brown's assistance, and Henry Knox's appeal to a higher calling, the Noble Train continued through the mountains, and news of the approaching artillery began to percolate across eastern Massachusetts. Ezekiel Price, in the town of Milton, would write in his diary: "It is reported that Colonel Henry Knox is on his return from Crown Point [Ticonderoga] and has with him a number of brass cannon and other ordinance stores and was expected at Cambridge last night with his artillery."[9] Henry Knox was still a long way from Cambridge, but he was moving again. That was enough for now, though the mountain still held the master card.

THE DEVIL'S
STAIRCASE

January 11, 1776

On January 11, snow fell in the mountains, giving the teamsters some relief as they worked their way down the mountain, winding ropes around trees with pulleys to prevent the sleds from sliding down the mountain or crushing the men in front of them. This was backbreaking, grueling work in frigid temperatures; many times the teamsters had to unyoke the oxen and feed out the line with the oxen providing ballast. "That the animals were equally conscious of the sharp hazards was evidenced by the fact that Knox himself had to see that—to prevent runaways and the slashing of weighted sleds downhill upon the men in front—drag chains and poles were thrust under the sled runners, with check ropes anchored to successive trees along the way to hold back the sleds when necessary."[1]

It was an engineer's nightmare: men hauling thousands of pounds of iron and brass cannons up the mountains and then down again. But Henry had headed off the crisis for now, as the Noble Train proceeded under a full moon that illuminated the snow crusting the distant peaks. Men swore, yelled, snapped whips, pushed, pulled, and fell. Knox's harrowing journey is hard to imagine based on the topography of the area today. As John D. Fiore writes,

> It takes less than twenty minutes for a modern automobile to travel from the state line at New York to Great Barrington, Massachusetts, another forty minutes will bring you to Springfield, but in 1776 this stretch was to challenge all of the

strength, courage, and ingenuity of Knox and his men. The road was treacherous, a part of it leading through a thick evergreen forest and then through a mountain pass that was a maze of all of nature's hazards for a traveler: lakes, swamps, chasms, valleys, and with it all, rocks everywhere.[2]

Even with this modern perspective it is difficult for people who rely on cars to understand the grueling, step-by-step, blood-freezing operation that Knox and his men undertook. Freezing weather slows down the blood, muscles tighten, fingers freeze, and iron becomes untouchable. Add to this the vortex of wind that cuts through the mountains, sending windchill indexes plummeting. In 1953 Robert Holcomb drew an illustration for *Springfield Union* magazine of the Noble Train ascending the mountains. The full moon is off to the side of the mountain. The oxen in their yokes haul the cannons on the large wooden sleds. Teamsters help to push the cannons along, holding on to the sides of the sled as the militiamen stalk through the snow, rifles at the ready. A man on a horse waves his arm, encouraging the men, a scarf trailing from his hand. The train of men and beast makes their way through deep snow at the night. It is an inspiring illustration that shows the Noble Train at its finest hour as the men struggled up the mountainside.

The fresh oxen were added to the teams and quickly tired from the constant pulling. A few lost their footing, falling down the mountainside. It was dangerous work and Knox rode up and down the line, helping, cajoling, playing the role of colonel and cheerleader. Finally, they reached the town of Great Barrington and began to follow a rugged road leading to Otis, Blandford, then Westfield.

> The road down from Blandford . . . is a steep one. Although Knox used a trail which was supposed to have been used by General Amherst in the French and Indian War 15 years earlier or so before to haul supplies from Boston to Albany and would have thereby avoided impossible climbs, the drovers did not hesitate to negotiate the steep grade down until Knox arranged for two spans of oxen to supplement their horses in controlling the sleds.[3]

Even today the original path can be seen, although it has not been used for many years. The route today is Route 23, and although it is a parallel trail, "Nevertheless, the narrow, winding, often steep modern highway will give . . . a feeling of kinship with those early drovers who had a more rugged forest path through which to haul the heavy guns under conditions which made Knox comment in wonder at how they have ever gotten their cargo up to Blandford."[4]

Indeed, the teamsters and their cannons were entering the Devil's Staircase, a series of cliffs above the south branch of the Westfield River. Some of these cliffs required the cannons to be lowered by block and tackle over the sheer face of the granite walls. The locals claim this was how Knox handled the cliffs. Even if Knox had veered around the cliffs, he had to descend elevations just as sheer, also part of the Devil's Staircase. It is not surprising that Knox's diary had essentially ended at this point, since the snow had disappeared once again so that the sleighs were being dragged over a frozen, rutted surface. In lowering the cannons, the teamsters used pulleys wrapped around trees, with ropes attached to the rear and front of the sleds, the oxen letting out the rope slowly. This was slow, painstaking work; surely Knox would have devised a workaround to get his cannons to the lower elevations. Knox had another problem, as well, as revealed by the letter he wrote before leaving Blandford on Sunday morning, January 14:

> To W. Twast
>
> Sir, I have waited at this place 2 days for some of your people to come up—but as the roads are so bad that they cannot come on till evening I have concluded to go to Springfield—I am afraid from some circumstances that they will not trust to go further than this place, if so I shall be obliged to get there and at Westfield—I had much rather they would go on to camp the roads are good and they can purchase fodder in the upper Towns for horses and in order to induce them to it offer them 14/yoke oxen a day for each span of horses that is after they leave Springfield—after they get down the next hill they will be able to travel much faster than oxen—I shall wait for you at Springfield in the interim.[5]

Knox was negotiating with a contractor for more oxen, horses, and men because he suspects the teamsters will head back to New York once they clear the mountains. John Becker Sr. had told him as much, so Henry Knox was once again scrambling to keep his train moving, hoping that the drovers would stay with him but entertaining the very real possibility that he might well be stuck without men, oxen, or horses.

Blandford was in the higher elevations of the mountains, but the train had reached an important milestone. No longer would the men be forced to sleep in tents or on the ground. From this point on, they could take shelter in towns along the way and rest. In the morning the Noble Train followed an Indian trail eastward. Two years later this same trail would be used by British General John Burgoyne after his defeat at Saratoga and before that was a trail that "provided ready communication between the Indians of the Hudson River and Connecticut River Valleys. . . . After the Indian custom, the trail ignored the easier village routes which modern road builders use and went across hill and dale in as direct line as possible, here and there being diverted by rivers, lakes, and swamps or some inaccessible mountains."[6]

News of Knox's train was now racing through colonial America as it entered western Massachusetts. The teamsters' work lessened as the elevation slowly flattened out. By the time they reached the town of Otis, the end of the Berkshire mountains was in sight. They rested the night of January 12. Henry Knox must have slept easier; he had just forded frozen snow-capped mountains in the dead of winter with 120,000 pounds of iron and brass in tow. The brute strength of the men and the oxen and providence had allowed his train to traverse impossible heights and then descend sheer cliffs. Knox did not want to get ahead of himself, but no one could blame him for thinking the worst was over and a straightforward run to Cambridge lay ahead.

As the expedition dropped to lower elevations, the snow had disappeared. The sleds were hauled over bare ground into the town of Westfield on the morning of January 13. Knox and his men were astounded to find people cheering them. Knox's mission had stirred the imagination of Americans up and down the colonies, and every town he passed now became a cheering crowd of men, women, and children. To the exhausted, frozen men, the attention must have been a welcome tonic after the brutal conditions they had endured for forty-five days.

These men had been exposed to freezing conditions in the mountains with no sleep while hauling sixty tons of cannons over peaks and into valleys. Even today, with all our modern excavating and hauling equipment, that would be a challenge. The men had only brute strength, oxen, pulleys, sleds, ropes, and the hope that they could make it off the mountains before a snowstorm or, worse, a blizzard occurred. Momentarily, they had been ready to give up but then they pushed on. Mountain climber A. Alvarez writes, "The more improbable the situation and the greater the demands made on the climber the more sweetly the blood flows later in release from all that tension."[7]

The isolated town had never seen a military operation, and the forty sleds, oxen, and horses paraded through the center of the town, the new Americans swelling with pride that it was for the deliverance of their own country. Few of the townspeople had ever seen cannons, much less five-thousand-pound cannons being sledded with oxen and horses. John Becker Jr. was amazed by the reception of cheering people and later recorded in his journal his impressions of that day. They are the impressions of a twelve-year-old boy witnessing a moment in history:

We then reached Westfield, Massachusetts, and were much amused with what seemed quaintness and honest simplicity of the people. Our armament here was a great curiosity. We found the very few, even among the oldest inhabitants, had ever seen a cannon. They were never tired of examining our desperate "big shooting irons" and guessing how many tons they weighed, others of the scientific order were measuring the dimensions of their muzzles and the circumference at the breech. The handles as they styled the trunnions, were reckoned rather too short, but they considered, overall, that the guns, must be pretty nice things at a long shot. We were great gainers by their curiosity, for while they were employed in remarking upon our guns, we were, with equal pleasure, discussing their cider and whiskey. These were generously brought out in great profusion, saying they would be darned if it was not their treat.[8]

A modern comparison might be that of astronauts returning from a moon mission. These strong, bearded men and their large, fearless leader, Henry Knox, along with the militia, the oxen, the large cannons, the horses, and the sheer movement of a military operation had an otherworldly appearance to a populace that generally never left the confines of the town. Yet from the mountains came a caravan of men and iron en route to Boston to save George Washington and the Continental Army and to defeat the British. It was a heroic, bigger-than-life undertaking, and the stories flowed about the various hazards the train had overcome to reach Westfield until myth supplanted truth. Hauling the cannons from Fort Ticonderoga already had all the makings of a legend.

The celebration was in full swing when the townspeople asked if one of the cannons might be fired. The teamsters seemed to realize at this moment what they had accomplished so far and had a new appreciation for the cannons as well. "The teamsters themselves were not idle. Indeed they had little opportunity to be. . . . The teamsters even took their turns at fondling and measuring the guns—as if they had not seen them before—then they were interrupted by the merry residents, by turns wishing to handle the guns and to show their hospitality, saying, 'they would be darned if it was not their treat.'"[9]

Knox selected a thirteen-inch mortar nicknamed Old Sow and fired it, using only powder but no shot. It was the first time that any of the cannons from Fort Ticonderoga had been fired, and Knox was not a little nervous as he lit the fuse. The cannon roared forth and "the resulting bellow which resounded across the snowy Massachusetts hills quieted the revelers for a serious moment. Had the British at Boston been able to hear it, the sound for them might have been a portentous signal."[10] Knox fired the gun again, and the concussion shook the windows of the town and elicited a cheering roar from the people. Knox did this several times, and each time the cannon seemed to fire louder than before.

People in the eighteenth century rarely had the opportunity to watch while a cannon was fired, and the sound must have been titanic to ears used to the silence of early rural America. Again, John Becker Jr. wrote later, "One old mortar, well known during the revolution as the old sow . . . was actually fired by the people of Westfield, for the novel pleasure of listening to its deep-toned thunders."[11]

It is highly doubtful that Knox would have allowed anyone but himself to fire the cannon. That night the party moved to the town inn where Knox was "surrounded by visitors . . . that evening." John Jr. recorded his impression of the moment.[12] "And the introduction [to the townspeople] that took place, gave to his acquaintance a host of militia officers of every rank and degree. Every man seemed to be an officer."[13] Knox would later tell John Becker Jr. "that what a pity our soldiers are not as numerous as our officers."[14] This, of course, was the result of towns creating their own militias. All men preferred to be officers, which Henry Knox knew full well, as he himself had advanced from civilian to colonel.

Henry Knox and his men turned in for the night with full bellies of food and spirits. They were only ninety-one miles from Cambridge, and Knox himself was basking in the glow of his newfound celebrity. He was not only a colonel in the American army, but he was also becoming famous for transporting cannons three hundred miles across lakes, rivers, and mountains, which might change the course of the war. He was so close that he would outrun any letter sent to Washington or Lucy. He was almost home.

28

CANNONS IN THE MUD, SPRINGFIELD

January 14, 1776

There was enough snow on January 14 to start heading for the trading town of Springfield, which was designated by George Washington as the site of the nation's first armory. It would take two days of sledding—and, at times, slogging through the mud with the heavy sleds. Knox wanted snow for much of the expedition, but when it came it was often too deep. Many times, the snow vanished, melting into the trails where the blades of the sleighs carved deep, muddy rivers and many times simply stopped. The oxen suffered the most, dragging thousands of pounds through muck that caused man and beast to slip and lose their footing.

Though Knox was less than a hundred miles from Cambridge, he could not take anything for granted. The countryside was honeycombed with Loyalists who could easily sabotage Washington's goal of bringing the cannons from Ticonderoga to train on the British in Boston. Knox set his eyes on reaching Springfield while the men slogged along the melting trail. He calculated a run of four or five days from Springfield to Cambridge, feeling the urgency of getting the cannons to "His Excellency," who surely had been wondering where he was.

Finally, the train of men, oxen, horses, and cannons reached Springfield and were once again treated to a celebration by the people of the town. As they passed west to east, Knox and his men reached more populous areas where news of their epic journey grew by the hour. The exhausted men once again partook in the festivities, but Knox now had to face that his New York teamsters were leaving and returning to their homes. John Becker Jr. records a final entry:

> We reached Springfield (the great place of deposit for arms) but could get no further. The sleighing failed and we had to leave our cannon lying ingloriously on the roadside, in the mud. I cannot give any further account of their travels. I believe they afterwards were not without effect in various fights and from having been intended by their first owners as the ultima ratio regum, they settled down on their beds the plain and forcible advocates of the doctrines of the continental congress.[1]

Hopefully the cannons weren't left in the mud as John Becker Jr. wrote, but the snow was gone and the sleds were sinking into the mire and muck. Knox had hoped to persuade the Beckers and the other teamsters to continue, but this time he could not. The original agreement had tacitly suggested Springfield as the place they would part, but clearly Knox had hoped their love of country and dedication to the glorious cause might persuade them to stay on to Cambridge to deliver the cannons to Washington. John Becker Jr. would have liked to see that final celebration, but his father was heading back to Saratoga, so they set off, parting with Henry Knox.

There were various reasons the teamsters from New York didn't stay. As historian North Callahan points out:

> Here Knox found he was able to get fresh oxen but discovered that he had a new problem. Most of his teamsters were from New York and were, of course, some distance from their homes. This fact, coupled with the increasingly difficult sledding conditions, discouraged many of the men and made them wish to return home. Had the weather been more favorable, Knox might have persuaded them to remain, as he had done before, but with the snow almost gone, the cannon lying forlornly in the mud by the roadside, he could hold out little promise to them of better conditions.[2]

Knox was within spitting distance of his destination, but the thaw combined with the men leaving his train again derailed his delivery of the artillery. This was the architecture of his journey: the unexpected threatening to destroy his mission at every turn. It is a litmus of Knox, as well as of the ethos of the American army—if not the revolution—to be able to react and problem solve on the spot. Historians point out time and again, all the way up to World War II, that the citizen soldier's ability to improvise made him superior to the enemies he faced.

The reason the British did not detect Knox's movement across Massachusetts, despite its seventeen thousand inhabitants, more than thirteen thousand British troops, and one thousand Tories, could be attributed to the rigidity of the hierarchy in the British army. Soldiers were not to think for themselves, and the British believed hard-and-fast rules governed warfare. Armies fought wars during the spring, summer, and fall and were dormant in the winter. No self-respecting army would journey forth in the dead of winter to bring back cannons across impassable terrain to be trained on an enemy. When this intelligence was received by the British—undoubtedly a soldier heard of the movement of this artillery train or a Tory told a British official—then the chain of command rejected it as spurious. The two armies could not have been more different in their approach to the use of talented young leaders. "If the desperate American need for leaders had thrust young men like Nathaniel Greene into positions beyond their experience, the British military system, wherein commissions were bought and aristocrats given preference, denied many men of ability the roles they should have played."[3]

Clearly, men like Henry Knox would never have been entrusted with a mission of such importance in the British military. And if the Americans had launched such a titanic military undertaking, then a British officer would have this knowledge, not an enlisted man or a Loyalist. This was where the British could have foiled Washington's plans with the train that was literally and figuratively stuck in the mud in Springfield while Henry Knox scouted frantically for more oxen, horses, teamsters, and sleds. Once again, the name Solomon Brown surfaces: "Brown was a veteran of the French and Indian War and knew the road networks and animal push transports very well. He was heavily involved with local trading since the war ended in 1763 and found the bustling markets of Springfield very pleasing. Based off Knox's intent he quickly found the suitable men, oxen and horses needed to fit the already configured sleds."[4]

Henry Knox was now in a populated area, so word of his predicament spread quickly. New England was a hotbed of patriots, and many rushed to help in the name of the cause. Becker and his team leaving was agreed upon, but there may have been other issues other than simply a desire to return home. Intense regional rivalries existed during this time and the Green Mountain boys had been declared outlaws, and perhaps the teamsters were fearful that the Green Mountain Boys might harm them if they remained.

Whatever the reason, John Becker and his father then returned to Albany where "our services were again imperiously required by the exigency of our northern affairs."[5] Although John Becker Jr. mentioned that the cannons laid in the mud by the side of the road, Knox never would have allowed the cannons to leave the sleds. "He had already insisted that the carriages they were put upon would carry them all the way and at most he would have allowed a direct transfer from the sleds to wagons, protecting his precious cannon in every conceivable way."[6] Henry Knox had not come this far to watch the expedition fall apart in Springfield. He would use the soldiers and the Massachusetts men to transport the cannons the rest of the way.

The temperature fell once more and snow descended, and on January 17, the Noble Train embarked again, making good time, heading for Worcester, Framingham, and just beyond, Cambridge.

29

DELIVERANCE

January 24, 1776

George Washington cradled his throbbing head in his hands and stared at the rug in his headquarters. He was surrounded by "Generals Ward, Putnam, Heath, Spencer, Sullivan, Greene, and Gates, . . . James Warren, head of the Massachusetts Assembly, and John Adams."[1] He had not been sleeping well and his wife Martha didn't sleep at all, the sound of guns keeping her on edge. Mount Vernon was vulnerable with his slaves in danger of running off any moment to join the British. The British captured one of his sentinels along the front lines and put his head on a pike facing the Americans. More British ships had just reached the harbor with reinforcements. Washington had spoken to his war council regarding the "indispensable necessity of making a bold attempt on Boston."[2]

He had been in this situation before. The council had listened to Washington and agreed that a "vigorous attempt" should be implemented but with the caveat: only when practical. This is what kept Washington up at night. He had no options; every time he contemplated a bold move, the council invoked caution and prudence, effectively tying his hands. He needed a break; he needed something to tip the balance in his favor. A rider had come in well after dark on January 18 with a message bearing hope. General Schuyler wrote that guns from Ticonderoga were on the way. Washington dared not make plans for the cannons in his siege campaign until he saw the cannons. But this was the most convincing piece of intelligence after the letters from Henry Knox that the twenty-five-year-old Boston bookseller might deliver on his promise made back in November to bring sixty tons of artillery three hundred miles across frozen lakes, rivers, mountains, and insurmountable wilderness.

The men around Washington had not thought it possible and voiced doubt that the young colonel would return with even one cannon in tow. General Lee was the fiercest critic of Washington for sending Knox on a fool's errand into the wilderness. Washington often suspected Lee saw himself as the more competent general and was irked that Washington had been appointed to head the Continental Army rather than Lee himself. Artemas Ward, the former commander of the colonial army during Bunker Hill, certainly saw himself as a man who had been unjustly passed over by the Continental Congress in its appointment of Washington.

George Washington had yet to produce even a hint of triumph and felt the "eyes of the whole continent were on him, fixed with anxious expectation."[3] There were few in whom he could truly confide, since his aide, Joseph Reed, had left in October for health reasons and to oversee his law practice. George Washington now spent days "chained to his desk with correspondence" from morning to night in his headquarters.[4] He had little privacy with his aides sleeping in adjoining rooms. He had procured a four-poster bed when Martha joined him in Cambridge in an attempt at marital propriety, but privacy was not to be; his residence and headquarters was bustling with people, riders, and entertainment for visiting senators and dignitaries. And there was always the paperwork. "At present my time is much taken up at my desk that I am obliged to neglect many other essential parts of my duty," he wrote to Reed, pleading for his return.[5]

Washington developed excruciating headaches that he attributed to working at his desk into the late hours. He had gone on walks to the harbor several times and jumped up and down on the ice, testing it to see if it could handle the weight of his troops. His days were not his own, and he took any opportunity to escape from councils, imploring aides, his wife's complaints about British shells that shattered her overwrought nerves, and his own continual frustration while the British planned their next move in Boston, which Washington now believed involved an invasion of New York.

The British could not be allowed to leave Boston at their leisure, but the American army was still short of gunpowder, and two thousand men lacked muskets. Benjamin Franklin had suggested to General Lee that soldiers be given bows and arrows. Washington had long since adopted a stoical front that he later told Reed he used "to conceal my weakness from the enemy and also conceals it from our friends and adds to their wonder."[6]

Still, Washington felt they must attack and force the British to abandon the city, taking the initiative away from the enemy. Anything else would be a defeat for the new army, the new general, and the new country. Washington pinned his hopes on Henry Knox and his artillery. He lifted his head, which throbbed from cerebral tension across his forehead, and nodded to his generals. He could only hope that Knox was on his way with the cannons.

Washington looked up at his generals.

"We will wait."

Washington left the room and went outside to breathe the clear, cool air. It had been snowing, but now the sky was clear and the moon shone down on the crisp new blanket lapping the land. George Washington had undergone a subtle transformation since the beginning of the revolution. He had become a gambler who had thrown convention to the wind. He had headed a token army fighting a revolution against an implacable foe. He had proclaimed that freed slaves could fight in the Continental Army. He had sent a man to retrieve cannons against impossible odds. And he had invited a former slave to visit him at his headquarters.

Her name was Phillis Wheatley and she had sent Washington a poem in honor of his new position as leader of the Revolution. "Proceed great chief, with virtuous thy side / Thy every action let the goddess guide / A crown, a mansion, and a throne that shine / With gold unfading, Washington! Be tine."[7] The twenty-one-year-old slave from Boston went on to laud America as "the land of freedoms heaven defended race!"[8] John Wheatley, a Boston tailor, had bought Phillis for his wife but recognized her talent and had her schooled in the classics. She lived with the Wheatley family and in 1773 published a book of verse, *Poems on Various Subjects, Religious and Moral.*[9]

She sent her verse to Washington, who responded with a letter, which was astonishing due to the fact that he was a Virginia slaveholder:

I thank you most sincerely for your polite notice of me in the elegant lines you enclosed. And however undeserving I may be of such encomium and panegyric, the style and manner exhibit a striking proof of your great poetical talents. . . . If you should ever come to Cambridge or near headquarters, I shall be happy to see a person so favored by the Muses and to whom nature has been so liberal and beneficent in her dispensations. I am with great respect, your obedient humble servant.[10]

Washington was engaged in a revolution, tipping over set ideas about government, societal norms, countries, as well as his own internal assumptions. It is safe to say that George Washington had become a work in progress as was the Revolution and like all great upheavals he was not sure what the breaking of convention would produce, but surely writing to a slave girl and inviting her to visit him was not something he would have contemplated even a year before. The American Revolution was a broad wave to which no one was immune, and few would remain unchanged at its end.

Washington took another deep breath of cool air then turned to go back in when he saw a rider approaching his headquarters from the woods. He waved off the sentinel and stepped off the porch, crunching through the freezing snow. A late express, perhaps, a messenger bearing news that Knox might be even closer. The man rode with a curious loping gait. He was a large man, a fat man, with a great beard flattened upon his chest. The rider was covered in snow and looked to Washington as if he had come many miles. Something about the man forced Washington to pause, his eyes on the scarf trailing the man's left hand.

30

THE FINAL LEG

January 17, 1776

After Springfield and the departure of the teamsters, the five groups of Henry Knox's Noble Train had broken up into pockets of men and animals moving at their own pace. The laboring oxen, horses, and men pulling thousands of pounds of cannons along snow-slicked roads in the brilliant sunshine was now a proud corps headed directly to George Washington at Cambridge. It had been more than fifty days since Knox had left for Ticonderoga, and the grueling nightmare of uncertainty, exhausting labor, frustration, and exposure that nearly resulted in death finally had coalesced into a route running through the villages of Wilbraham, Monson, Palmer, Brimfield, Spencer, Leicester, Cherry Valley, and Worcester.

Knox was impatient now. He could see victory in the fresh packed snow, the frozen Worcester pond, and Lake Quinsigamond, which they still must cross. But the recent freeze provided stable ice on the pond and the river, allowing the men, sleds, and oxen to pass without incident. After traversing the mountains and losing the teamsters and oxen, Knox felt as if they had passed their final tests. The towns they passed through during the next seven days had more people turning out to cheer them on. The teamsters and militia made use of the inns and the roadside taverns, and Henry sometimes set up unofficial headquarters in the local churches during stopovers. But speed was of the essence.

This part of Knox's journey would be laid out two hundred years later with markers spaced six miles apart. It is the most accessible part of Knox's journey, where the final run across Massachusetts along the main highway led to West-borough, Marlborough, Newton, then Watertown—and eventually to Worchester, where Lucy was staying, on January 20. Knox once again fired "Old Sow" for the townspeople who celebrated the arrival of the cannons headed for Boston. Knox was becoming more and more famous the closer he got to Boston. Word traveled from town to town extolling the exploits of Henry Knox's Noble Train and growing with each retelling. Rich in mythology, the story of Knox's journey across mountains, frozen rivers, and lakes with sixty tons of iron and brass cannons would take its place in the annals of history along with Washington's crossing of the Delaware. It was becoming apparent that George Washington's faith was well placed in the young Boston bookseller.

There are no letters commemorating Lucy and Henry's reunion. Nor should there be. They were newlyweds who had been separated by circumstance for long periods of time. Henry Knox had just returned from the wilderness not only victorious, but now a bona fide war hero. People gathered around and listened, enraptured, by the tale of hardship and endurance that Knox recounted to them. Months later, Lucy would later write Henry, apparently when he had a cold, and describe the cloud of misery their separations caused her:

> This is indeed hard. My Harry is sick, and I cannot see him. Let me beg and entreat of you, as you value my peace, to take care of your precious health. Do not expose yourself in this manner. If you do, you will soon make an end to your life and mine, for I trust our affection is too deep riveted to admit the life of one after the other is gone. God grant us to live to meet again. . . . Pray for your little girl. My Harry, she is half distracted. I have more fortitude than I thought I had, but there are times when every other consideration gives way to the soul racking idea of my friend, my husband, my all, exposed to a dangerous enemy.[1]

Henry Knox finally was reunited with Lucy after risking his life many times over in the name of a cause that had forever altered his life. But now, with the snow falling outside the windows, Knox knew a contentment he had felt only a few times in his life; since they escaped Boston under the cover of night, contentment had been elusive. He was an officer in an army fighting a revolution against the British in which freedom was in the balance, and he was part of that equation. Even as he slept, Knox understood the urgency of the moment, and he knew at dawn's light he must be on his way with no knowledge of when he might return to his wife.

Old Sow once again shook the windows in Worcester as the men touched the fuse and fired off the powder charge over and over. After spending the night with Lucy, Henry was up early once again, as was his custom, and pulling out of Worchester. The townspeople came to see the train of artillery off. By now, many of the oxen had been replaced by horses. They needed speed now rather than brute strength, and the horses followed the roads through Shrewsbury, Northborough, Marlborough, Southborough, and then finally Framingham, where they stopped on January 24, 1776.

After securing the artillery, Knox could hold himself back no longer. He was fifteen miles from Cambridge and George Washington's headquarters. Knox rode off on his horse into the winter night by the light of the cold moon. He had made a promise to General Washington two months before that he would return with the cannons from Fort Ticonderoga, and the twenty-five-year-old bookseller had done just that. He wanted to inform "his excellency" immediately that the cannons were in Framingham and that he planned to bring them into camp, return them to their carriages, and most importantly, to train them on the British at Boston.

Knox galloped his horse, his cape flying, breathing the cold air, bent over the neck of his steed, a young man on a crusade to deliver his promised treasure. He hit the outskirts of Cambridge with his horse winded from the full gallop and his face numb. He felt the beating of blood in his arms and legs and the full vitality of a man wedded to a cause and victorious in that cause. He came into view of Washington's headquarters with candles burning in the windows. A sentinel approached as Knox prepared to identify himself, but suddenly the man turned and Henry Knox saw a tall man striding through the crisp January snow. His white hair was pulled back tight, his demeanor ramrod straight. Knox felt tears come to his eyes. None other than His Excellency George Washington himself was coming to greet the pilgrim at end of his long journey.

THE HEIGHTS

31

COLONEL OF
THE ARTILLERY

February 11, 1776

Colonel Knox galloped next to George Washington, Colonel Putnam, and several other officers. They were going to inspect the narrow causeway leading to Boston. A cold blast of air had finally frozen the ice in Boston Harbor and that, along with the arrival of Knox's artillery, had for the first time allowed George Washington to go on the offensive. The minute Henry Knox appeared outside Washington's headquarters on January 24, the momentum had shifted to the Americans; but there was not a moment to lose. "Washington felt tremendous pressure from Congress and many leaders around the country to order a strike at Boston. He also was desperate to attack and felt a golden opportunity was slipping away."[1]

Washington immediately had guns placed at Roxbury, Cobble Hill, and Lechmere Point. Messengers sped off from headquarters with increased activity in the American camp. "Great activity and animation are observed among our officers and soldiers who manifest an anxious desire to have a conflict with the enemy," wrote Dr. James Thatcher.[2]

Washington was like a child with a new toy. He traveled to Framingham after Knox arrived to inspect the guns with other officers and was impressed. John Adams saw the guns on January 25 and wrote in his diary, "Thursday, about 10 a.m. Mr. Elbridge Gerry called for me and we rode to Framingham where we dined. Colonel Buckminster after dinner showed us the train of artillery brought from Ticonderoga by Colonel Knox."[3] The question quickly became how best to use these massive cannons to break the stalemate at Boston. Washington still pursued an idea of a straightforward invasion supported by the new cannons. The lack of powder convinced him that an artillery bombardment would be ineffective and would not dislodge the British.

To that end, on February 11 Knox accompanied Washington and his staff to Boston Neck for a firsthand look at British fortifications and the approaches to Dorchester. The group left their horses and advanced on foot when they spotted two British officers. One began riding toward them. They were within range of the British artillery, and the officers signaled their batteries to open fire. Washington and his officers ran and narrowly escaped being killed. Knox, for his part, was ready to follow "his excellency" anywhere, and to that end he supported Washington's proposal of an invasion of Boston on February 16.

Since Knox's arrival, he had been the toast of the American army as he assumed his role as colonel of the artillery. As his Noble Train of Artillery flowed in from Framingham, Knox sent off his first letter as colonel to General Lee in New York requesting more cannons:

> His excellency General Washington informs me that he has written you in general terms expecting a quantity of shot and shells that were ordered from New York some time since, also desires me to write more particularly,—I do myself the honor to enclose a list of these articles which were to have been forwarded to camp by the provincial congress of the committee who sit during the recess of Congress—why they have not the reasons for it are unknown to me—the stores at Turtle Bay, the cannon at Kings Bridge excepting the 2 brass six pounders which belong to the city and were promised as a loan—if they could be put on board some small vessel and sent through the East River to New London or Norwich the expense of carting would be very much diminished although I brought 11 very fine field pieces from Ticonderoga. Yet without the additional ones from New York we shall be deficient in field artillery—the shells are much wanted—The General has desired me to send an officer of artillery. Accordingly, I have ordered Capt. Badlam an officer of merit considering his experience to serve you immediately. I have the honor to be with the greatest respect sir. Your most obedient humble servant.
>
> Henry Knox Colonel of the Regiment of Artillery[4]

This is the first document dated January 25 in which Knox is acting in his official capacity. He clearly wants to round up as many cannons as possible. After presenting his expenses to Washington for the expedition of 520 pounds, 15 shillings, 8¾ pence, he received an invitation in kind from Washington recognizing his achievement and his new status in the army. "The General and

Mrs. Washington present their compliments to Colonel Knox and Lady. Beg the favor of their company at dinner, on Friday half after 2 o'clock. Thursday Evening Feb. 4, 1776."[5]

Henry Knox had arrived. But there was much to do. Knox was present at the meeting of the war council when Washington proposed "a bold and resolute assault upon the troops in Boston."[6] Although it seems curious that Washington did not immediately turn to Dorchester Heights, he was a man who took a conclusion to its logical end and he was daring the war council to block him once again now that the harbor had frozen and he had Knox's artillery. Washington was desperate to strike before British reinforcements arrived. He understood the gunpowder situation and reasoned that a bombardment would destroy part of the town and use up the powder without dislodging the British. He wanted to move across the ice between Dorchester Heights and avoid British fortifications and cannons at Boston Neck.

Washington's generals once again vetoed his plan. They still lacked gunpowder, and they believed that the artillery would accomplish little in weakening the British behind their fortifications. The general accepted the verdict but had pointed out that "a stroke well aimed at this juncture might put a final end to the war."[7] General Israel Putnam had been lamenting the lack of gunpowder for weeks. One of Washington's staff later wrote of the general's intransigence, "He is still as hard as ever, crying out for powder, powder, ye gods, give us powder!"[8] This was the fourth time the war council had turned down Washington, who later vented to Joseph Reed that they had waited all year for the bay to freeze and now "the enterprise was thought too dangerous!"[9]

But necessity is the mother of invention, and Washington's disappointment at having his original land assault campaign on Boston turned down once again by the war council turned Washington to the logical use of Henry Knox's cannons. He told Knox on February 18 that Connecticut was sending three thousand pounds of powder, "which Henry said would provide his guns with enough ammunition to force the king's men from the city."[10] The twin hills of Dorchester Heights "loomed over Boston from the south and could be used to defeat the British if . . . fortified. This strategic bluff, more than one hundred feet high, had remained unarmed."[11] General Howe swore he would attack if he detected the Americans trying to fortify the Heights, and Washington's plan quickly took shape. They would fortify the hill, taking the guns from Ticonderoga to the top, under the cover of night. This would force the British to attack, drawing them out into the open. Washington wrote Reed again, admitting that "perhaps the irksomeness of my situation led me to undertake more than could be warranted by prudence."[12] He saw the folly of his original plan when compared to the brilliance of the Dorchester maneuver. "I am preparing to take post on Dorchester."[13]

The high guns would threaten not only Boston, but the British fleet in the harbor. Howe would have no choice but to act. Of course, the execution of the plan required great planning and skill, for if the British detected what the Americans were up to, they would attack immediately. Washington had no way of knowing if the British were aware of the arrival of Knox's cannons, and he didn't want to give them a chance to attack before he could implement his plan to move them to the Heights.

Moving the guns to Dorchester depended on a classic feint. The Americans would open with a salvo from Roxbury, Cobble Hill, and Lechmere Point. The cannonade would screen the sounds of the oxen and wagons that would be used to move the cannons and men up the hills. The 112-feet elevation of the Heights was steeper than Bunker Hill and would put the cannons out of reach of the British guns. However, the long winter had made the ground "impenetrable as a rock," as Washington wrote.[14] This proved problematic in digging trenches and constructing traditional fortifications to protect the men.

The solution was prefabrication, which made its first appearance during the American Revolution. Rufus Putnam was a resourceful lieutenant who had helped construct the fortifications at Roxbury. He was a farmer and a surveyor who came up with a solution to Washington's problem after reading a military text on artillery, "Mueller's Field Engineer" by British professor John Muller. Putnam presented his idea to Knox and to his cousin Israel Putnam.

Putnam suggested constructing the fortifications off-site and then hauling them along with the cannons up Dorchester Heights. Washington approved the plan, and immediately "hundreds of men were at work building chandeliers, great timber frames that could be filled with screwed hay [hay twisted into bales] or compact bundles of brushwood called fascines."[15] Washington also ordered barrels filled with earth hauled up to the top of the hills to roll down on the British when they approached. Wagon wheels would be wrapped with hay for silence, and to block the view of the British, the American soldiers shielded the movement of the train up the hill with bales of hay. The undertaking depended on stealth and on the British assumption that the Americans still had no artillery.

Timing and use of all available men and materials would be crucial, as the entire operation had to be completed by dawn. "Three thousand men under General Thomas were to take part in fortifying the Heights. Another four thousand were to stand by at Cambridge for an amphibious assault on Boston once the British launched their assault on the Heights. General Putnam had overall command of the Boston attack. Generals Greene and Sullivan would lead the crossing. On the Charles River at Cambridge, 60 flatboats stood ready."[16]

Washington called up two thousand Massachusetts militia, and work details rounded up eight hundred oxen and wagons to haul the cannons and the prefabricated fortifications. Thousands of bandages were procured for the army hospital in Cambridge and hundreds of beds made ready for wounded. "Notices in the *Boston Gazette* called for volunteer nurses."[17] The buzz around Boston intensified. "It is generally thought that there will be something done amongst you very soon," Sarah Hodgkin wrote from Ipswich to her husband, Joseph, in the army.[18] Abigail Adams wrote to a friend, "The preparations increase and something is daily expected, something terrible it will be."[19]

It is surprising that George Washington didn't immediately recognize the overwhelming advantage the Heights gave him. The British lines were a mile and a half from Dorchester Heights, well within the range of Knox's twelve or eighteen pounder cannons. The distance to the British fleet off Long Wharf was two miles, but this was still within range of the three five-thousand-pound cannons. It was just barely in range, but a lucky shot could sink a ship. Still, Washington anticipated the battle being won on the ground when the British attacked the Heights.

The night of March 4 would begin the movement of the cannons, men, and fortifications up to the twin hills of Dorchester. It was bold, decisive, and possible only because Henry Knox had brought the cannons from Ticonderoga to Concord. On the eve of the attack, Washington wrote a Virginia friend that he was preparing "to bring on a rumpus" with the redcoats.[20] It was a classic Washington understatement, concealing the fact he was rolling the dice on a single maneuver to change the course of the American Revolution. Fittingly, on the same date of the Boston Massacre—March 5—the Americans would open fire on the British to retake Boston.

32

THE CANNONS
OF TICONDEROGA

March 4, 1776

It is amazing that the British didn't know what the Americans were up to on Dorchester Heights. Secrecy was pivotal to Washington's plan, but many did know what was unfolding. Washington could only hope that the British would not act in time. Washington ordered a stop to all secret communications with Boston. Generals Heath and Sullivan "personally inspected the lines to verify the vigilance of the guards on duty."[1] Regiments stood ready to march at a moment's notice should the British discover the movement of troops and cannons. Many Loyalists who gladly would have informed the British of the plan simply had no idea. Deserters did tell British officers on February 29 of the plan to occupy the Heights, and a spy named "Junis" confirmed that the rebels "intended to bombard the town from Dorchester."[2] Despite their thrashing at Bunker Hill, the British still clung to hard-and-fast ideas about the way in which wars were fought and chose to ignore the warnings.

George Washington knew what was at stake: the fate of the American Revolution. If the British could reinforce and launch an assault against New York or route the Americans from the Heights, the war could be lost. The world was waiting to see if a rebel army could outfight the most powerful nation on earth, and the cradle of the American Revolution was in the offing. Washington issued final orders to his men, letting them know what was at stake.

As the season is now fast approaching where every man must expect to be drawn into the field of action, it is highly necessary that he should prepare his mind, as well as everything necessary for it. It is a noble cause we are engaged in, it is the cause of virtue and mankind, every temporal advantage and comfort to us, and our posterity depends upon the vigor or our exertions. . . . But it may not be amiss for the troops to know that if any man in action shall presume to skulk, hide himself, or retreat from the enemy, without the orders of his commanding officer, he will be instantly shot down as an example of cowardice.[3]

This was an all-or-none proposition for Washington and for the army—every man had to do his part. On the eve of the bombardment, Washington wrote a final letter to Artemas Ward "that everything must be set and ready to go on Monday night, March 4th." Washington folded and sealed the letter then wrote on the back, "Remember the barrels."[4]

Henry Knox readied his cannons to shell his hometown. He would fire from three directions: "Roxbury from the south, Lechmere's Point from the north, and Cobble Hill on the west."[5] At midnight on March 2, he began his cannonade and unleashed a ferocious bombardment of Boston. The cannonballs rained on the city while soldiers and panicked citizens ran for any shelter they could find. The sky filled with streaks of fire as Knox artillerymen coolly loaded and fired in rapid succession. This was the first time the guns of Ticonderoga had been used by the Americans against the British. "The shots and shells were heard to make a great crashing in the town," the *Pennsylvania Journal* reported.[6]

Then the British opened fire from fortifications on the Neck and from the western side of Boston. The sky was filled with fire. Three of Knox's mortars exploded due to inept loading, a rookie mistake for the new artillerymen, but it didn't slow down the cannonade. The firing continued through the night, doing little damage to Boston and ending sometime in the morning. Then on Sunday night Knox opened fire again, and the British responded. On Monday night, Knox let loose with everything he had, and the British responded in kind. Abigail Adams wrote from ten miles away, "The house shakes . . . with the roar of the cannon. . . . No sleep for me tonight."[7]

A British captain, Charles Stuart, wrote about the bombardment: "The inhabitants were in a horrid situation, particularly the women, who were several times drove from their houses by shot, and crying for protection."[8] American Lieutenant Samuel Webb later wrote, "Our shells raked the houses and the cries of the poor women and children frequently reached our ears." But the attack was going as planned, and as the guns crashed through the night, General Thomas and two thousand men hurried across the Dorchester causeway, shielded by the barrier of hay bales. They moved silently and quickly; the men were forbidden to talk. The race was on against first light and a "covering party" of eight hundred riflemen spread out along Dorchester shores should any British come to see what was happening. Then twelve hundred men tasked with creating the fortifications followed and then "came hundreds of carts and heavy wagons loaded with chandeliers, fascines, hay bales, barrels, and most importantly the cannons from Ticonderoga."[9]

Henry Knox led a procession of four hundred men with oxen and wagons hauling the heaviest guns up the hills. It was the Noble Train all over again with the men urging the oxen up the steep incline and the five-thousand-pound cannons becoming heavier with each step. "The whole procession moved on in solemn silence and with perfect order and regularity, while the continued roar of the cannons served to engage the attention and divert the enemy," wrote Dr. Thatcher, who crossing the causeway with the troops, noted the "vast number of large bundles of screwed hay arranged in a line next to the enemy . . . to which we would have been greatly exposed while passing."[10]

The same daring that pushed Knox to drag the cannons three hundred miles though mountains in winter now propelled him to haul those same cannons to heights overlooking the city under the noses of the British. Stealth, cunning, and the desperate, unexpected act of necessity by men with their backs against the wall while General Howe and his officers slept were the secret weapons of the Americans. The men driving the oxen swore under their breath, whipping on the oxen that strained under the steep ascent. The movement up the steep hills reminded Knox of Devil's Canyon in the Berkshires. But Mother Nature assisted, and the night was unseasonably mild with a full moon to light the way for the soldiers. Reverend William Gordon later wrote, "a finer night for work could not have been taken out of the whole 365. . . . It was hazy below the Heights so that our people could not be seen, though it was a bright moonlit night above on the hills."[11]

Many trips were made up and down the hills to get all the cannons and supplies to the top. Knox kept the men and oxen moving and then orchestrated the positioning and setting up of the cannons on top of the Heights. "The oxcarts and wagons with their entrenching tools, timbers, hay, barrels, and fascines crawled snakelike and steadily up the heights. . . . All night long men and animals labored like clockwork. Had the British sentries posted on Boston Neck, only a mile away, been alert enough to look up, they would have observed the weird snaking procession of men and steers moving dimly and ominously along the southern horizon."[12]

General Thomas reported that as of ten o'clock the fortifications could withstand "small arms and grapeshot." At the same time, Sir John Campbell, a British lieutenant, told Brigadier General Francis Smith, "The rebels were at work on Dorchester Heights."[13] At this moment the British could have foiled Washington's covert operation, but General Smith, a veteran of thirty years, believed less in surprise than regularity when it came to warfare. He simply did not believe the rebels could mount a threat to the British and ignored the warning.

The work continued on the Heights of Dorchester with men breaking frozen ground with picks, axes, and shovels to fill the chandeliers and barrels with hardened dirt. "The unforgiving ground had ice two feet thick and was hard as rock."[14] Another relief force of three thousand men ascended the heights around 4:00 a.m. and continued the work unabated. The cannons were positioned and the ammunition brought forth as the artillery crews worked smoothly and methodically under Knox's watchful eyes. His men readied themselves for the opening salvo that would commence with the dawn. Five more regiments lined up on the shore, and by early light twenty cannons were in place atop Dorchester.

The fortifications were finished as the first rays of light streaked across Boston Harbor. George Washington walked quietly among the men and stared toward the Boston spires and rooftops pink in the morning light. He had left his home to lead a rebel army that had become an American Revolution for a new country. It all came down to this moment. Henry Knox waited for the signal to begin the bombardment of a town where a year before he had been a bookseller.

Each man had come to this juncture of history from very different origins, but they were both part of the Noble Train that had swept up the nation and they were risking all. Knox stared at the dew glistening on the barrels of the black iron cannons, which had led him to this moment. George Washington stood ramrod straight, his profile against the brimming dawn breaking over the city, wind picking at his waistcoat as he turned to the men and "asked them to remember this day." He then nodded to Knox.

Colonel Henry Knox lit the cannon fuse and opened fire.

33

AT DAWN'S LIGHT

March 5, 1776

General Howe was a man who enjoyed life's pleasures. Since the disaster at Bunker Hill, he had come to assume the rebels would still be there in the spring when he would move on New York and either burn Boston or leave a small occupying force. Either way, the timetable was his, and he took George Washington and the rebel army not at all seriously. He had been enjoying elegant dinners and long nights at the faro table, always in the company of a beautiful young woman who was another's wife.

She would become known as "Billy Howe's Cleopatra" but her real name was Elizabeth Lloyd Loring, and her husband, Joshua Loring Jr., was from a prominent Loyalist family whom Howe had hired to supervise the commissary for rebel prisoners. "Joshua had a handsome wife. The general . . . was fond of her. Joshua had no objections. He fingered the cash, the general enjoyed madam," wrote a Loyalist chronicler of the war.[1]

On March 5, Howe awoke to shrieking howls of mortars and cannons lobbing shells into the center of Boston. He was fairly thrown out of the bed he shared with his concubine, and he rushed to the windows. He saw "the missiles ripping through houses, sending chunks of brick and splintered wood flying."[2] The shells seemed to be falling from directly above and the concussion was ear splitting. Howe pulled on his pants, not understanding where the shells were coming from. The rebels had no real artillery to speak of, yet Boston seemed to be under severe attack from all sides as exploding shells shattered windows and set houses on fire. The British were turning out on the double, and Howe rushed into the street and stared up at a sight he would not forget.

Other British commanders stared at the cannons breaking the dawn sky. Howe shook his head. "My God, these fellows have done more work in one night than I could make my army do in three months!"[3] Panic was everywhere as citizens ran for cover from the raining mortar shells. Another British general, General Heath, later wrote, "Perhaps there was never so much done in so short a space of time."[4] A British engineering officer, Archibald Robertson, had calculated that to have created the fortifications and hauled the cannons up to the Heights it was a "most astonishing night's work and must have required at least 15,000 to 20,000 men."

A London paper would later carry a letter by an "officer of distinction":

5th March This I believe, likely to prove an important day to the British empire as any in our annals. We underwent last night a very severe cannonade, which damaged several houses, and killed some men. This morning at daybreak we discovered two redoubts on the hills of Dorchester Point and two smaller works on their flanks. They were all raised during the night, with an expedition equal to that of the genie belonging to Aladdin's wonderful lamp. From these hills they command the whole, so that we must drive them from their post, or desert the place.[5]

The surprise was total. The British had been asleep at the wheel for months as Henry Knox dragged sixty tons of cannons from Ticonderoga and then in one night performed the ultimate checkmate by hoisting the cannons to the Heights of Dorchester and shelling the British in their beds. It was a precursor to Washington's crossing of the Delaware, in which assumed rules of engagement were thrown to the wind, and the British suffered for their complacency. Henry Knox and his artillerymen did not pause. Their powder-blackened faces shined with early light as they touched off the eighteen pounders that lobbed exploding cannonballs into the center of Boston. There was a real chance that Knox might shell his own London Bookstore, blowing it to bits.

The British lost no time in returning fire, aiming all their cannons on the Heights. The two-hour cannonade did nothing, as the guns couldn't be elevated sufficiently to hit the fortifications or Knox's cannons. Washington wrote Congress after the attack that "this tactical victory was equal to our most sanguine expectations."[6] An American captain who was held prisoner by the British managed to escape during the bombardment related that the "bombardment and cannonade caused much surprise in town as many of the soldiery said they had never heard or thought we had mortars or shells."[7] The situation was very clear when Admiral Molyneux Shuldham sent a message to Howe stating that no ship could stay in the harbor unless the guns were removed from the Heights. Although the ships were at the far range of the guns, approximately two miles, a lucky shot could still take out a warship, an unacceptable risk to the admiral.

Howe had to act at once. He gathered his generals at Province House before noon and announced his decision to attack. He had no long-term plans of staying in Boston; it was a matter of pride and honor, and Howe would not be chased from the city by a ragtag rebel army. He ordered two thousand troops to the harbor and into flatboats at Castle Island, where the attack on Dorchester Heights would be launched. Captain Archibald Robertson had doubts about Howe's plan and wrote about it in his diary later, calling it "the most serious step ever an army of this strength in such a situation took, considering the state the rebels work in and the number of men they appear to have under arms."[8] Robertson saw the plan to move on the fortified Heights as a slaughter for the British and went on to say the fate of the town was at stake, if "not to say the fate of America."[9]

It didn't matter. General Howe would not leave Boston without defeating the rebels first. The large transports pushed off from Long Wharf around noon while the men on the Heights watched the entire operation. "We saw distinctly the preparations which the enemy were making to dislodge us," wrote John Trumbull.[10] "The entire waterfront of Boston lay open to our observation and we saw the embarkation of troops form the various wharves. . . . We were in high spirits, well prepared to receive the threatened attack."[11]

Dr. Thatcher, an army doctor, would later cite the swarms of spectators on the hills gathering to watch the battle. "His excellency George Washington is present animating and encouraging the soldiers."[12] Knox was ready to decimate the British with lethal fire once they reached the shores of Dorchester. Thatcher described the Americans waiting for the approach of the British:

> Each man knows his place and is resolute to execute his duty. Our breastworks are strengthened and among the mean of defense are a great number of barrels, filled with stone and sand, arranged in front of our works, which are to be put into motion and made to roll down the hill, to break the ranks and legs of assailants as they advance. These are the preparations for blood and slaughter! Gracious God! If I be determined in thy Providence that thousands of our fellow creatures shall this day be slain, let thy wrath be appeased, and in mercy grant that victory be on the side of our suffering bleeding country.[13]

Washington called on the men to "remember it is the fifth of March and avenge the death of your brethren."[14] His words were passed from man to man, and the general said he "never saw spirits higher."[15] As the British troops pushed off from Castle Island, the man who had been focused on attacking for months could now almost taste the blood. Washington had laid a perfect trap; all that was left was for the British to sail into the crosshairs. But providence intervened. A strong headwind was the first sign of a changing weather pattern. The warm pleasant day gave way to a strong southeastern wind that pushed back against the boats. John Trumbull would later write, "Soon after Washington's visit, the rain, which had already commenced, increased to a violent storm and a heavy gale of wind, which deranged all the enemy's plan of debarkation, driving the ships foul of each other."[16]

By night the rain had turned to snow and sleet as house windows were smashed, roofs torn off, and several of the transports were blown ashore. Issac Bangs, an American lieutenant on the high ground of Dorchester, wrote that it was the worst storm "that ever I was exposed to."[17] The British assault was postponed for the night. In the morning the winds continued along with the sleet and rain. General Howe pondered the situation while George Washington felt that his prey had slipped his snare at the last minute. He later told General Lee that the storm "was the most fortunate circumstance for them and unfortunate for us that could have happened. As we had everything so well prepared for their reception. . . . I am confident we should have given a very good account of them."[18]

In a meeting, several of General Howe's officers pleaded with him to call off the attack. Some would later say the storm gave Howe an easy out. Captain Robertson wrote in his diary of a final meeting with Howe.

> It is now eight o'clock in the evening. We went to headquarters at seven. After waiting some time Captain Montresor came down from the general and told me had been in the council and had advised the going off [embarkation] altogether, that Lord Percy and some others ascended to him, and that the general said it was his own sentiments from the first, but thought the honor of the troops concerned. So, it is agreed immediately to embark everything.[19]

The man whom George III had chosen to quell his rebellious colonies gave the order to evacuate Boston and turn it over to the Americans. General Howe's argument that his original plan for attack was to preserve honor among his troops rings hollow; an American who saw the British waiting to board the boats observed that "they looked in general pale and dejected, and said to one another it would be another Bunker Hill or worse."[20] General Howe later wrote that the weather had given the enemy more time to reinforce the Heights and "I could promise myself little success by attacking them under all the disadvantages I had to encounter; wherefore I judged it most advisable to prepare for the evacuation of the town."[21]

Howe's capitulation likely spared Washington terrible casualties as well. To take Boston, the Americans would have to cross a half mile of open water in boats against the well-entrenched British. After landing, they would head into British fire—without being able to return to their boats—forcing them to either route the British or be vanquished.

On Friday, March 8, four men flying a white flag approached the Neck at Boston. It was Deacon Newell and three selectmen carrying a message stating that General Howe "had no intention of destroying the town, unless the troops under his command are molested during the embarkation."[22] The note was intended for Washington but wasn't specifically addressed to him, so there was no official reply. Still, it was understood that if the British were allowed to evacuate, the city wouldn't be burned. To cover his evacuation of the city, Howe fired on the Heights on March 9 with seven hundred cannons, killing one American. The next day the men on the Heights collected seven hundred cannonballs to reuse them. Washington monitored the activities in the city as

> the town deteriorated into a sense of tumultuous disorder; British troops pitched disabled cannons and produce barrels into the harbor. . . . Debris bobbed in the water everywhere or lay heaped upon the shore. Crowds of desperate Loyalists surged into overloaded ships in a chaotic spectacle. The sense of shock was palpable among these refugees, prompting some to dive to their death in the chilly waters.[23]

Washington wrote to his brother, taking some pleasure in the turn of events after months of having to endure Loyalists informing the British of his every move. "One or two have done what a great many ought to have done a long ago—committed suicide. By all accounts there never existed a more miserable set of human beings than these wretched creatures now are, taught to believe that the power of Great Britain was superior to all opposition."[24] One can't blame George Washington for crowing after taking on the most powerful army and navy in the world and forcing the ships to abandon the harbor and the army to leave the city.

"Nothing but hurry and confusion, every person striving to get out of this place," wrote American merchant John Rowe.[25] The problem was General Howe had no real evacuation plan and had received no orders from London. He was on his own. British General James Grant would tell Howe "that I had been in many scrapes but that I was never in so thick a wood with all the branches like thorns, but that we must look forward and get out."[26] Americans watched from the hills as Bostonians loyal to the crown scrambled for ships lest they face retribution when the town fell to the Americans.

Even General Howe's coach was dumped in the harbor to make room for men, women, and children. Cannons were either loaded or destroyed before being sent overboard. Washington later wrote that the streets were "full of great movements and confusion among the troops night and day . . . in hurrying down their cannon, artillery and other stores to the wharves with utmost precipitation."[27]

On March 10, the Loyalists began boarding, leaving their belongings, their homes, and their former lives behind. The refugees who had fled Cambridge or Lexington had already left everything behind, and boarding the British ships was the next logical step to leaving their country behind. Lucy Flucker's parents were one of the many Loyalist families who would leave Boston and never return. "It is not easy to paint the distress and confusion of the inhabitants on this occasion. I had but six or seven hours allowed to prepare for this measure, being obliged to embark the same day," wrote Reverend Henry Caner.[28]

The Tories never saw this day coming. They assumed the British would be victorious and that "in their allegiance to King and to the rule of law they saw themselves as the true American patriots. They had wanted no part of the rebellion . . . and had trusted, not unrealistically, in the wealth and power of the British nation to protect them."[29] As many as eleven hundred Loyalists from every walk of life would board British ships and sail away from families and friends, many never to return.

As the British pulled back, gangs and outlaws plundered the town, smashing store windows and breaking into homes. Howe told the town leaders that all citizens must remain indoors as the army evacuated. If there was any interference, he would burn the town. On Sunday, March 17, Saint Patrick's Day, the wind turned favorable and at four in the morning, "more than 8,000 redcoats marched through the dark, narrows streets of Boston as if on parade. By seven the sun was up, and ships thronged at the wharves began lifting sail. By nine o'clock they were on their way."[30]

Henry Knox watched from the Heights as the flotilla got underway. Seventy-eight ships dotted the horizon as nearly nine thousand soldiers and more than a thousand Loyalists left Boston to sail for Nova Scotia. Henry Knox stood by his cannons with the ocean breeze ruffling his hair, watching the army that had imprisoned his town evacuate. Not one person on the British ships understood that the man with the wind nipping at the scarf on his left hand was responsible for their loss of home and hearth. They would have been astounded to learn that a Boston bookseller with no military experience was behind the defeat of the British army.

34

THE PRODIGAL SON RETURNS

March 18, 1776

Knox wasn't the only one watching the British depart. People on shore watched the British fleet depart from the harbor, sailing toward the horizon. "In the course of the forenoon," wrote James Thatcher, "we enjoyed the unspeakable satisfaction of beholding their whole fleet under sail, wafting from our shores the dreadful scourge of war."[1] Bostonians on shore began weeping, some cheering. "Surely, it is the Lord's doing and it is marvelous in our eyes," wrote Abigail Adams.[2] Small boys ran from the British fortifications across the Neck and proclaimed that the lobsterbacks were gone.

General Sullivan wasn't so sure. He saw sentinels still manning the fortifications at Bunker Hill, and mounting his horse for a closer look, discovered that the British had left straw dummies behind. It was true; the British were gone. In the early afternoon five hundred men from Roxbury who had been inoculated against smallpox entered Boston with Artemas Ward leading the way. Washington stayed back, allowing the former commander and New Englander the honor of entering the liberated town first. Washington stayed in Cambridge and attended Sunday service held by the chaplain in Knox's artillery regiment, Reverend Abiel Leonard, who read from Exodus 14:25: "And they took off their chariot wheels, that they drove them heavily, so that the Egyptians said, Let us flee from the face of Israel, for the Lord fighteeth for them against the Egyptians."[3]

On Monday, March 18, George Washington led his victorious army into Boston. The mood was jubilant, and the people cheered mightily as the troops marched down the main street with Henry Knox beside Washington as the prodigal son who has returned after liberating his hometown. Washington noted that the town was not in ruins, and he wrote later to John Adams that "I have particular pleasure in being able to inform you, sir, that your house has received no damage worth mentioning."[4]

But many homes had been severely damaged by the British, with windows smashed, furniture bayonetted, books thrown from shelves. These desperate last acts of destruction could be seen in the buildings torn down for firewood and the destroyed cannons, gun carriages, and wagons. Ships in the harbors had been sunk with their masts sawed off, and enormous amounts of barrels, furniture, animals, carriages, floated in the harbor.

Washington, however, was amazed by how much had been preserved. The quartermaster general, Thomas Mifflin, compiled a list of "5,000 bushels of wheat at the Hancock wharf, 1,000 bushels of beans and 10 tons of hay at the town granary, 35,000 feet of good planks at one of the lumberyards. There were more than a hundred horses left by the British."[5] Washington also noted the town's fortifications, describing Boston as "almost impregnable, every avenue fortified." Washington immediately set the tone for the occupation of Boston, threatening severe punishment for looting. His men guarded the Tories still in the city until their futures were decided by the Massachusetts legislature. "If any officer or soldier shall presume to strike, imprison, or otherwise ill-treat any of the inhabitants, they may depend on being punished with utmost severity."[6] He then returned a horse that had been given to him when he learned that it had been taken from a Tory.

Knox for his part explored his hometown on his own and found 250 pieces of large-caliber artillery left behind by the British. The trunnions of some of the cannons had been knocked off and some had been spiked, but Knox found New England gunsmiths who could repair the cannons, and they were added to his growing arsenal. When Knox had come down the main avenue with Washington, a Tory clergyman, Dr. Mather Byles, who was an old friend from his bookselling days, proclaimed, "I never saw Knox fatter in my life!"[7] Knox took it in stride, knowing the adage that we are never as famous in our hometown. And he probably saw the cannonballs still lodged in the church towers, so maybe that evened the score.

Knox then headed to Cornhill with his heart pounding. He stopped at his London Bookstore. He dismounted his horse while his men waited as the colonel inspected his former store, surveying the damage. "Volumes were scattered around the floor, thrown open to the weather, damaged, water soaked, and destroyed. The windows had been shattered and glass lay upon the floor.

The shelves were broken up."[8] The old, pulpy smell of books still lingered, and Knox could hardly believe that less than a year before he had been waiting for Lucy so that they could slip out of Boston under the cover of darkness.

Knox looked around at the remaining books and remembered that he still owed money on the inventory, which was a total loss. He stared at his former life. He had left Boston as a bookseller and returned a colonel of the artillery in a new army representing a new country. The speed of events was dizzying. In the quiet of his bookstore, he tried to account what had happened during the last year. He left his family to embark on an impossible journey in which he traveled three hundred miles to bring back sixty tons of cannons to dislodge the British from the town he had fled in fear of his life. He dragged those cannons across frozen lakes, rivers, wilderness, and mountains in the dead of winter and he had prevailed. He promised George Washington a Noble Train of Artillery, and he had risked everything for it. Knox paused and looked around his old bookstore one last time. Despite all the books he had read, he had never really understood nobility. He now knew what nobility really was: a willingness to sacrifice every-thing for something not yet seen.

THE UNBORN
MILLIONS

When Henry Knox wrote to George Washington from Fort George in the winter of 1775 and said he was bringing his "Noble Train of Artillery," he chose an interesting turn of phrase. A train of artillery was a collection of cannons and this was common nomenclature of the time. In fact, Henry Knox had trained with an artillery train in Boston. But he added another word that changed the meaning of his caravan of cannons forever.

Noble.

We don't have much use for the word "nobility" today. It sounds a bit trite, old fashioned, overblown. One might argue that nobility has vanished from national discourse. But in 1775, this was all that the small group of men had who were fighting for a new way of organizing government, a new way of *being*. George Washington called it the "glorious cause"; Henry Knox saw the fight for liberty as nothing less, often citing God as being behind their cause in his letters. There is no doubt that George Washington was a noble man. His nobility of spirit pushed him to leave Mount Vernon and risk everything on a patchwork army comprised of colonial militias. Only nobility would empower him to take on the most powerful nation and risk his very life to fight a revolution that would lead to the formation of a new country based on freedom and liberty.

Henry Knox was much the same. Although he was a Boston bookseller, he left his business and his friends and took his wife from her family forever for a cause that could cost him his life. He was twenty-five and he had a long life ahead of him, but it was providential that he should meet the forty-three-year-old general who had taken over the army and who inspired him with his willingness to risk all. George Washington was an inspirational man and a born leader. He held high ideals if not for life, then for mankind, and when the cause quivered on the horizon, he transferred those ideals to the creation of a nation based on the same unwavering bar by which he lived.

Why did Henry Knox volunteer to retrieve the cannons from Ticonderoga when he had no experience at all with moving artillery, when he had trained only with militia in Boston, and when most of his knowledge came from books? He was an irrepressible person who wanted to command an artillery unit but needed cannons. His actions would make sense, except that the risk of leaving his pregnant wife behind, whom he had already separated from her parents due to his political beliefs, was a high price to pay in order to impress the new general and secure his position as commander of the artillery.

The Revolution was a young man's ideal. Jefferson, Knox, Adams, and Washington at forty-three were young men in their prime, and young men believe in causes and the nobility of those causes. The cause of freedom and liberty was like the wind for Henry Knox, and to ride that wind, no price was too great. Transporting cannons from Fort Ticonderoga over lakes, rivers, and mountains was the price for a new nation founded on the belief that all men are created equal and have inalienable rights endowed by their creator. Therefore everything associated with this holy quest was holy by nature, and that included the Noble Train of cannons. Because the men who were fighting this revolution did it for the "unborn millions" who might enjoy a world where liberty and freedom would not be snuffed out.

Knox has taken his place among the people in American history who have, by individual effort, made a difference for those yet to come: Washington crossing the Delaware, Lincoln holding the nation together, Henry Knox retrieving the cannons that would save the American Revolution. Many colonies had not sent delegates yet to the Continental Congress, taking a wait-and-see approach to what was unfolding at Boston. The first American victory quieted the people who said the British could never be defeated, and France considered supporting the Americans against the British. The victory at Boston legitimized the American Revolution. "Without the victory at Boston support for nationhood would have seemed a hollow cry based on unrealistic expectations. . . . The triumph remains one of the most significant military victories in U.S. history, for it boosted hopes for independence in that heady spring of 1776 that would lead to the Declaration of Independence."[1]

In writing to George Washington from the frozen confines of Fort George and promising more than he could deliver, Knox embodied that emerging American ethos. He nearly had lost the cannons in the lake and he had no oxen or sleds to transport the artillery across the frozen rivers, wilderness, and mountains ahead of him. He had no idea how he would do it. Yet he declared that in seventeen days Washington would have his "Noble Train of Artillery." Knox reflected the nobility of a country founded on an ideal that still shines back at us today. By putting something above his own life, Knox hitched himself to the train that began in the frozen snows in 1775 and continues today, a train of nobility shining the way for the yet unborn millions.

EPILOGUE

To the right of George Washington was Henry Knox, who was with him in every battle of the American Revolution from Boston to Yorktown. They were not only brothers-in-arms, but they became fast friends. Washington had no children, and there was a paternal quality to their friendship. Lucy even stayed at Mount Vernon during one of her pregnancies. When Washington took his leave at the end of the war and said good-bye to Knox, "he wept openly as he wrapped his arms around Henry and embraced him, kissing him on the cheek."[1]

Henry Knox would follow Washington and take his artillery to New York after the battle of Boston as commander of the Continental Army's Artillery Corps, and he would direct the evacuation from Brooklyn Heights in 1776. During the famous crossing of the Delaware, Knox oversaw getting the men across the river and then led the way with his cannons on that icy Christmas night. Knox never led troops, but at the battle of Yorktown he personally directed the guns and was "an exceptionally versatile commander, an expert in every branch of the service, and a skilled engineer, artilleryman, strategist, and ordinance master."[2] Henry Knox was never formally trained, but taught himself all his life in "strategy, tactics, and the calculus in firing cannons."[3] As a commander of men, he was well liked and respected during his tenure during the Revolution. To his credit, "the American artillery corps performed on par with the formidable French at Yorktown and outdueled the British."[4]

In 1778 he set up a military academy to train officers in strategy, tactics, logistics, and engineering. The school eventually would become West Point. After the war, he was one of the leading voices calling for a constitution to replace the Articles of Confederation and served as the secretary of war in the first administration of the nation, alongside Thomas Jefferson and Alexander Hamilton. He helped create the U.S. Navy, oversaw the construction of frontier forts, and negotiated treaties with the Indians.

In 1795 he left government service and moved to Thomaston, Maine, where he built a three-story mansion called Montpelier. Knox tried his hand at many businesses including shipbuilding, brick making, and real estate speculation. The businesses faltered, and Knox incurred large debts that forced him to sell land. On October 25, 1806, Knox swallowed a chicken bone that lodged in his throat. Three days later he died from an accompanying infection. He was fifty-six. He and Lucy would have thirteen children, of which only three would survive to adulthood. Lucy would become reclusive after Knox's death and was forced to sell off the family home to satisfy creditors. She died eighteen years later on June 20, 1824.

Henry Knox is known today primarily by his name on Fort Knox. Since 1937 it has been the repository for the nation's gold reserves, the U.S. Bullion Depository, and is one of the largest installations in the U.S. Army. Few know the story of the twenty-five-year-old bookseller who went into the wilderness in 1775 to retrieve sixty tons of cannons and take them to Boston to win the first battle of the American Revolution. In a storied life, this certainly was Henry Knox's finest hour; he is forever that self-taught man who dared the impossible: to bring forth a new nation based on liberty and freedom. Then again, for all his military accomplishments, perhaps he is forever a bookseller. After returning to Boston and finding his bookstore looted and vandalized by the British, Knox made his last payment of £1,000 pounds to Longman Printers in London for a shipment of books he would never receive.

George Washington would later turn the tide of war with his brilliant crossing of the Delaware on Christmas Eve, a feat that mirrored the audacity of Henry Knox's dash to retrieve the cannons. Washington, of course, would go on to become the nation's first president and is revered today as half deity and half father of our country. The unsettled and unproven man who sent Henry Knox on his journey in 1775 hides behind the towering figure of American history. It is hard for people to imagine that he had doubts, foibles, and often made poor decisions in the early days of the Revolution. But to Washington's credit, he was a man who learned from his mistakes and saw the gifts in others that could bring about a desired result.

John Becker Jr. and his father continued freighting supplies throughout the war, and the twelve-year-old's journal reads like an adventure story, telling the tale of what American families endured during the Revolutionary War years.

Chased out of their homes and many times in danger of attack from the Indians who aligned with the British, young John Becker Jr. and his family made several harrowing, narrow escapes that easily could have resulted in the horrible deaths that befell their neighbors.

After the war, his father returned to farming and still moved freight as a wagon master. At the end of his life, John Becker Jr. published a journal of his adventures, and when his father died, he inherited his farm and proclaimed, "Blessings seemed to rest upon my head."[5] He became a prosperous farmer but eventually lost everything when "investments which promised a certain return, melted away from grasp."[6] He lent money to family members that was never repaid and, like Henry Knox, found that "all my fair prospects vanished away."[7] In the end, the man of sixty-four lamented that "every hope deserted me, and I have only a few more days of life to anticipate, which, while they seem a narrow space, bring with them at least the consolation of a speedy refuge from poverty and a desolate old age."[8]

On April 6, 1779, Henry Knox received $2,500 from the government for his Noble Train expedition to Fort Ticonderoga to retrieve the sixty tons of cannon in 1775. From the proceeds, he paid his brother William, as well. Ultimately, Henry Knox earned $3 dollars a day to save the American Revolution with his Noble Train, a small price for nobility.

ACKNOWLEDGMENTS

Thanks to the good folks at Prometheus as always for their expertise and intuition in bringing this story to life. Also thanks to my agent Leticia Gomez at Savvy Literary who sells just about everything I come up with. To all of the people who endured the questions about the construction and cannons of Fort Ticonderoga at the Fort Ticonderoga National Museum in New York, and to the people who had to drive around the man pulling over to look at every marker along the Massachusetts and New York highways that designate the path Henry Knox followed in 1775. And, of course, to my family, who have watched me disappear into books and onto the road in the pursuit of each historical discovery.

NOTES

PROLOGUE

1. David McCullough, *1776* (New York: Simon and Shuster, 2005), 11.
2. McCullough, *1776*, 11.

CHAPTER 1: FORT TICONDEROGA/LAKE GEORGE

1. James Perry, *A Mere Matter of Marching* (New York: Xlibris, 2011), 25.

CHAPTER 2: BOSTON ON EDGE

1. Mark Puls, *Henry Knox* (New York: Macmillan, 2008), 2.
2. Puls, *Henry Knox*, 2.
3. Puls, *Henry Knox*, 2.
4. Puls, *Henry Knox*, 3.
5. Puls, *Henry Knox*, 4.
6. Puls, *Henry Knox*, 4.
7. Puls, *Henry Knox*, 5.
8. Puls, *Henry Knox*, 5.
9. Puls, *Henry Knox*, 5.
10. Puls, *Henry Knox*, 5.
11. Puls, *Henry Knox*, 7.
12. Puls, *Henry Knox*, 7.
13. Puls, *Henry Knox*, 8.
14. Puls, *Henry Knox*, 8.
15. Puls, *Henry Knox*, 8.

16. Puls, *Henry Knox*, 8.
17. Puls, *Henry Knox*, 8.
18. Puls, *Henry Knox*, 9.
19. Puls, *Henry Knox*, 9.
20. Puls, *Henry Knox*, 9.
21. Puls, *Henry Knox*, 9.
22. Puls, *Henry Knox*, 9.
23. Puls, *Henry Knox*, 9.
24. Puls, *Henry Knox*, 9.
25. Puls, *Henry Knox*, 9.
26. Puls, *Henry Knox*, 10.
27. Puls, *Henry Knox*, 10.
28. Puls, *Henry Knox*, 11.
29. Puls, *Henry Knox*, 11.
30. Puls, *Henry Knox*, 11.

CHAPTER 3: HIS EXCELLENCY

1. Nathaniel Philbrick, *Bunker Hill* (New York: Penguin Books, 2013), 240.
2. Philbrick, *Bunker Hill*, 240.
3. Robert Middlekauff, *The Glorious Cause* (Oxford: Oxford University Press, 2007), 293.
4. Robert Harvey, *Maverick Military Leaders* (New York: Skyhorse Publishing, 2008), 42.
5. David McCullough, *1776* (New York: Simon and Schuster, 2005), 49.
6. Michael Shea, *In God We Trust* (New York: Liberty Quest, 2012), 54.
7. McCullough, *1776*, 44.
8. Ron Chernow, *Washington: A Life* (New York: Penguin, 2010), 13.
9. McCullough, *1776*, 44.
10. Middlekauff, *The Glorious Cause*, 294.
11. Chernow, *Washington*, 13, 44.
12. Philbrick, *Bunker Hill*, 239.
13. Philbrick, *Bunker Hill*, 239.
14. McCullough, *1776*, 45.
15. McCullough, *1776*, 47.
16. McCullough, *1776*, 47.
17. McCullough, *1776*, 47.
18. McCullough, *1776*, 46.
19. Robert Daizell, *George Washington's Mount Vernon* (Oxford: Oxford University Press, 2000), 103.
20. Chernow, *Washington*, 13, 124.
21. McCullough, *1776*, 48.

22. McCullough, *1776*, 48.

23. Middlekauff, *The Glorious Cause*, 296.

24. Middlekauff, *The Glorious Cause*, 296.

25. McCullough, *1776*, 28.

26. Merill Jensen, *The Founding of a Nation* (New York: Hackett, 2004), 634.

27. Chernow, *Washington*, 189.

28. McCullough, *1776*, 25.

29. McCullough, *1776*, 26.

30. McCullough, *1776*, 28.

31. Middlekauff, *The Glorious Cause*, 297.

32. Middlekauff, *The Glorious Cause*, 298.

33. Middlekauff, *The Glorious Cause*, 299.

34. McCullough, *1776*, 42.

35. McCullough, *1776*, 42.

36. Middlekauff, *The Glorious Cause*, 300.

37. Philbrick, *Bunker Hill*, 241.

38. Middlekauff, *The Glorious Cause*, 301.

39. Middlekauff, *The Glorious Cause*, 301.

40. McCullough, *1776*, 31.

41. McCullough, *1776*, 33.

42. McCullough, *1776*, 33.

43. Joseph Ellis, *His Excellency, George Washington* (New York: Vintage Books, 2005), 272.

44. Washington Irving, *The Life and Times of George Washington* (New York: Putnam and Sons, 1876), 169.

45. Chernow, *Washington*, 198.

46. Philbrick, *Bunker Hill*, 243.

47. George Washington, *The Writings of George Washington*, vol. 3 (New York: American Stationers, 1834), 48.

48. Burke Davis, *George Washington and the American Revolution* (New York: Random House, 1975), 25.

49. McCullough, *1776*, 70.

CHAPTER 4: THE REBEL BOOKSELLER

1. Noah Brooks, *Henry Knox: Soldier of the Revolution* (New York: Cosimo, 2007), 9.

2. North Callahan, *Henry Knox: General Washington's General* (South Brunswick, NY: Rinehart, 1958), 21.

3. Callahan, *Henry Knox*, 22.

4. Callahan, *Henry Knox*, 24.

5. Callahan, *Henry Knox*, 24.

6. Callahan, *Henry Knox*, 23.

7. Mark Puls, *Henry Knox: Visionary General of the Revolution* (New York: Macmillan, 2010), 14.

8. Puls, *Henry Knox*, 15.

9. Callahan, *Henry Knox*, 25.

10. Callahan, *Henry Knox*, 25.

11. Puls, *Henry Knox*, 14.

12. Puls, *Henry Knox*, 17.

13. Phillip Hamilton, *The Revolutionary War Lives and Letters of Lucy and Henry Knox* (Baltimore: Johns Hopkins University Press, 2017), 12.

14. Hamilton, *The Revolutionary War Lives and Letters of Lucy and Henry Knox*, 12.

15. Hamilton, *The Revolutionary War Lives and Letters of Lucy and Henry Knox*, 13.

16. Puls, *Henry Knox*, 18.

17. Puls, *Henry Knox*, 19.

18. Callahan, *Henry Knox*, 25.

19. Puls, *Henry Knox*, 20.

20. Francis Drake, *Life and Correspondence of Henry Knox* (New York: 1873), 13.

21. Puls, *Henry Knox*, 24.

22. Puls, *Henry Knox*, 24.

23. Puls, *Henry Knox*, 24.

CHAPTER 5: THE FRUSTRATED GENERAL

1. Ron Chernow, *Washington: A Life* (New York: Penguin, 2010), 206.

2. David McCullough, *John Adams* (New York: Simon and Schuster, 2001), 413.

3. George Washington, *The Writings of George Washington*, vol. 3 (New York: John B. Russell, 1834), 48.

4. Robert O'Connell, *Revolutionary: George Washington at War* (New York: Random House, 2019), 107.

5. McCullough, *John Adams*, 51.

6. McCullough, *John Adams*, 52.

7. McCullough, *John Adams*, 52.

8. Phillip Papas, *Renegade Revolutionary: The Life of Charles Lee* (New York: New York University Press, 2014), 5.

9. McCullough, *John Adams*, 52.

10. McCullough, *John Adams*, 52.

11. John Fitzpatrick, ed., *The Writings of George Washington from the Original Manuscript Sources* (New York: Best Books, 1935), 484.

12. McCullough, *1776* (New York: Simon and Schuster, 2005), 54.

13. McCullough, *1776*, 80.

14. Fitzpatrick, *The Writings of George Washington*, 512.

15. Mark Puls, *Henry Knox: Visionary General of the Revolution* (New York: Macmillan, 2010), 28.

16. McCullough, *1776*, 56.

17. McCullough, *1776*, 56.

18. Puls, *Henry Knox*, 34.

19. Chernow, *Washington*, 208.

CHAPTER 6: THE BOOKSELLER MEETS THE GENERAL

1. Mark Puls, *Henry Knox: Visionary General of the Revolution* (New York: Macmillan, 2010), 27.

2. Puls, *Henry Knox*, 28.

3. Puls, *Henry Knox*, 27.

4. Puls, *Henry Knox*, 28.

5. Puls, *Henry Knox*, 28.

6. Puls, *Henry Knox*, 29.

7. Puls, *Henry Knox*, 29.

8. Francis Drake, *Life and Correspondence of Henry Knox* (Boston: S. G. Drake, 1873), 18.

9. Ron Chernow, *Washington: A Life* (New York: Penguin, 2010), 203.

10. Puls, *Henry Knox*, 30.

11. Puls, *Henry Knox*, 30.

12. Puls, *Henry Knox*, 31.

13. Phillip Hamilton, *The Revolutionary War Lives and Letters of Lucy and Henry Knox* (Baltimore: Johns Hopkins University Press, 2017), 20.

14. Hamilton, *The Revolutionary War Lives and Letters of Lucy and Henry Knox*, 21.

15. Puls, *Henry Knox*, 32.

16. Puls, *Henry Knox*, 32.

17. George Washington, *The Writings of George Washington*, vol. 3 (New York: John B. Russell, 1834), 148.

18. Chernow, *Washington*, 204.

19. Puls, *Henry Knox*, 34.

20. Puls, *Henry Knox*, 35.

21. Puls, *Henry Knox*, 35.

22. Puls, *Henry Knox*, 36.

23. John Fitzpatrick, ed., *The Writings of George Washington from the Original Manuscript Sources* (New York: Best Books, 1935), 122.

24. Washington, *The Writings of George Washington*, vol. 3, 179.

CHAPTER 7: THE HEIGHTS OF DORCHESTER

1. Nathaniel Philbrick, *Bunker Hill* (New York: Penguin, 2013), 255.
2. David McCullough, *1776* (New York: Simon and Schuster, 2005), 72.
3. McCullough, *1776*, 70.
4. McCullough, *1776*, 71.
5. McCullough, *1776*, 74.
6. McCullough, *1776*, 74.
7. McCullough, *1776*, 77.
8. McCullough, *1776*, 77.
9. McCullough, *1776*, 76.
10. McCullough, *1776*, 76.
11. McCullough, *1776*, 76.
12. Richard Frothingham, *History of the Siege of Boston and of the Battles of Lexington and Concord* (New York: n.p., 1896), 137.

CHAPTER 8: STARTING OUT

1. Phillip Hamilton, *The Revolutionary War Lives and Letters of Lucy and Henry Knox* (Baltimore: Johns Hopkins University Press, 2017), 22.
2. Hamilton, *The Revolutionary War Lives and Letters of Lucy and Henry Knox*, 27.
3. Ron Chernow, *Washington: A Life* (New York: Penguin, 2010), 204.
4. Chernow, *Washington*, 204.
5. Chernow, *Washington*, 204.
6. Charles Bolton, *The Private Soldier under Washington* (New York: Charles Scribner's Sons, 1902), 79.
7. Liz Sonneborn, *Chronology of American Indian History* (New York: Infobase Publishing, ca. 2007), 88.
8. Henry Knox, *Diary of Henry Knox* (n.p.: n.p., 1775), 1.
9. Hamilton, *The Revolutionary War Lives and Letters of Lucy and Henry Knox*, 22.

CHAPTER 9: ON TO NEW YORK AND ALBANY

1. Mark Puls, *Henry Knox: Visionary General of the Revolution* (New York: Macmillan, 2010), 36.
2. David McCullough, *1776* (New York: Simon and Schuster, 2005), 73.
3. Henry Knox, *Diary of Henry Knox* (n.p.: n.p., 1775), 8.
4. William Browne, *Ye Cohorn Caravan* (Schuylerville, NY: NoPaul Publishers, 1975), 15.
5. Puls, *Henry Knox*, 37.
6. Puls, *Henry Knox*, 37.

7. Phillip Hamilton, *The Revolutionary War Lives and Letters of Lucy and Henry Knox* (Baltimore: Johns Hopkins University Press, 2017), 25.

8. Knox, *Diary of Henry Knox*, 8.

9. Hamilton, *The Revolutionary War Lives and Letters of Lucy and Henry Knox*, 25.

10. Thomas Campeau, *The Noble Train of Artillery* (Fort Leavenworth, KS: U.S. Government Department of Defense, 2015), 22.

11. Campeau, *The Noble Train of Artillery*, 22.

12. John Becker, *Reminiscences of the American Revolution* (Albany, NY: Leopold Classic Library, 1806), 10.

13. Becker, *Reminiscences of the American Revolution*, 20.

14. Becker, *Reminiscences of the American Revolution*, 20.

15. Becker, *Reminiscences of the American Revolution*, 21.

16. Becker, *Reminiscences of the American Revolution*, 21.

17. Campeau, *The Noble Train of Artillery*, 22.

18. Campeau, *The Noble Train of Artillery*, 22.

19. Hamilton, *The Revolutionary War Lives and Letters of Lucy and Henry Knox*, 25.

CHAPTER 10: WASHINGTON ON ICE

1. John Fitzpatrick, ed., *The Writings of George Washington from the Original Manuscript Sources* (New York: Best Books, 1935), 512.

2. Washington Irving, *The Life and Times of George Washington* (New York: Putnam, 1876), 366.

3. Ron Chernow, *Washington: A Life* (New York: Penguin, 2010), 210.

4. Chernow, *Washington*, 210.

5. Chernow, *Washington*, 210.

6. Irving, *The Life and Times of George Washington*, 243.

7. Chernow, *Washington*, 208.

8. Chernow, *Washington*, 209.

9. Chernow, *Washington*, 209.

10. Chernow, *Washington*, 209.

11. Chernow, *Washington*, 209.

12. Chernow, *Washington*, 209.

13. Fitzpatrick, *The Writings of George Washington*, 7.

14. Fitzpatrick, *The Writings of George Washington*, 398.

15. Fitzpatrick, *The Writings of George Washington*, 28.

16. Chernow, *Washington*, 216.

17. Chernow, *Washington*, 219.

18. Chernow, *Washington*, 219.

19. Chernow, *Washington*, 218.

20. Chernow, *Washington*, 218.

21. Chernow, *Washington*, 218.

22. Chernow, *Washington*, 218.
23. David McCullough, *1776* (New York: Simon and Schuster, 2005), 63.

CHAPTER 11: FORT GEORGE

1. Thomas Campeau, *The Noble Train of Artillery* (Fort Leavenworth, KS: U.S. Government, Department of Defense, 2015), 22.
2. Campeau, *The Noble Train of Artillery*, 22.
3. John Becker, *Reminiscences of the American Revolution* (Albany, NY: Leopold Classic Library, 1806), 25.
4. William Browne, *Ye Cohorn Caravan* (Schuylerville, NY: NoPaul Publishers, 1975), 14.
5. Browne, *Ye Cohorn Caravan*, 16.
6. Becker, *Reminiscences of the American Revolution*, 25.
7. Browne, *Ye Cohorn Caravan*, 16.
8. Becker, *Reminiscences of the American Revolution*, 24.
9. Browne, *Ye Cohorn Caravan*, 17.
10. Browne, *Ye Cohorn Caravan*, 17.
11. Browne, *Ye Cohorn Caravan*, 34.
12. Campeau, *The Noble Train of Artillery*, 23.
13. Browne, *Ye Cohorn Caravan*, 18.
14. Campeau, *The Noble Train of Artillery*, 26.

CHAPTER 12: FORT TICONDEROGA

1. John Becker, *Reminiscences of the American Revolution* (Albany, NY: Leopold Classic Library, 1806), 23.
2. William Browne, *Ye Cohorn Caravan* (Schuylerville, NY: NoPaul Publishers, 1975), 18.
3. Browne, *Ye Cohorn Caravan*, 20.
4. North Callahan, *Henry Knox: General Washington's General* (South Brunswick, NY: Rinehart, 1958), 40.
5. Browne, *Ye Cohorn Caravan*, 27.
6. Thomas Campeau, *The Noble Train of Artillery* (Fort Leavenworth, KS: U.S. Government, Department of Defense, 2015), 25.
7. Campeau, *The Noble Train of Artillery*, 47.
8. Browne, *Ye Cohorn Caravan*, 21.
9. Campeau, *The Noble Train of Artillery*, 25.
10. Browne, *Ye Cohorn Caravan*, 22.
11. Browne, *Ye Cohorn Caravan*, 22.
12. Browne, *Ye Cohorn Caravan*, 22.
13. Browne, *Ye Cohorn Caravan*, 21.

CHAPTER 13: THE HELL OF LAKE GEORGE

1. Thomas Campeau, *The Noble Train of Artillery* (Fort Leavenworth, KS: U.S. Government, Department of Defense, 2015), 26.

2. William Browne, *Ye Cohorn Caravan* (Schuylerville, NY: NoPaul Publishers, 1975), 22.

3. Browne, *Ye Cohorn Caravan*, 21.

4. Henry Knox, *Diary of Henry Knox* (n.p.: n.p., 1775), 9.

5. Browne, *Ye Cohorn Caravan*, 21.

6. Campeau, *The Noble Train of Artillery*, 27.

7. Michael Alexander, *Discovering the New World* (New York: Harper and Row, 1976), 201.

8. William Standard, *Virginia Magazine of History and Biography* 66 (1958): 47.

9. Browne, *Ye Cohorn Caravan*, 21.

10. Browne, *Ye Cohorn Caravan*, 23.

11. Campeau, *The Noble Train of Artillery*, 27.

12. Knox, *Diary of Henry Knox*, 10.

13. Browne, *Ye Cohorn Caravan*, 24.

14. Browne, *Ye Cohorn Caravan*, 24.

15. Knox, *Diary of Henry Knox*, 11.

16. Browne, *Ye Cohorn Caravan*, 25.

17. Browne, *Ye Cohorn Caravan*, 26.

CHAPTER 14: THE MAN WHO STARTED THE FRENCH AND INDIAN WAR

1. William Baker, *Washington after the Revolution* (Philadelphia: J. B. Lippincott, 1897), 40.

2. Ron Chernow, *Washington: A Life* (New York: Penguin, 2010), 119.

3. Chernow, *Washington*, 119.

4. John Rhodehamel, *George Washington: The Wonder of the Age* (New Haven, NJ: Yale University Press, 2017), 37.

5. Chernow, *Washington*, 32.

6. Chernow, *Washington*, 32.

7. Chernow, *Washington*, 32.

8. Chernow, *Washington*, 32.

9. Chernow, *Washington*, 33.

10. Chernow, *Washington*, 34.

11. Chernow, *Washington*, 35.

12. Chernow, *Washington*, 36.

13. Chernow, *Washington*, 36.

14. Chernow, *Washington*, 37.

15. Chernow, *Washington*, 37.

16. George Washington, *The Writings of George Washington*, vol. 3 (New York: American Stationers Company, 1834), 42.

17. George Washington, *The Journal of Colonel Washington* (New York: J. Munsell's Sons, 1893), 17.

18. Chernow, *Washington*, 40.

19. Chernow, *Washington*, 41.

20. Chernow, *Washington*, 42.

21. Chernow, *Washington*, 42.

22. Chernow, *Washington*, 47.

23. Chernow, *Washington*, 49.

24. Chernow, *Washington*, 49.

25. Chernow, *Washington*, 49.

26. Rock DiLiso, *American Advance: Westward from the French and Indian War* (N.p.: iUniverse, 2008), 5.

CHAPTER 15: A NOBLE TRAIN

1. *Harvard Illustrated Magazine*, vol. 1, 1900.

2. William Browne, *Ye Cohorn Caravan* (Schuylerville, NY: NoPaul Publishers, 1975), 28.

3. Browne, *Ye Cohorn Caravan*, 29.

4. Francis Drake, *Memorials of the Society of the Cincinnati of Massachusetts* (Boston: Society of the Cincinnati, 1873), 545.

5. Browne, *Ye Cohorn Caravan*, 31.

6. Henry Knox, *Diary of Henry Knox* (n.p.: n.p., 1775), 7.

7. Phillip Hamilton, *The Revolutionary War Lives and Letters of Lucy and Henry Knox* (Baltimore: Johns Hopkins University Press, 2017), 22.

8. Hamilton, *The Revolutionary War Lives and Letters of Lucy and Henry Knox*, 68.

9. Browne, *Ye Cohorn Caravan*, 32.

10. Browne, *Ye Cohorn Caravan*, 32.

11. Browne, *Ye Cohorn Caravan*, 25.

12. Browne, *Ye Cohorn Caravan*, 32.

13. Browne, *Ye Cohorn Caravan*, 32.

14. Browne, *Ye Cohorn Caravan*, 32.

15. Mark Puls, *Henry Knox: Visionary General of the Revolution* (New York: Macmillan, 2010), 39.

16. Browne, *Ye Cohorn Caravan*, 31.

17. Browne, *Ye Cohorn Caravan*, 31.

18. Browne, *Ye Cohorn Caravan*, 32.

19. Browne, *Ye Cohorn Caravan*, 32.

20. Browne, *Ye Cohorn Caravan*, 31.

21. Browne, *Ye Cohorn Caravan*, 31.

22. Browne, *Ye Cohorn Caravan*, 36.

CHAPTER 16: THE BEST LAID PLANS

1. William Browne, *Ye Cohorn Caravan* (Schuylerville, NY: NoPaul Publishers, 1975), 36.

2. Browne, *Ye Cohorn Caravan*, 38.

3. Browne, *Ye Cohorn Caravan*, 39.

4. North Callahan, *Henry Knox: General Washington's General* (New York: Rinehart, 1958), 47.

5. Browne, *Ye Cohorn Caravan*, 39.

6. Browne, *Ye Cohorn Caravan*, 39.

7. Browne, *Ye Cohorn Caravan*, 39.

8. Browne, *Ye Cohorn Caravan*, 39.

9. Browne, *Ye Cohorn Caravan*, 40.

10. Browne, *Ye Cohorn Caravan*, 40.

11. Browne, *Ye Cohorn Caravan*, 40.

12. Browne, *Ye Cohorn Caravan*, 40.

13. Browne, *Ye Cohorn Caravan*, 40.

14. Browne, *Ye Cohorn Caravan*, 40.

15. Callahan, *Henry Knox*, 47.

16. Browne, *Ye Cohorn Caravan*, 42.

17. Browne, *Ye Cohorn Caravan*, 41.

18. Browne, *Ye Cohorn Caravan*, 41.

19. Browne, *Ye Cohorn Caravan*, 41.

20. Browne, *Ye Cohorn Caravan*, 41.

21. *Proceedings of the New York State Historical Association*, 18: 231.

22. Browne, *Ye Cohorn Caravan*, 36.

23. Browne, *Ye Cohorn Caravan*, 37.

24. John Becker, *Reminiscences of the American Revolution* (Albany, NY: Leopold Classic Library, 1806), 8.

25. Becker, *Reminiscences of the American Revolution*, 26.

26. Becker, *Reminiscences of the American Revolution*, 49.

27. Becker, *Reminiscences of the American Revolution*, 27.

28. Becker, *Reminiscences of the American Revolution*, 27.

29. Becker, *Reminiscences of the American Revolution*, 28.

30. Thomas Campeau, *The Noble Train of Artillery* (Fort Leavenworth, KS: U.S. Government, Department of Defense, 2015), 27.

31. Campeau, *The Noble Train of Artillery*, 28.

32. Campeau, *The Noble Train of Artillery*, 63.

33. Campeau, *The Noble Train of Artillery*, 63.

34. Campeau, *The Noble Train of Artillery*, 28.
35. Browne, *Ye Cohorn Caravan*, 41.

CHAPTER 17: THE BAD GENERAL

1. Benson Lossing, *Washington and the American Republic*, vol. 2 (New York: Virtue and Yorston, 1870), 3.
2. Lossing, *Washington and the American Republic*, 3.
3. Lossing, *Washington and the American Republic*, 3.
4. Mark Puls, *Henry Knox: Visionary General of the Revolution* (New York: Macmillan, 2010), 241.
5. Gordon Wood, *Friends Divided: John Adams and Thomas Jefferson* (New York: Penguin, 2017), 29.
6. *Magazine of American History*, vol. 6, 1881, 133.
7. Puls, *Henry Knox*, 242.
8. Puls, *Henry Knox*, 242.
9. Puls, *Henry Knox*, 249.
10. Puls, *Henry Knox*, 250.
11. John Fitzpatrick, ed., *The Writings of George Washington from the Original Manuscript Sources* (New York: Best Books, 1935), 167.
12. Richard Frothingham, *History of the Siege of Boston and of the Battles of Lexington and Concord* (New York: n.p.,1896), 271.
13. Frothingham, *History of the Siege of Boston*, 271.
14. Puls, *Henry Knox*, 251.
15. Puls, *Henry Knox*, 251.
16. Puls, *Henry Knox*, 251.
17. Puls, *Henry Knox*, 257.
18. Puls, *Henry Knox*, 260.
19. Puls, *Henry Knox*, 261.
20. Puls, *Henry Knox*, 261.
21. Puls, *Henry Knox*, 261.
22. Ron Chernow, *Washington: A Life* (New York: Penguin, 2010), 201.
23. Chernow, *Washington*, 157.
24. Chernow, *Washington*, 423.
25. David McCullough, *1776* (New York: Simon and Schuster, 2005), 75.
26. McCullough, *1776*.

CHAPTER 18: HEADING BACK DOWN

1. Thomas Campeau, *The Noble Train of Artillery* (Fort Leavenworth, KS: U.S. Government, Department of Defense, 2015), 32.

2. William Browne, *Ye Cohorn Caravan* (Schuylerville, NY: NoPaul Publishers, 1975), 50.

3. Browne, *Ye Cohorn Caravan*, 50.

4. John Becker, *Reminiscences of the American Revolution* (Albany, NY: Leopold Classic Library, 1806), 30.

5. Campeau, *The Noble Train of Artillery*, 31.

6. Browne, *Ye Cohorn Caravan*, 43.

7. Becker, *Reminiscences of the American Revolution*, 27.

CHAPTER 19: CROSSING THE ICE

1. Mark Puls, *Henry Knox: Visionary General of the Revolution* (New York: Macmillan, 2010), 40.

2. Puls, *Henry Knox*, 40.

3. Henry Knox, *Diary of Henry Knox* (n.p.: n.p., 1775), 17.

4. John Becker, *Reminiscences of the American Revolution* (Albany, NY: Leopold Classic Library, 1806), 30.

5. Thomas Campeau, *The Noble Train of Artillery* (Fort Leavenworth, KS: U.S. Government, Department of Defense, 2015), 31.

6. Campeau, *The Noble Train of Artillery*, 32.

7. Campeau, *The Noble Train of Artillery*, 32.

8. David McCullough, *1776* (New York: Simon and Schuster, 2005), 33.

9. Campeau, *The Noble Train of Artillery*, 32.

CHAPTER 20: THE LIFE AND TIMES OF A TEAMSTER

1. John Becker, *Reminiscences of the American Revolution* (Albany, NY: Leopold Classic Library, 1806), 11.

2. Becker, *Reminiscences of the American Revolution*, 11.

3. Becker, *Reminiscences of the American Revolution*, 12.

4. Becker, *Reminiscences of the American Revolution*, 12.

5. Becker, *Reminiscences of the American Revolution*, 49.

6. Becker, *Reminiscences of the American Revolution*, 24.

7. Becker, *Reminiscences of the American Revolution*, 21.

8. Becker, *Reminiscences of the American Revolution*, 37.

9. Becker, *Reminiscences of the American Revolution*, 37.

10. Becker, *Reminiscences of the American Revolution*, 52.

11. Becker, *Reminiscences of the American Revolution*, 52.

12. Becker, *Reminiscences of the American Revolution*, 54.

13. Becker, *Reminiscences of the American Revolution*, 56.

14. Becker, *Reminiscences of the American Revolution*, 56.

15. Becker, *Reminiscences of the American Revolution*, 59.
16. Becker, *Reminiscences of the American Revolution*, 59.
17. Becker, *Reminiscences of the American Revolution*, 94.
18. Becker, *Reminiscences of the American Revolution*, 67.
19. Becker, *Reminiscences of the American Revolution*, 69.
20. Becker, *Reminiscences of the American Revolution*, 158.
21. Becker, *Reminiscences of the American Revolution*, 158.
22. Becker, *Reminiscences of the American Revolution*, 70.
23. Becker, *Reminiscences of the American Revolution*, 72.
24. Becker, *Reminiscences of the American Revolution*, 73.
25. Becker, *Reminiscences of the American Revolution*, 74.
26. Becker, *Reminiscences of the American Revolution*, 67.

CHAPTER 21: CANNON DOWN, HALF MOON

1. John Becker, *Reminiscences of the American Revolution* (Albany, NY: Leopold Classic Library, 1806), 31.
2. Becker, *Reminiscences of the American Revolution*, 31.
3. Becker, *Reminiscences of the American Revolution*, 32.
4. Becker, *Reminiscences of the American Revolution*, 32.
5. Becker, *Reminiscences of the American Revolution*, 32.
6. William Browne, *Ye Cohorn Caravan* (Schuylerville, NY: NoPaul Publishers, 1975), 52.
7. Browne, *Ye Cohorn Caravan*, 52.
8. Browne, *Ye Cohorn Caravan*, 52.
9. Becker, *Reminiscences of the American Revolution*, 31.
10. Browne, *Ye Cohorn Caravan*, 42.
11. Browne, *Ye Cohorn Caravan*, 43.
12. Browne, *Ye Cohorn Caravan*, 45.
13. Browne, *Ye Cohorn Caravan*, 45.
14. Browne, *Ye Cohorn Caravan*, 45.
15. Browne, *Ye Cohorn Caravan*, 46.
16. Browne, *Ye Cohorn Caravan*, 46.
17. Browne, *Ye Cohorn Caravan*, 46.
18. Browne, *Ye Cohorn Caravan*, 46.
19. Browne, *Ye Cohorn Caravan*, 46.
20. Browne, *Ye Cohorn Caravan*, 47.
21. Browne, *Ye Cohorn Caravan*, 48.
22. Browne, *Ye Cohorn Caravan*, 48.
23. Browne, *Ye Cohorn Caravan*, 48.
24. Browne, *Ye Cohorn Caravan*, 48.

CHAPTER 22: THE THIRD COLUMN

1. Thomas Jefferson, *The Life and Writings of Thomas Jefferson* (New York: Putnam, 1900), 290.

2. Paul Longmore, *The Invention of George Washington* (Charlottesville: University Press of Virginia, 1999), 138.

3. David McCullough, *John Adams* (New York: Simon and Schuster, 2001), 86.

4. James Tyson, *An Outline of the Political and Social Life of George Washington* (n.p.: Pacific Press Company, 1895), 327.

5. Ron Chernow, *Washington: A Life* (New York: Penguin, 2010), 174.

6. Frank Grizzard, *George Washington: A Biographical Companion* (Santa Barbara, CA: ABC-CLIO, 2002), 308.

7. David McCullough, *1776* (New York: Simon and Schuster, 2005), 36.

8. McCullough, *1776*, 36.

9. George Washington, *The Writings of George Washington, 1775–1776* (New York: Putnam, 1889), 162.

10. Washington, *The Writings of George Washington*, 308.

11. Chernow, *Washington*, 176.

12. *Peterson Magazine*, vol. 106, 1895, 907.

13. Michael Lee Lanning, *African Americans in the Revolutionary War* (New York: Citadel Press, 2005), 48.

14. Chernow, *Washington*, 213.

CHAPTER 23: THE ALBANY

1. John Becker, *Reminiscences of the American Revolution* (Albany, NY: Leopold Classic Library, 1806), 32.

2. Mark Puls, *Henry Knox: Visionary General of the Revolution* (New York: Macmillan, 2010), 41.

3. Becker, *Reminiscences of the American Revolution*, 33.

4. Becker, *Reminiscences of the American Revolution*, 33.

5. William Browne, *Ye Cohorn Caravan* (Schuylerville, NY: NoPaul Publishers, 1975), 55.

6. Browne, *Ye Cohorn Caravan*, 55.

7. Browne, *Ye Cohorn Caravan*, 55.

8. Puls, *Henry Knox*, 41.

9. Browne, *Ye Cohorn Caravan*, 56.

10. Browne, *Ye Cohorn Caravan*, 56.

11. Browne, *Ye Cohorn Caravan*, 56.

12. North Callahan, *Henry Knox: General Washington's General* (South Brunswick, NY: Rinehart, 1958), 50.

13. Callahan, *Henry Knox*, 50.

14. Callahan, *Henry Knox*, 50.

15. Browne, *Ye Cohorn Caravan*, 56.

16. Thomas Campeau, *The Noble Train of Artillery* (Fort Leavenworth, KS: U.S. Government, Department of Defense, 2015), 33.

17. Browne, *Ye Cohorn Caravan*, 56.

CHAPTER 24: ALL THE KINGDOMS OF THE EARTH

1. William Browne, *Ye Cohorn Caravan* (Schuylerville, NY: NoPaul Publishers, 1975), 56.

2. John Becker, *Reminiscences of the American Revolution* (Albany, NY: Leopold Classic Library, 1806), 33.

3. Phillip Hamilton, *The Revolutionary War Lives and Letters of Lucy and Henry Knox* (Baltimore: Johns Hopkins University Press, 2017), 26.

4. Browne, *Ye Cohorn Caravan*, 62.

5. Browne, *Ye Cohorn Caravan*, 62.

6. Browne, *Ye Cohorn Caravan*, 62.

7. North Callahan, *Henry Knox: General Washington's General* (South Brunswick, NY: Rinehart, 1958), 51.

8. Thomas Campeau, *The Noble Train of Artillery* (Fort Leavenworth, KS: U.S. Government, Department of Defense, 2015), 34.

9. Callahan, *Henry Knox*, 51.

10. Brian Daly, *The White Climb* (India: Partridge, 2014), 44.

11. Campeau, *The Noble Train of Artillery*, 34.

12. Browne, *Ye Cohorn Caravan*, 62.

13. Jon Krakauer, *Into Thin Air* (New York: Doubleday, 1998), 185.

14. Krakauer, *Into Thin Air*, 41.

CHAPTER 25: COMMON SENSE

1. David McCullough, *1776* (New York: Simon and Schuster, 2005), 65.

2. McCullough, *1776*, 65.

3. McCullough, *1776*, 67.

4. George Washington, *The Writings of George Washington*, vol. 3 (New York: American Stationers, 1834), 286.

5. Francis Greene, *General Greene* (New York: Appleton, 1897), 31.

6. Ron Chernow, *Washington: A Life* (New York: Penguin, 2010), 214.

7. Thomas Paine, *Common Sense* (Boston: n.p., 1776), 1.

8. Diane Ravitch, *The American Reader: Words That Moved a Nation* (New York: Putnam, 2010), 47.

9. Paine, *Common Sense*, 23.

10. Chernow, *Washington*, 215.

11. Chernow, *Washington*, 215.
12. Paine, *Common Sense*, 27.
13. Chernow, *Washington*, 215.
14. Richard Frothingham, *The Rise of the Republic of the United States* (Boston: Little Brown, 1872), 480.
15. Chernow, *Washington*, 215.
16. George Washington, *The Writings of George Washington*, vol. 4 (Washington, DC: The United States Government Printing Office, 1834), 234.

CHAPTER 26: A SINISTER VIOLENCE OF INTENTION

1. Jon Krakauer, *Into Thin Air* (New York: Doubleday, 1998), 57.
2. Mark Puls, *Henry Knox: Visionary General of the Revolution* (New York: Macmillan, 2010), 159.
3. William Browne, *Ye Cohorn Caravan* (Schuylerville, NY: NoPaul Publishers, 1975), 62.
4. Joseph Conrad, *Lord Jim* (New York: Strebinsky Media, 2015), 10.
5. Browne, *Ye Cohorn Caravan*, 62.
6. Puls, *Henry Knox*, 161.
7. Browne, *Ye Cohorn Caravan*, 62.
8. Krakauer, *Into Thin Air*, 5.
9. Bernard Drew, *Henry Knox and the Revolutionary War Trail* (Boston: McFarland, 2012), 163.

CHAPTER 27: THE DEVIL'S STAIRCASE

1. North Callahan, *Henry Knox: General Washington's General* (South Brunswick, NY: Rinehart, 1958), 52.
2. Jordan Fiore, *The Noble Train of Artillery* (Boston: Commonwealth Bicentennial Publication, 1976), 16.
3. William Browne, *Ye Cohorn Caravan* (Schuylerville, NY: NoPaul Publishers, 1975), 65.
4. Browne, *Ye Cohorn Caravan*, 65.
5. Browne, *Ye Cohorn Caravan*, 63.
6. Callahan, *Henry Knox*, 52.
7. Jon Krakauer, *Into Thin Air* (New York: Doubleday, 1998), 73.
8. John Becker, *Reminiscences of the American Revolution* (Albany, NY: Leopold Classic Library, 1806), 33.
9. Callahan, *Henry Knox*, 53.
10. Callahan, *Henry Knox*, 54.
11. Becker, *Reminiscences of the American Revolution*, 34.
12. Becker, *Reminiscences of the American Revolution*, 35.

13. Becker, *Reminiscences of the American Revolution*, 35.
14. Becker, *Reminiscences of the American Revolution*, 35.

CHAPTER 28: CANNONS IN THE MUD: SPRINGFIELD

1. John Becker, *Reminiscences of the American Revolution* (Albany, NY: Leopold Classic Library, 1806), 35.
2. North Callahan, *Henry Knox: General Washington's General* (New York: Rinehart, 1958), 54.
3. David McCullough, *1776* (New York: Simon and Schuster, 2005), 78.
4. Thomas Campeau, *The Noble Train of Artillery* (Fort Leavenworth, KS: U.S. Government, Department of Defense, 2015), 36.
5. Becker, *Reminiscences of the American Revolution*, 35.
6. William Browne, *Ye Cohorn Caravan* (Schuylerville, NY: NoPaul Publishers, 1975), 66.

CHAPTER 29: DELIVERANCE

1. David McCullough, *1776* (New York: Simon and Schuster, 2005), 81.
2. McCullough, *1776*, 81.
3. McCullough, *1776*, 81.
4. Ron Chernow, *Washington: A Life* (New York: Penguin, 2010), 217.
5. Chernow, *Washington*, 217.
6. Mark Puls, *Henry Knox: Visionary General of the Revolution* (New York: Macmillan, 2010), 274.
7. Chernow, *Washington*, 217, 220.
8. Chernow, *Washington*, 217, 220.
9. Chernow, *Washington*, 217, 220.
10. Chernow, *Washington*, 217, 220.

CHAPTER 30: THE FINAL LEG

1. Phillip Hamilton, *The Revolutionary War Lives and Letters of Lucy and Henry Knox* (Baltimore: Johns Hopkins University Press, 2017), 50.

CHAPTER 31: COLONEL OF THE ARTILLERY

1. Mark Puls, *Henry Knox: Visionary General of the Revolution* (New York: Macmillan, 2010), 43.
2. David McCullough, *1776* (New York: Simon and Schuster, 2005), 86.
3. John Adams, *The Works of John Adams*, vol. 2 (New York: Verlag, 1910), 220.

4. William Browne, *Ye Cohorn Caravan* (Schuylerville, NY: NoPaul Publishers, 1975), 67.

5. Browne, *Ye Cohorn Caravan*, 68.

6. George Washington, *The Writings of George Washington, 1775–1776* (New York: Putnam, 1889), 425.

7. Puls, *Henry Knox*, 43.

8. McCullough, *1776*, 87.

9. McCullough, *1776*, 87.

10. Puls, *Henry Knox*, 44.

11. Ron Chernow, *Washington: A Life* (New York: Penguin, 2010), 224.

12. McCullough, *1776*, 87.

13. McCullough, *1776*, 87.

14. Washington, *The Writings of George Washington*, 425.

15. McCullough, *1776*, 87.

16. McCullough, *1776*, 89.

17. McCullough, *1776*, 89.

18. McCullough, *1776*, 89.

19. McCullough, *1776*, 89.

20. McCullough, *1776*, 89.

CHAPTER 32: THE CANNONS OF TICONDEROGA

1. David McCullough, *1776* (New York: Simon and Schuster, 2005), 90.

2. McCullough, *1776*, 91.

3. McCullough, *1776*, 91.

4. McCullough, *1776*, 91.

5. Mark Puls, *Henry Knox: Visionary General of the Revolution* (New York: Macmillan, 2010), 44.

6. Puls, *Henry Knox*, 44.

7. McCullough, *1776*, 91.

8. McCullough, *1776*, 92.

9. McCullough, *1776*, 92.

10. McCullough, *1776*, 92.

11. McCullough, *1776*, 92.

12. North Callahan, *Henry Knox: General Washington's General* (New York: Rinehart, 1958), 57.

13. Nathaniel Philbrick, *Bunker Hill* (New York: Penguin, 2013), 280.

14. Ron Chernow, *Washington: A Life* (New York: Penguin, 2010), 226.

CHAPTER 33: AT DAWN'S LIGHT

1. David McCullough, *1776* (New York: Simon and Schuster, 2005), 75.

2. McCullough, *1776*, 75.

3. McCullough, *1776*, 93.

4. McCullough, *1776*, 93.

5. McCullough, *1776*, 94.

6. Mark Puls, *Henry Knox: Visionary General of the Revolution* (New York: Macmillan, 2010), 44.

7. Puls, *Henry Knox*, 44.

8. McCullough, *1776*, 94.

9. McCullough, *1776*, 94.

10. McCullough, *1776*, 95.

11. McCullough, *1776*, 95.

12. McCullough, *1776*, 95.

13. McCullough, *1776*, 95.

14. McCullough, *1776*, 95.

15. McCullough, *1776*, 95.

16. Ron Chernow, *Washington: A Life* (New York: Penguin, 2010), 226.

17. McCullough, *1776*, 96.

18. Chernow, *Washington*, 226.

19. McCullough, *1776*, 96.

20. McCullough, *1776*, 97.

21. McCullough, *1776*, 97.

22. McCullough, *1776*, 99.

23. Chernow, *Washington*, 227.

24. Chernow, *Washington*, 227.

25. McCullough, *1776*, 98.

26. McCullough, *1776*, 98.

27. McCullough, *1776*, 99.

28. McCullough, *1776*, 100.

29. McCullough, *1776*, 100.

30. McCullough, *1776*, 104.

CHAPTER 34: THE PRODIGAL SON RETURNS

1. David McCullough, *1776* (New York: Simon and Schuster, 2005), 105.

2. McCullough, *1776*, 84.

3. McCullough, *1776*, 106.

4. McCullough, *1776*, 106.

5. McCullough, *1776*, 106.

6. George Washington, *The Writings of George Washington*, vol. 3 (New York: American Stationers Company, 1834), 323.

7. James McNabney, *Born in Brotherhood* (New York: Authorhouse, 2006), 398.

8. Mark Puls, *Henry Knox: Visionary General of the Revolution* (New York: Macmillan, 2010), 47.

CHAPTER 35: THE UNBORN MILLIONS

1. Mark Puls, *Henry Knox: Visionary General of the Revolution* (New York: Macmillan, 2010), 46.

EPILOGUE

1. Mark Puls, *Henry Knox: Visionary General of the Revolution* (New York: Macmillan, 2010), 186.

2. Puls, *Henry Knox*, 254.

3. Puls, *Henry Knox*, 254.

4. Puls, *Henry Knox*, 254.

5. John Becker, *Reminiscences of the American Revolution* (Albany, NY: Leopold Classic Library, 1806), 199.

6. Becker, *Reminiscences of the American Revolution*, 199.

7. Becker, *Reminiscences of the American Revolution*, 199.

8. Becker, *Reminiscences of the American Revolution*, 199.

BIBLIOGRAPHY

Adams, John. *The Works of John Adams*. Vol. 2. New York: Verlag, 1910.

Alexander, Michael. *Discovering the New World*. New York: Harper and Row, 1976.

Allan, Herbert S. *John Hancock: Patriot in Purple*. New York: Macmillan, 1948.

American State Papers, Foreign, Indian and Military Affairs. Washington, DC: Library of Congress, n.d.

Baker, William. *Washington after the Revolution*. Philadelphia: Lippincott, 1897.

Bancroft, George. *History of the United States from the Discovery of the American Continent*. New York: Harper, 1882.

Becker, John. *Reminiscences of the American Revolution*. Albany, NY: Leopold Classic Library, 1806.

Bolton, Charles. *The Private Soldier under Washington*. New York: C. Scribner's Sons, 1902.

Brookhiser, Richard. *Founding Fathers Rediscovering George Washington*. New York: Free Press, 1996.

Brooks, Noah. *Henry Knox: George Washington's General*. New York: A. S. Barnes, 1958.

———. *Henry Knox: Soldier of the Revolution*. New York: Cosimo, 2007.

Brooks, Victor. *The Boston Campaign*. Conshohocken, PA: Combined Publishing, ca.1999.

Browne, William. *Ye Cohorn Caravan*. Schuylerville, NY: NoPaul Publishers, 1975.

Burns, James McGregor. *George Washington*. New York: Times Books, 2004.

Callahan, North. *Henry Knox: General Washington's General*. New York: Rinehart, 1958.

Campeau, Thomas. *The Noble Train of Artillery*. Fort Leavenworth, KS: U.S. Government, Department of Defense, 2015.

Carrington, Henry B. *Battles of the American Revolution 1775–1781*. New York: Promontory Press, 1877.

Chernow, Ron. *Alexander Hamilton*. New York: Penguin Press, 2004.

———. *Washington: A Life*. New York: Penguin, 2010.

Conkling, Margaret C. *Memoirs of the Mother and Wife of Washington*. Auburn, NY: Derby Miller, 1850.

Conrad, Joseph. *Lord Jim*. New York: Strebinsky Media, 2015.

Copeland, David A. *Debating the Issues in Colonial Newspapers: Primary Documents on Events of the Period*. Westport, CT: Greenwood Press, 2000.

Custis, George Washington Parke. *Recollections and Private Memoirs of Washington*. New York: Derby Jackson, 1860.

Daizell, Robert. *George Washington's Mount Vernon*. Oxford: Oxford University Press, 2000.

Darnton, Robert. *George Washington's False Teeth: An Unconventional Guide to the Eighteenth Century*. New York: W. W. Norton, 2003.

Davis, Burke. *George Washington and the American Revolution*. New York: Random House, 1975.

Decatur, Stephan, Jr. *Private Affairs of George Washington, from the Records and Accounts of Tobias Lear, Esquire, His Secretary*. Boston: Houghton Mifflin, 1933.

DiLiso, Rock. *American Advance Westward from the French and Indian War*. N.p.: iUniverse, 2008.

Drake, Francis. *Memorials of the Society of the Cincinnati of Massachusetts*. Boston: Massachusetts Society of the Cincinnati, 1873.

Drake, Francis Samuel. *Life and Correspondence of Henry Knox*. Boston: Samuel G. Drake, 1873.

Drew, Bernard. *Henry Knox and the Revolutionary War Trail*. Boston: McFarland, 2012.

Ellis Joseph. *Founding Brothers: The Revolutionary Generation*. New York: Albert A. Knopf, 2000.

———. *His Excellency, George Washington*. New York: Vintage Books, 2005.

Ferling, John E. *The Ascent of George Washington: The Hidden Political Genius of an American Icon*. New York: Bloomsbury Press, 2009.

Fiore, Jordan. *The Noble Train of Artillery*. Boston: Commonwealth Bicentennial Publication, 1976.

Fitzpatrick, John, ed. *The Writings of George Washington from the Original Manuscript Sources*. New York: Best Books, 1935.

Flexner, James Thomas. *George Washington*. 4 vols. Boston: Little Brown, 1965–1972.

Ford, Washington, ed. *Journals of the Continental Congress, 1774–1789*. 34 vols. Washington, DC: Library of Congress, 1904.

Freeman, Douglas Southall. *George Washington: A Biography*. 7 vols. New York: Charles Scribner's Sons, 1948.

French, Allen. *The Siege of Boston*. New York: Macmillan, 1911.

Frothingham, Richard. *History of the Siege of Boston and of the Battles of Lexington and Concord*. New York: n.p., 1896.

———. *The Rise of the Republic of the United States*. Boston: Little Brown, 1872.

Furstenberg, Francois. *In the Name of the Father: Washington's Legacy, Slavery, and the Making of a Nation*. New York: Penguin, 2006.

Golway, Terry. *Washington's General: Nathanael Greene and the Triumph of the American Revolution*. New York: Henry Holt, 2006.

Gilder Lehrman Collection on Deposit at the New York Historical Society.

Greene, Francis. *General Greene*. New York: Appleton, 1897.

Grizzard, Frank. *George Washington: A Biographical Companion*. Santa Barbara, CA: ABC–CLIO, 2002.

The Harvard Illustrated Magazine, vol. 1, 1900.

Harvey, Robert. *Maverick Military Leaders*. New York: Skyhorse Publishing, 2008.

Hamilton, Phillip. *The Revolutionary War Lives and Letters of Lucy and Henry Knox*. Baltimore: Johns Hopkins University Press, 2017.

Hayden, Sidney. *Washington and His Masonic Compeers*. New York: Masonic Publishing, 1866.

Henriques, Peter. *Realistic Visionary: A Portrait of George Washington*. Charlottesville: University of Virginia Press, 2006.

Higgenbotham, Don, ed. *George Washington Reconsidered*. Charlottesville: University of Virginia Press, 2001.

Irving, Washington. *The Life and Times of George Washington*. New York: Putnam and Sons, 1876.

———. *The Life of George Washington*. New York: William L. Allison, 1859.

Jackman, William J., Jacob H. Patton, and Rossiter Johnson. *History of the American Nation*. 9 vols. Chicago: K. Gaynor, 1911.

Jefferson, Thomas. *The Life and Writings of Thomas Jefferson*. New York: Putnam 1900.

Jensen, Merill. *The Founding of a Nation*. New York: Hackett Publishing, 2004.

Kagan, Robert. *Dangerous Nation: America's Place in the World from the Earliest Days to the Dawn of the Twentieth Century*. New York: Alfred A Knopf, 2006.

Knox, Henry. *Diary*. N.p.: New England Historical and Genealogical Register, Diary of the Ticonderoga Expedition, n.d.

———. *Diary of Henry Knox*. N.p.: n.p., 1775.

———. *Henry Knox Papers*. 65 vols. Boston: Massachusetts Historical Society; New York: Henry Knox Papers.

———. Letter to George Washington. December 17, 1775. Henry Knox Papers, 1736–1823. Boston: Massachusetts Historical Society.

———. Letter to Lucy Knox. January 5, 1776. Henry Knox Papers, 1736–1823. Boston: Massachusetts Historical Society.

"Knox Journey." *Springfield Union*. January 16, 1976.

"Knox Trail New Berkshire Scenic Highway Will Cut off Twenty Miles." *Springfield Republican*. September 26, 1926.

Krakauer, Jon. *Into Thin Air*. New York: Doubleday, 1998.

Lanning, Michael Lee. *African Americans in the Revolutionary War*. New York: Citadel Press, 2005.

Larabee, Benjamin Woods. *The Boston Tea Party*. Boston: Northeastern University Press, 1979.

Lee, Jean B. *Experiencing Mount Vernon: Eyewitness Accounts 1784–1865*. Charlottesville: University of Virginia Press, 2006.

Lengel, Edward G. *General George Washington: A Military Life*. New York: Random House 2005.

Longmore, Paul. *The Invention of George Washington*. Charlottesville: University of Virginia, 1999.

Lossing, Benson. *Washington and the American Republic*. Vol. 2. New York: Virtue and Yorston, 1870.

Lossing, Benson J. *Martha Washington*. New York: J. C. Buttre, 1861.

Magazine of American History, vol. 6, 1881.

Marshall, John. *The Life of George Washington*. Indianapolis, IN: Liberty Fund, 2000.

McCullough, David. *1776*. New York: Simon and Shuster, 2005.

———. *John Adams*. New York: Simon and Schuster, 2001.

McNabney, James. *Born in Brotherhood*. New York: Authorhouse, 2006.

Messages and Papers of the Presidents: George Washington. Washington, DC: Federal Register Division, National Archives and Records Service, Government Printing Office, 1956.

Middlekauff, Robert. *The Glorious Cause*. Oxford: Oxford University Press, 2007.

Moore, Frank, ed. *Diary of the American Revolution from Newspapers and Original Documents*. Vol. 1–2. New York: Charles Scribner, 1860.

Morgan, Philip D. "To Get Quit of Negroes, George Washington and Slavery." *Journal of American Studies* 39, no. 3 (2005).

Morgan, Edmund, S. *The Genius of George Washington*. New York: W. W. Norton, 1980.

Nelson, Craig. *Thomas Paine, Enlightenment, Revolution, and the Birth of the Modern Nation*. New York: Viking, 2006.

O'Connell, Robert. *Revolutionary: George Washington at War*. New York: Random House, 2019.

Paine, Thomas. *Common Sense*. Boston: n.p., 1776.

Papas, Phillip. *Renegade Revolutionary: The Life of Charles Lee*. New York: New York University Press, 2014.

Perry, James. *A Mere Matter of Marching*. New York: Xlibris, 2011.

Peterson Magazine, vol. 106, 1895.

Philbrick, Nathaniel. *Bunker Hill*. New York: Penguin Books, 2013.

Proceedings of the New York State Historical Association, vol. 18, 1890.

Puls, Mark. *Henry Knox*. New York: Macmillan, 2008.

———. *Henry Knox: Visionary General of the Revolution*. New York: Macmillan, 2010.

Ramsey, David. *The Life of George Washington*. London: T. Cadell and W. Davies, 1807.

Rhodehamel, John. *George Washington: The Wonder of the Age*. New Haven, NJ: Yale University Press, 2017.

Richard, Alexander. *Hamilton American*. New York: Free Press Touchstone, 2000.

Schwarz, Philip, ed. *Slavery at the Home of George Washington*. Mount Vernon, VA: Mount Vernon Ladies Association, 2002.

Shea, Michael. *In God We Trust*. New York: Liberty Quest, 2012.

Smith, Paul, ed. *Letters of Delegates to the Continental Congress 1774–1789*. 25 vols. Summerfield, FL: Historical Database, 1998.

Sonneborn, Liz. *Chronology of American Indian History*. New York: Infobase, ca. 2007.

Thayer, William Roscoe. *George Washington*. New York: Houghton Mifflin, 1922.

Tyson, James. *An Outline of the Political and Social Life of George Washington*. N.p.: Pacific Press Company, 1895.

The Virginia Magazine of History and Biography, vol. 66, 1958.

Ware, Susan. *Forgotten Heroes Inspiring American Portraits from Our Leading Historians*. New York: Penguin, 2006.

Wills, Gary. *Cincinnatus: George Washington and the Enlightenment*. Garden City, NY: Doubleday 1984.

Weems, Mason. *The Life of Washington*. Cambridge, MA: Belknap Press, 1962.

Washington, George. *George Washington Writings*. Edited by John Rhodehamel. New York: Library of America, 1997.

———. *The Writings of George Washington*. Vol. 3. New York: American Stationers, 1834.

Wood, Gordon. *Friends Divided: John Adams and Thomas Jefferson*. New York: Penguin, 2017.

INDEX